arién

Sancti Spíritus

○ Camagüey

○ Holguín

Santiago
de Cuba

Sierra Maestra ◉

# Vida Clandestina

## My Life in the Cuban Revolution

ENRIQUE OLTUSKI

FOREWORD BY EDUARDO TORRES-CUEVAS

*Translated by Thomas and Carol Christensen*

wiley.com

Published by

wiley.com

Copyright © 2002 by John Wiley & Sons, Inc.

This book has been developed and produced by the staff of Jossey-Bass, a Wiley Company.

Internal design by Lisa Buckley.

Both A Brief History of Cuba and the Glossary are provided by the publisher and are not written by the author.

An earlier and shorter version of this book was published in 2000 as *Gente Del Llano* by Ediciones Imagen Contemporanea, Casa de Altos Estudios Don Fernando Ortiz, Universidad de La Habana, Cuba.

**Library of Congress Cataloging-in-Publication Data**

Oltuski, Enrique, date.
  Vida clandestina : my life in the Cuban Revolution / Enrique
Oltuski ; translated by Thomas and Carol Christensen.—1st ed.
    p. cm.
Includes index.
  ISBN 0–7879–6169–8 (alk. paper)
  1. Cuba—History—Revolution, 1959—Personal narratives. 2.
Cuba—History—1933–1959. 3. Oltuski, Enrique, date. I. Title.
  F1788 .O48 2002
  972.9106'4—dc21                                                                    2002002223

FIRST EDITION
*HB Printing*   10   9   8   7   6   5   4   3   2   1

# Contents

*Foreword*  ∘  Eduardo Torres-Cuevas        vii
*Preface: Why I Wrote This Book*        xvii
*A Brief History of Cuba*        xxiii
*Map of Cuba*        xxxiii

## Before the Plains and the Sierra

ONE  ∘  Batista's Coup d'État        3

TWO  ∘  First Revolutionary Impulses        15

THREE  ∘  Student in the United States        25

FOUR  ∘  Journey to Latin America        35

FIVE  ∘  Attack on the Moncada Barracks        45

SIX  ∘  Return to Cuba        55

SEVEN  ∘  Revolutionary Quest        63

EIGHT  ∘  Joining the 26th of July Movement        75

## The Plains

NINE  ∘  Conspiracy in Havana        89

TEN  ∘  The Civil Resistance Movement        105

ELEVEN  ∘  The Fight in Las Villas        121

TWELVE  ∘  Strike of April 9        139

THIRTEEN  ∘  The Sierra Assumes Command        155

## Photographs   173

## The Sierra

FOURTEEN  ∘  Che in Las Villas   189

FIFTEEN  ∘  The Sierra Maestra   205

## After the Plains and the Sierra

SIXTEEN ∘ Batista Flees   229

SEVENTEEN ∘ Fidel Marches on Havana   239

EIGHTEEN ∘ Government Minister   253

NINETEEN ∘ The Revolution Takes Power   267

## Epilogue   275

*Glossary*   290

*About the Author*   295

*About the Translators*   296

*Index*   297

I DEDICATE MY BOOK
TO THE YOUNG PEOPLE OF THE WORLD.

# Foreword

Thanks to my work as writer and publisher, I had the good fortune to review the manuscript of this book prior to its publication. Its pages, which I devoured in a single night, were part of a living legend that is now becoming written history, the history of the men who made and who sustain the Cuban revolution today.

I first heard the author of these pages speak in the days of the triumph of the insurrectionary movement in January 1959. Until then he was only known, among a very tight circle, in his role as the Coordinator of the Revolutionary Movement of the 26th of July in the central Cuban province of Las Villas—a territory in which the fight against the dictatorship of Fulgencio Batista had been especially intense, as much in the mountains as in the cities, a territory where the columns of legendary guerrilla commanders Camilo Cienfuegos and Ernesto "Che" Guevara had destroyed the tyrant's troops.

Enrique Oltuski was a mysterious figure who was known only by his nom de guerre, Sierra. He was the only leader of the 26th of July whom the punitive forces of the regime had not been able to identify, and, for many, it was a real surprise that this architect, who had gotten his degree in the United States and was an employee of Shell Oil—in which capacity he was able to move around the country—was the noted underground fighter. The sincerity, the honesty, and the courage of Oltuski have become proverbial, and they strike the reader even in the way he has written his work and in the modesty with which its main character, the author, downplays his role as protagonist, in order to relay what he saw, felt, and lived, the personal experience through which he observes and shares his relations

with the men of a generation that was able to transform a world, the world of his homeland.

Oltuski says that this is not a work of history. Written in the style of a novel, with a real element of suspense, all the actions, situations, and atmosphere of the time are brought to life by the faithful memory of his annotations, documents, and experiences. What does not interest Oltuski is to fossilize, sanctify, or abstract these experiences at the cost of true lived history. He would rather let the men be known as they really were without hiding or sugarcoating, without denying others the right to write their own stories. In fact, this type of essentially testimonial literature, by observing the conventions of fiction, brings alive the exciting spirit of a time, through its men and women, better than dense, rigid, and preconceived academic history texts. It is a work that delights from beginning to end, that draws us in through the simplicity of its language and the clarity of its story line.

The events of the book take place between 1952 and the early months of 1959: the period of Cuban history in which the revolutionary movement was born, developed, and triumphed, a period when honest and brave young people faced well-established, vastly superior, repressive troops, in spite of all the established ideas that caused some older men to view the struggle with skepticism. That underground movement not only overthrew the dictatorship but also changed a country where crime, indolence, apathy, and betrayal had drowned out democracy and corrupted the public institutions and the political parties to the point of allowing the most violent tyranny the country had ever endured.

On March 10, 1952, by means of a military coup d'état, Fulgencio Batista overturned the constitutional process and installed his illegal regime, propped up by the bayonets of the army. The tyrant became a symbol, the personification of all the evils of republican Cuba: he was, in fact, the negation of the dream and philosophy of the apostle of Cuban independence, José Martí, and of the men and women who, for more than a century, had fought and given their lives for a Cuba "free, sovereign, and with social justice." Thus there would be two types of opposition to the tyranny—that of the old politicians who sought a return to the conditions prior to the military coup, and that of the young people who wanted to radically change all that had demoralized and impoverished the country.

Before March 10, the political and social atmosphere had been marked by corruption, public scandals, and the rule of the gun (including organized crime). To that was added the divisiveness and confusion of the progressive and revolutionary forces. The people were mired in skepticism and impotence, in a country of strong contrasts between the misery of the many and the opulence of a few, whose wealth was often the result of illegality and the plundering of public funds. An audacious politician, Eduardo Chibás, had tried to confront this situation. With the motto "Shame against money," he founded the Cuban People's Party (the Ortodoxos), which took as its symbol the broom, indicating that it intended to sweep away all the prevailing corruption. It attracted a large number of the young people of Cuba, among them a young lawyer, Fidel Castro.

One tragic day, Chibás committed suicide. Yet, in spite of clear internal divisions, his party's chances of winning the next election seemed guaranteed. It was under those conditions that Batista took action and staged his military coup.

On July 26, 1953, Fidel Castro, with a group of young people, in a shift from the tactics previously employed, attacked one of the country's largest military strongholds, the Moncada barracks in the city of Santiago de Cuba. Although the attempt did not achieve its objectives, it became a call to combat. Around the figure of the revolutionary leader, the main rebel movement began to form, taking its name from the date of the attack on Moncada.

The 26th of July Movement began to mobilize nationally in 1955, and soon it had divisions throughout the country. After being imprisoned, then freed for only a few months, then persecuted and harassed by the repressive organs of the tyranny, Fidel traveled to Mexico to prepare the expeditionary nucleus that would land in Cuba to begin the armed rebellion. Another part of the leadership of the movement, the underground branch, had to recruit members, arms, and money, to develop an effective propaganda, and to ensure the conditions for the beginning of the insurrection.

The movement attracted more and more young people of all social and political backgrounds through its rejection of the manipulative policies of the old politicians, its revolutionary direction, and the honesty of its leaders. Once the guerrilla war had begun in the Sierra Maestra, under the leadership of Fidel himself, the repression increased, and so, in turn, did the acts of sabotage, propaganda, and preparation for a general revolutionary national strike by the underground movement. Thereafter a particular structure arose in which two fighting forces were recognized: the rebel army of the *Sierra,* or mountains, and the underground fighters of the cities, the *Llano,* or plains. This explains the way that Enrique Oltuski divides his book into four parts; he was a man of the plains—and, by the way, one of the most outstanding.

An interesting thing about *Vida Clandestina* is that it allows us, seemingly bit by bit, to grow in experience, to become increasingly clear in our understanding of the actions and, more fundamentally, of the policies. During the better part of its development, the underground movement in the plains believed that the ultimate triumph would be achieved by means of a general strike, while the armed forces in the Sierra believed in the necessity of destroying the central apparatus of the dictatorship, the army, in order to initiate a true revolutionary process.

The failure of the strike of April 1958 demonstrated that the cities were not the weakest point of the Batista regime and that an action of this kind would not easily lead to triumph. Fidel, with a more historical vision, had taken as reference the wars of Cuban independence from the Spanish colonial power, in which guerrilla warfare had worn down vastly superior troops, better trained and better armed; he had noticed that the weak points of the dictatorship's military apparatus were in the field and in its conventional training. And so, the Sierra faction was recognized as the driving force of the revolution, and the revolutionary group in the plains consolidated its role as an actively engaged rear guard.

These strategic differences have sometimes been exaggerated, even to the extent of a politicized imbalance. The incomplete image of a rural guerrilla without an urban network has made it difficult to understand the Cuban revolutionary process. Oltuski, a man of the plains, helps us achieve a more balanced point of view by taking us inside the rich human universe of this urban network, in which he knew many who, with the passage of years, have had diverse destinies. He portrays them as he saw them, as they were in their youth, far from the lapses of age.

The Cuban revolution, to prevail, destroyed two myths: first, the invincibility of the army, and second, the primary role of the U.S. government in any political action. It also destroyed a corollary to these myths, on which a mediocre republic had been based, a corollary added by the Stalinists, according to whom the revolution had to prevail first in the United States and only then in Latin America. The first notion, that a revolution can be made either with or without the army but never against the army, vanished in Cuba. The success of the revolution confirmed the Fidelist idea that it was necessary—and possible—to destroy that repressive apparatus, whose function was more internal than for national defense. The second myth was more difficult to eradicate, because of its long history and the strength of the internal and external forces by which it was maintained.

The last of the Cuban wars of independence from the Spanish colonial power began in 1895. Its principal organizer, José Martí, had created a rich body of work comprising articles, pamphlets, letters, and speeches, in which he summed up all the aspirations of Cubans, not just for independence but for a republic "of everyone and for the good of everyone" in which "the total dignity of man" was the first law. At first, Spain insisted it would hold on to Cuba "to the last man and the last peseta," but the human and material cost was so high that in 1897 there were desperate shouts of "not one more man nor one more peseta." In those circumstances, the United States declared war on Spain and soon, with the aid of the Cuban forces, defeated it. This was one of the most complex moments of twentieth-century Cuban history.

The U.S. forces occupied Cuba for three and a half years; in the end, they left it organized as a dependent republic. The United States government succeeded in attaching an appendix to the Cuban constitution that became known as the Platt Amendment, which was approved by the U.S. Congress and which authorized U.S. intervention in Cuba—and offended the sensibilities of Cubans of all classes. The United States also compelled the new government to sign a predatory economic exchange treaty that barred trade with other nations. As a result, Cuba was neither externally nor internally independent. Thus began the theory of geographic fatalism, which held that Cuba could take no sovereign action because everything would happen, for better or worse, according to the dictates of the North Americans. The direct, vulgar, and disdainful way they treated Cuba and the Cubans was a very bitter pill. And yet—and this must be emphasized—relations between Cubans and many North Americans were quite brotherly. They were two peoples who enjoyed knowing each other.

The support of the U.S. government for the bloodthirsty dictatorships of the time—Batista, Trujillo, and Somoza, to name a few—and its obstruction of all reformist, nationalistic, and populist movements, or even, in many cases, purely democratic ones, such as that of Jacobo Arbenz in Guatemala, was consistent with its lack of support and its harassment of the Cuban revolutionary movement. The revolutionary leadership was not the enemy of the United States—

it was merely independent. Decisions without previous consultation with Washington were taken for the first time. But that was not to be tolerated.

Two factors were decisive in the revolutionary strategy and gave it a profoundly innovative stamp. First, in direct opposition to the motto "divide and conquer," which was used against those who were fighting Batista's regime, Fidel insisted that all acknowledge the essential unity of the revolutionary forces. No one was excluded because of his previous political affiliations. Various political groups—Auténticos, Ortodoxos, Communists, Trotskyites, Apristas, and those without a party—all joined the ranks of the movement in the fight for a revolutionary agenda that sprang from the most deep-seated of Cuban aspirations. But unity as a strategic concept went beyond that. Its foundation was the people, the only force that could confront the great transformation of the country and the forces that, inevitably, would rise up against a process of radical change.

The second decisive factor was that the concept of revolution was not based on a fixed program but was an organic process based on the exigencies that developed along the way, always with the Cuban reality as strategy and guide—the physical and spiritual needs of the people and the total fulfillment of man in a society that, once the obstructing mechanisms were destroyed, would be released, once and for all, to become new and completely free, with a freedom born of culture and knowledge, the bases of true understanding.

Fidel's choices were informed by his study of revolutionary practice. The Cuban revolution, seen with eyes free of prejudice and self-interest, was clearly a heresy against all the dogmas that had bound the hands and feet and gagged the mouths of generations of Cubans; it was a new creation born of the tradition of the Cuban independence movement. Its guiding light was José Martí, the greatest figure of the longest struggle for independence in Latin America. Martí, whom Fidel credits as the "intellectual author of Moncada," had said that "Humanity is the homeland . . . the sweetest union of loves and hopes." He proclaimed that "with the poor people of the land I choose to cast my lot," and he dreamed of a totally sovereign republic within the Latin American and global community.

Those words inspired the men of the Cuban revolution, who gave with love the generous offering of their lives to change an unjust world, who were free of the hatreds that blind and had the courage that is needed if the seed of love is to be planted, from which a new, free, right, sovereign, and humane society may flower. These men, whom he knew, their passions and their realities, are the true subject of this memoir by Enrique Oltuski.

Eduardo Torres-Cuevas
*President*
*Imagen Contemporanea*
*University of Havana*

# Preface: Why I Wrote This Book

If you don't agree, write your own," said Che.

We were working late one night at the Ministry of Industries in 1962, when I criticized something he had written about the revolution. I had objected because I felt that Che underestimated the importance and the danger of the underground fight in the plains and the cities, where I was working during the struggle against the Batista regime from 1952 to 1959. For him the guerrilla forces in the Sierra Maestra were the reason for everything, but I believed that without the clandestine support of those of us in the plains and the cities, the revolution could not have prevailed.

This reminded me of another discussion we had had one night in 1958 when I went to visit him in the Sierra de Escambray. He had recently arrived from the Sierra Maestra; I was leading a double life as both an executive of Shell Oil and also the secret leader of the 26th of July Movement in the central plains.

It was raining torrentially that night, so he said to me with his characteristic ironic humor, "I'm sorry, but tonight you will not be able to sleep in your bed with its white sheets. Here you will have to sleep in a hammock, under the rain and the mosquitoes."

"Yes, that is true," I answered, "but at least I will *sleep* here, because in my bed at home with its white sheets, the danger that follows us every minute is so great that I can never sleep well. Here at least I feel safe."

We would often get into such discussions, in which everyone saw everything with different eyes and experienced the same events differently. And this was quite natural. It was not just the different social backgrounds of the insurgents; it was the battleground, the type of fight that shaped their thoughts and actions. The two fields of battle—the Sierra and the plains (the *Llano*)—marked different approaches, during the fight and after the victory.

We of the plains admired the struggle in the Sierra, with reservations, and finally we were swept along by it. Those in the Sierra did not really understand our work in the plains, and likely underestimated it. But we were all important—the campesinos in the mountains and the small businessmen, students, and workers of the plains.

After Fidel and his men landed in the *Granma* on December 2, 1956, it seemed in the early stages that victory would be won on the plains and that the Sierra would be mainly a symbol. Reality disproved this theory. From the failure of the struggle in the plains, a winning approach emerged: the guerrillas of the Sierra became the backbone of an armed struggle, and the plains shifted to playing a supporting role: collecting money, supplying arms and clothing, committing acts of sabotage, executing enemies, producing underground newspapers, recruiting and organizing members of the revolutionary movement.

The shift of strategic significance from the plains to the Sierra, and the final triumph of the Sierra, meant that the political thought of the Sierra dominated, along with its leaders.

The privations in the mountains, the suffering of the campesinos, and the shared life of the guerrillas contributed to an ongoing discussion and dissemination of the most advanced political ideas. In the plains, in contrast, the movement was led by and mostly made up of small businessmen, young people, and students—along with a Marxist vanguard that was opposed to armed warfare almost until the end. There was also a corrupt labor movement whose leaders had fallen into an alliance with the dictator Batista. There was also a style of struggle in which distrust, dispersion, and constant danger hampered the discussion and development of progressive ideas.

And the best leaders—Fidel, his brother Raúl, and Che—were in the Sierra, as we who were engaged in the struggle in the plains would be first to admit.

But everything was not always so clear. Nothing was absolute, black and white. We faced a complicated situation. How these obstacles were overcome, how forces moving in opposite directions converged, how a successful path was taken—this is the amazing story of the revolution, of the genius of Fidel. Luckily for the revolution, Fidel never relied on any one man, but took the best from all.

That is why I was sure that each of us would have—and did have—his own version of the same story, and that as participants we were biased by our own experience, even if we denied that this was so. The story was complicated, composed of many small events. Che was right to say that we should each tell our part of the story. In this way, later—much later—the full picture might emerge.

So this is not the definitive story of the revolution, just my own particular version; not the most important, but the one I lived, the one I remember.

I do not intend the material in this book to be used as a historical source. I do not want to talk so much about specific dates, places, words, people. I want to go back to my youth. I want to show the unjust society in which we lived, the atmosphere in our country, who we were, why we rebelled, how we became revolutionaries. I want to speak of the suffering of our mothers and our lovers, the desire to have a son, the fear, the torture and death. And, mainly, I want to speak of the dedication of idealistic, decent, and honest youth to the cause of the people. I may be mistaken about some dates and about who exactly was in each scene that I describe, but I believe everything here is accurate in its ideas and general information. Every word of the dialogue, of course, cannot be as precise as a recording, but here again, I believe it is true and accurate overall. I have chosen to describe the roles of people who were representatives of certain types rather than simply those who were "major figures."

This book includes only the revolutionary period, so it cannot tell the full story of how situations and characters developed over time. As I intend to describe in future books, with the revolution in power, with evolving ideas and shifting values, some friends became enemies and old enemies, allies.

All I can say, and not from any false modesty, is that the story I have written is only a pale reflection of reality and that no book can ever convey the greatness of a people in revolt.

I am told that every book must contain acknowledgments. I did not want to include them because it would be a very long list of people and still many would be missing, but if I have to, this is what I have to say:

To Fidel Castro, who made the history.

To Alan Rinzler, my editor, from whom I have learned how a book is made.

To Joan Goldsmith, my American friend, who has worked so hard to get this book published in the United States.

To Martha, my wife, who has accompanied me throughout the story.

July 2002
Enrique Oltuski<br>*Havana*

# A Brief
# History of Cuba

**3500 B.C.–1100 A.D.** | Various indigenous peoples inhabit the island now known as Cuba, first hunter-gatherers, then farmers and fishermen.

**1100** | The Taino people settle on the island, forming villages of thatched circular huts. Before the arrival of the Europeans, there are between 100,000 and 500,000 Tainos, who fish, weave hammocks, and grow yucca, corn, yams, and peppers. They are skilled potters and boatbuilders.

**1492** | After first landing in what is now the Bahamas, Christopher Columbus, guided by natives, first sees the island on October 27 and claims it as a Spanish colony. He writes in his journal that the people living there "are the best people in the world, without knowledge of what is evil; nor do they murder or steal. . . . All the people show the most singular loving behavior . . . and are gentle and always laughing." Within fifty years, all the natives are enslaved and destroyed; they eventually disappear, with only faint traces of mixed ancestry among the conquering Spanish settlers.

**1492–1762** | Cuba is the shipyard, center of commerce, and military base for the Spanish treasure fleets from South and Central America. Because of their vulnerability as well as their wealth and other attractions, Cuba's primary port, Havana, and other Cuban ports are frequent targets of piracy. Nevertheless, Havana prospers and by 1760 is larger than either New York or Boston.

1762 | On August 13, an armada of two hundred English warships captures Havana to open up the island to free trade. Within a year, England makes a treaty with Spain that trades Cuba for Florida but also ensures its commercial interests in the coffee, tobacco, sugar, and slave trade on the island.

1808 | Thomas Jefferson expresses a desire to purchase the island of Cuba from Napoleon Bonaparte, who was in control of Spain and her empire at the time, but the initiative does not succeed. Nevertheless, merchants from North America, France, Spain, England, and elsewhere arrive in Havana during this period to develop flourishing businesses and plantations throughout the island.

1823 | An independence movement arises, led by José Francisco Lemus, appealing primarily to students, poor white Cubans, and Negroes, both slave and free. A brief revolt fails. Subsequent insurrections in 1826 and 1827 were smashed, their leaders hanged by 40,000 Spanish troops who throng the island.

1826 | On December 9, Simón Bolívar defeats the last Spanish army in South America, and turns toward Cuba. Strong opposition from the United States, however, dissuades him from further military intervention. Many U.S. politicians fear that Cuban independence would lead to a slave insurrection similar to that in Haiti, and lobby to annex the island as a slave state.

1825–1868 | Supported by slavery and the slave trade, the wealth of Cuba, based partially on coffee but mostly on sugar, increases greatly under the dictatorship of a series of captains-general.

1848 | On May 30, prompted by a strong pro-slavery campaign led by politicians in the Southern states, President Polk proposes the purchase of Cuba. He begins negotiation with the queen of Spain, but the initiative fails when the Spanish regime is overthrown. Nevertheless, a vocal movement for annexation continues. Later, in 1857, another president, James Buchanan, promises to add Cuba to the Union, but cannot get financial backing.

**1860** | Jefferson Davis announces that if a Republican is elected president, the South will secede and simply conquer Cuba to add another slave state. Abraham Lincoln is elected and announces that the United States will not acquire Cuba so long as slavery remains there.

**1868** | A coalition of Cuban planters, freed slaves, merchants, reformists, and veterans of prior battles declare a war of independence against Spain. Their numbers grow to between 10,000 and 20,000, but they succeed only in the eastern part of the island.

**1869** | A sixteen-year-old student named José Martí founds his first newspaper, *Patria Libre,* but is arrested for a letter accusing an old friend of backing Spain. Sentenced to six years of hard labor, Martí is transferred to the Isle of Pines, then exiled to Spain in 1871. In 1879, he moves to New York City, where he works as a journalist, also producing dozens of speeches, essays, stories, and poems on the theme of independence and freedom for Cuba, and founding La Liga de Instruccion, a training school for revolutionaries.

**1880** | The civil war leaves the Cuban sugar mills and plantations in financial jeopardy as the new sugar beet also reduces prices worldwide. This brings down the old sugar oligarchy and weakens the economy and social structure, leaving the island vulnerable for North American financial, political, and cultural penetration.

**1895** | Martí returns from exile to lead a new revolutionary uprising, but is ambushed in a skirmish on May 19 and shot dead at forty-two. He remains a mythical revolutionary hero whose large body of writings has inspired generations since.

**1896** | Spain continues to oppress the rebel forces. But U.S. political opinion—fueled by a newspaper circulation war between the *Journal,* published by interventionist William Randolph Hearst, and the *Sun,* published by Martí's friend Charles Anderson Dana—strongly favors a U.S. military invasion of Cuba against Spain.

**1898** | On the evening of February 15, the U.S. battleship *Maine,* sent ostensibly on a mission of security, is blown up in the Havana harbor by unknown parties. President McKinley, reluctant to declare war, first attempts again to buy Cuba for $300 million, but negotiations break down.

In April of the same year, Spain announces an armistice in Cuba and attempts to enlist the revolutionary leader Maximo Gomez in a common cause against the North Americans. The seventy-three-year-old veteran replies that he would prefer military support from the United States (hoping for only shipments of arms), a statement that would affect U.S.-Cuban relations for the next sixty years.

Shortly thereafter, President McKinley authorizes an expedition of 70,000 U.S. soldiers to invade Cuba on the side of the rebels against Spain. At the same time, Commodore Dewey sails into Manila harbor in the Philippines to seize that island from Spain, signaling the beginning of the Spanish-American War.

On July 1, Teddy Roosevelt, McKinley's assistant secretary of the navy and a zealous supporter of U.S. military intervention in Cuba, charges up San Juan Hill near Santiago de Cuba with his Rough Riders. Ultimately the Spanish troops surrender, and U.S. forces negotiate a peace without consulting the Cuban rebel leadership. As a result, the United States assumes dominance, and the rebels remain powerless in a backseat role.

1899–1902 | Cuba is run by a U.S. military government.

1901 | In March, President McKinley signs the Platt Amendment, which guarantees the United States the right of intervention in Cuban affairs and acquires the title to land for naval stations at Guantánamo Bay for one hundred years. Cubans protest at all levels of society but remain powerless and defeated.

1902 | The U.S. military government officially withdraws, leaving the government in the control of corrupt cronies and entrepreneurs. During the first three years of so-called independence, an estimated 60 percent of Cuban land is bought by speculators and investors from North America. U.S. interests in the sugar industry increase from 15 percent to 75 percent. By 1905, however, a new serious group of liberal rebels emerge.

1906 | President Theodore Roosevelt intervenes in the chaotic and violent political situation by sending in Judge Charles Magoon as civilian governor of Cuba. By 1909, Magoon hands over office to the democratically elected José Miguel Gomez, who presides over a period of great scandals and corruption, marked by increasing violence.

1913 | Gomez is replaced by the even more venal and corrupt General Mario Garcia Menocal, who suppresses, with U.S. backing, all attempts at liberal reform.

1925 | Gerardo Machado, a former butcher, cattle robber, and member of Menocal's cabinet, emerges after a long period of disarray as a strong-arm president, who admires Mussolini and imprisons his opposition. By 1928, he has assumed dictatorial powers and regularly assassinates his enemies.

1933 | After years of violence and corruption, Machado is forced from office with the intervention of the U.S. ambassador, Sumner Welles. His handpicked successor, Carlos Miguel Cespedes, is shortly overcome by the Sergeants' Revolution, which is led by, among others, a thirty-two-year-old sergeant stenographer from the Oriente named Fulgencio Batista.

A coalition of the sergeants and university students form a new republic under a new president, Dr. Grau San Martín. Batista, now in command of the army, leads an attack on a counterrevolutionary group of officers besieged in Havana's Hotel Nacional. After a bloody shootout with heavy causalities on both sides, his troops emerge victorious. As a result, Batista's popularity and power are consolidated.

1934 | Batista takes over the government, operating behind the scenes as the greatest power in the country, while a series of figureheads hold office as president.

1940 | Batista himself is elected president. He sustains his hold on the office through violent repression of broad opposition and by alliance with the United States and with criminal elements. He offers Cuba as a valuable air and naval base during World War II.

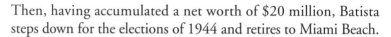

Then, having accumulated a net worth of $20 million, Batista steps down for the elections of 1944 and retires to Miami Beach.

**1944** | Ramon Grau San Martín is elected again, but betrays the democratic ideals of his supporters by presiding over a corrupt regime based on bribery and fraud. Among his most prominent early advocates is Eduardo Chibás, who attempts to keep alive the revolutionary dreams of the liberals and university students who originally backed the regime. Eventually Chibás breaks with Grau San Martín and decides to run for office himself.

**1948** | Carlos Prío, Grau's Minister of Labor, defeats Chibás and two other candidates for the office of president. Prío and his brothers amass a fortune in office through corruption, bribery, and graft, while Chibás rails against them on the radio as a popular leader of the opposition. Increasingly unbalanced, however, Chibás shoots himself after an incendiary broadcast and dies ten days later, leaving the left liberal movement in disorder and despair.

**1952** | Instead of participating in free elections, Batista returns from his exile in Miami to seize power by force with a coalition of conspirators who overthrow Prío in a coup d'état.

An era of still greater and unprecedented oppression, violence, and gangsterism begins. One of the reform candidates for Congress in the election that Batista has canceled is a twenty-three-year-old law student named Fidel Castro.

**1953** | On July 26, Castro leads an armed attack on the Moncada barracks in Santiago de Cuba. Quickly defeated, arrested, and sentenced to the Isle of Pines, Castro escapes death with the protection of a sympathetic judge, having pled his case with the dramatic two-hour speech "History Will Absolve Me." Now a national hero, Castro is freed in 1955 and flees the country for Mexico. Later that year, he meets Che Guevara, an Argentinean doctor, intellectual, and revolutionary.

**1956** | On November 28, Fidel, Che, and eighty other poorly armed revolutionaries sail on the *Granma,* a 58-foot-long wooden yacht they have bought from an American for $15,000. Overcrowded, seasick, and often lost at sea, they finally land on the southwest corner of the Oriente province on December 2.

**1957** | Batista claims that Castro has been killed and the rebellion destroyed, but on January 17, Fidel leads a surviving group of about twenty men on an attack on La Plata barracks, which results in a military victory and the capture of a small cache of arms.

Exactly one month later, on February 17, the *New York Times* correspondent Herbert Matthews finds Fidel Castro in the Sierra Maestra and interviews him at length, a report that fills the front page of the *Times* for several days and electrifies the world. Castro is universally hailed as a hero in his struggle against the draconian dictator Batista. At the time, Castro has only eighteen surviving followers, but during this interview he exaggerates the number of men under his command by marching the same troops back and forth before the eyes of Matthews.

Meanwhile, the 26th of July and other revolutionary movements throughout the rest of the island create increasing mayhem in the cities and countryside, blowing up buildings, calling strikes, attacking the presidential palace, burning crops, raising money, and starting underground newspapers. Batista responds with increasingly brutal oppression, which draws more and more supporters to the revolution, and Castro gradually emerges as the primary leader of a broad spectrum of revolutionary groups.

**1958** | Castro organizes his growing band of rebels into separate military columns commanded by his brother Raúl, Che Guevara, and Camilo Cienfuegos. At the start they are successful in carefully planned guerilla attacks on hapless Batista outposts. Eventually they are able to achieve major military victories against larger numbers of the regular army.

Batista suspends all civil rights and attempts to maintain power through increasingly repressive measures. The United States begins to lose faith and suspends all arms shipment to the Cuban dictatorship. Nevertheless, on May 24, Batista attempts one last "Big Push" against the Sierra Maestra. Thousands of his well-armed troops, led by demoralized, corrupt, cruel, and lazy officers, are soundly defeated, and the dictatorship is in shock.

In August, Castro sends a column of rebel troops led by Camilo Cienfuegos toward Havana, while Che Guevara leads a second column further westward to Las Villas, where he eventually wins a ferocious battle for the city of Santa Clara early in December.

The war is basically over and the revolution triumphant. Batista and his cronies flee the country by airplane after celebrating New Year's Eve, December 31, 1958. He takes with him an estimated $300 million.

1959 | Fidel Castro arrives in Havana on January 8. During an evening speech at an old fortress before a crowd of hundreds of thousands of hysterically happy people, two white doves alight on his shoulder.

The honeymoon is brief. The revolution remains a tremendous threat to U.S. business interests: U.S. companies own 80 to 100 percent of Cuba's utilities, mines, cattle ranches, and oil refineries; 40 percent of the sugar industry; and 50 percent of the public railways. As Castro sets up a nationwide system of education, housing, and land distribution to landless peasants, the Eisenhower administration—particularly Secretary of State John Foster Dulles and his brother, Allen Dulles, the head of the CIA—become increasingly uncomfortable with the new revolutionary government.

1960 | Castro nationalizes the telephone company, banks, sugar mills, distilleries, rice and textile mills, hotels, insurance companies, and 382 other U.S. businesses. When the United States refuses to purchase any more Cuban sugar or sell Cuba any oil, the Soviet Union begins purchasing the entire Cuban sugar crop at inflated prices and selling oil to Cuba at prices well below the market.

Later the same year, outgoing President Eisenhower approves a plan by the Dulles brothers to arm and train a secret expedition of antirevolutionary Cubans and mercenaries to attack Cuba under U.S. military protection.

**1961** | President Kennedy, assured by the CIA that no American military forces would participate and that the Cuban people would rise up in arms to overthrow Castro, approves the inherited plan to invade the Bay of Pigs on April 17. Within seventy-two hours, the attacking troops are defeated, with Castro personally leading the defense.

On December 1 of the same year, Castro informs Cuba and the world that Cuba is officially a Marxist-Leninist state.

**1962** | On October 14, a U-2 spy plane flying over western Cuba reports Soviet-built missile sites with potential to deliver nuclear warheads to the United States within minutes of launch. President Kennedy demands that they be removed, but Nikita Kruschev, premier of the Soviet Union, refuses. On the verge of a full-scale nuclear war, Kruschev ultimately relents and withdraws the missiles, without consulting Castro.

**1963** | Under the Trading with the Enemy Act, the United States begins a long policy of an embargo against Cuba that prevents any American from exporting or importing medical supplies, technology, commodities, or other goods to or from Cuba.

**1989** | With the fall of the Soviet Union, Cuba is unable to sell its sugar at high prices or buy oil at low prices. Castro declares a "special period" of economic hardship and rebuilding.

**1996** | The U.S. Senate and House of Representatives pass the Helms-Burton bill, which punishes any U.S. citizen or foreign country who trades with Cuba, and eliminates the power of the president to respond to political and economic changes by limiting any Cuban policy decisions directly to Congress.

By the end of the 1990s, the Cuban government declares that Cuba's economy has recovered nearly to the level it had reached in 1989.

**2002** | Fidel Castro celebrates his forty-third year in office.

# Before the Plains and the Sierra

## chapter 1

# Batista's Coup d'État

I looked up from the drawing and stared out the window of my classroom. On benches under the trees, students sat and talked or read between classes. I looked back at the drawing board. I took out a T-square and went over the plan: the parking was off; not enough cars would fit. I would have to redo part of it to enlarge the parking lot. I scanned the drawing, trying out different proportions, reviewing the requirements. No use! My head was pounding, and sweat was pouring off of me. I checked my watch: the bell was about to ring. I lit a cigar and stared out the window again.

It was early March, 1952—only three months until summer vacation at the University of Miami. Then I could go back to Cuba. I pictured the airplane making its descent to Rancho Boyeros Airport. Soon the coastline would appear and then Havana, block after block of streets and buildings, as orderly as a map. Then bright green fields of sugarcane, studded with royal palms, the rows interrupted by fields.

I would go straight to Santa Clara, the capital of the province of Las Villas in the central part of Cuba, about two hundred miles east of Havana. I would stay home a few weeks, get spoiled by my mother. I would spend the day in bed, reading the many books I had acquired over the course of the year.

Afterward I would start going out, visiting my friends. We would spend evenings in the park, talking about a thousand things: school, politics, girls. Then a month in Varadero: the beach and nights at the Bolera.

And what was I doing here? Whatever possessed me to go to school in the North? How could I have left Cuba!

The bell rang. I packed up my drafting tools, rolled up the drawings, and went down the stairs. Beyond the shade of the huge trees, the glare of midday awaited me. The street was in the sun. I hurried along to the student apartment I lived in just a block and a half away. When I got there, the living room was full of students, most of them Cuban. They were all silent, listening to the radio.

My roommate Manolo, a young man from Havana, turned to me and said, "Did you hear the news? Batista has taken power!"

In those days there was no large or vocal community of Cuban exiles in Miami. Only a few Cubans were living there at that time, most of whom were young and impoverished. They had come to the States in the hope of finding more economic opportunities to improve their financial condition than they could in the oppressive, corrupt, and discriminatory society of Cuba. And of course there was also a handful of Cuban students, such as myself and my friends, who were studying at the university.

Two days later, the Cuban students were still talking about Batista's coup. I joined a group standing around the living room sofa. At its center, Manolo was leafing through *Bohemia,* a magazine just in from Cuba. It had pages of pictures. There was one of officials at the presidential palace surrounded by tanks. Another was captioned, "The president leaving the palace." It showed President Prío—who had been a distinguished student leader in his youth but had become just another corrupt politician when he achieved office—with a worried expression. During those terrible moments, he looked ridiculous wrapped up in a teenager's sweater. His brothers Paco and Antonio were with him. For some reason Prío was smiling in one of the pictures.

Manolo finished looking at those pages and started reading the section "On Cuba."

The third Sunday of Carnival, with its popular celebrations, was over. Just after midnight, on the 10th, the Havana night seemed quiet as usual.

But it didn't last: some people were not sleeping. Shortly after 2 A.M. a pair of cars pulled out of a well-known estate in Arroyo Arenas. The first car held armed men in civilian clothing; in the second, accompanied by an army officer, was a medium-sized, dark-skinned man dressed in sports clothes.

"What a son of a bitch!" someone shouted.
Manolo continued reading:

A few blocks before arriving at the Columbia National Military Headquarters—where the general staff of the army was located—the mystery man ordered the escort car preceding him to stop, telling his companion:
"Captain Robaina, we'll change cars here."
"But General, they're expecting us to be in this car . . ."
"Yes, but we'll take the other."
The order of General Fulgencio Batista was carried out before the vehicles drove on.
His co-conspirators inside the garrison—lieutenants and captains—welcomed their old boss, who did not conceal his emotion, his gratitude for their show of enthusiasm.

Manolo read on, interrupted constantly by comments and exclamations from his companions.

At 4 A.M. the presidential palace learned that Batista was at the military base. Paco and Antonio Prío hurried to alert their brother, quietly sleeping in La Chata, the presidential retreat on the outskirts of Havana where he usually spent the weekend with his family. A few minutes after five, a worried-looking Carlos Prío arrived at the palace, accompanied by his brothers and several friends and government officials.

All of them realized the gravity of the situation, and each offered his advice to the shaky president.

"What you should do, Carlos," one suggested, "is move your government to some province that is still loyal and put up a fight. The people will follow you."

Shouts of opposition went up, arguments arose, and Prío looked around the group indecisively.

"Gentlemen," said Eduardo Suárez Rivas, "let us think carefully before we act."

"What a bunch of jerks!" Everyone talked at once. Manolo yelled, "Let me go on."

At 7:30 A.M., a committee from the Students Federation (known as the FEU) arrived at the door of the presidential palace. They were worried about the national situation. The delegation of students was anxious to speak with the president:

"Mr. President, as you know the FEU has sometimes disapproved of your acts and has often criticized your government, but we are here today to offer our help. The university, faithful to its revolutionary tradition, must uphold democratic rights, and so we will support you."

Prío seemed moved by their generous offer, but made some vague response. One of the student leaders asked:

"Mr. President, are you going to lead the fight?"

"Yes, I am going to fight, of course."

"Do you have a plan to develop resistance?"

"We are studying the situation."

The students pressed him: "Mr. President, we are here to discuss ways to resist the takeover. We don't have any weapons. They should be distributed at the university. We want to fight!"

Carlos Prío tried to shake off his inertia: "Yes, that's right, we will send guns where they're needed." The students set off for the university.

The telephone rang: a long-distance call. Prío took it. Then, without emotion: "The city of Matanzas still supports us."

"Let's get out of here!" A hysterical shout from Paco Prío.

Prío was stunned again. Finally they left. The head of the palace guard asked for instructions. One of Prío's aides answered in a low voice: "Do not fight."

Prío then left the presidential palace, sought refuge in a foreign embassy, and finally left the country, heading for Miami.

"Holy Mary, what faggots!" Again everyone talked at once. Manolo turned the page. Close-ups of Batista. More photos. The Havana candidate for governor, Partido Accion Unitaria leader Alberto Salas Amaro, talking to Batista. General Batista surrounded by sympathizers. Papo, son of the new head of the state, standing by his father, wearing a smug smile. The first meeting of the new cabinet at the military headquarters. Batista giving them a little lecture. Politicians and friends arriving on the scene. The wife of General Batista, with several friends, entering the garrison. The offices of the general staff, all abustle.

All of us were truly disgusted with what we saw. Once again the forces of corruption, greed, and violence had been victorious in our nation.

We had founded a fraternity not too long before. Superficially a social group, it brought together students from every country in Latin America. Our hero was the great South American revolutionary Simón Bolívar, and our objective was to unite all the Latin peoples of the continent into a great nation or federation of states. The organization had certain conspiratorial aspects. Some members came from the highest ranks of the Latin American bourgeoisie. Others, like me, came from backgrounds that had been originally quite humble but had gradually achieved the wealth, status, and education that led us to cross the line in social standing and qualify for a North American university.

My parents had married in Poland when they were nineteen years old. Cousins who had already emigrated to Cuba wrote to them about the beauties of the island and the opportunities for work. As Jews in Poland, they were discriminated against and isolated in ghettos, so they left for the New World, arriving in the year 1929.

My father, Bernardo Oltuski, was an enterprising man; in Cuba, beginning as a simple shoemaker, he rose to become the owner of several shoe factories, retail stores, warehouses, and tanneries. His brand of footwear was distributed all over the country, and he had as many as two hundred employees. He was never a millionaire, but he had achieved some hundreds of thousands of dollars in capital, which was a huge amount of money at that time. Because upper-middle-class people were accustomed to sending their children to study "in the North," I went along with the idea and came to the University of Miami in Florida, where the weather was similar to that of Cuba.

We Latin American students were split in two groups: the majority, from the upper class, were reactionaries and recalcitrant Catholics; the minority group, which I led, was middle class, containing business and professional people. What united us was a strong nationalistic sentiment, our language, our customs, and the distance from home.

A few days after Batista's coup, I was straightening the bow tie on my dinner jacket when I heard Manolo's croon: "Let's go, let's go, let's go, get into the conga line, get into the conga line . . ."

We got into Roberto's Oldsmobile convertible and drove off. We were going out with the three Urdaneta sisters. They were daughters of a former minister of Pérez Jiménez—the horrible Venezuelan dictator who had stolen millions. Mr. Urdaneta had bought a small palace on Biscayne Boulevard, joined the flourishing Miami social scene, and became a developer, building new homes on the islands around the city.

I had some qualms about dating the Urdaneta sisters. But they were so pretty! Tonight I was taking Ana, the oldest sister, who was twenty, almost as old as me, at twenty-two. There was an unspoken affection between us. We waited in the living room for the girls to come down. Finally they appeared at the top of the stairs.

It was the usual fraternity party. A lot of drinking and fooling around. A few people were already dancing. The band started playing "Autumn Leaves," and Ana and I got up to dance. We made a smooth couple, dancing with eyes closed, just barely avoiding bumping into the other couples. The music stopped, and I took her hand and led her out to the garden.

When we came back, the party was in full swing. My fraternity brothers were in charge, and the band was playing Latin American music. I saw Manolo at the head of a conga line, which immediately surrounded me and separated me from Ana. We kept changing partners. One of the turns threw me together with Peggy.

"Enrique," she said, "I'll be waiting for you at home after the dance."

"I'm going with Manolo and Roberto."

"Bring them along, but only men."

"Only men for lonely women?"

"Yes, single men for single women." And she smiled with pleasure, in anticipation.

The party was almost over when Ana and I got back together. At our table there were a few jokes about our new relationships. When we dropped off the sisters, I passed along Peggy's invitation to Robert and Manolo.

"That American is too much!" Manolo declared, rubbing his hands together.

We put the roof of the car down and sped off to the south. The early morning air could not dry our sweaty faces. Robert stopped the car in front of the huge white building. We went into the house. There were several girls, and Roberto and Manolo stayed in the living room while I went to the kitchen in search of a drink. It was warm, and I went out to the large patio. A quiet splash caught my attention—somebody was swimming in the pool.

"Come on in!" I heard Peggy's voice.

"I don't have a swimsuit," I replied.

"That doesn't matter. Come on!" Peggy repeated.

I undressed quickly and dove into the water. When I came up, a body encircled me.

Now it was June, and the summer vacation was approaching. On one Sunday, my friends and I were watching a baseball game on television.

"Strike two!" the announcer said.

"Miñosa slugged it," Roberto exclaimed.

"Incredible! That black put a lot on the ball," said Manolo.

Between innings, Manolo said, "Gentlemen, vacation time at last. We were always talking about it, and now it's here. I'm looking forward to three months of fishing!"

"For what?" Roberto asked.

"Boy, all kinds of fish. But the one I like best is the marlin."

"This summer I am going to spend some time with you, Manolo," I said.

"Of course! We'll have some fun." He thought for a while. "If Batista lets us. There have already been some protests, and the University of Havana is fired up."

"Good, but I don't think it will go any further," Roberto said. "Batista is Batista. He'll crush them."

"Maybe you're right, " Manolo replied, "but what I want is to catch some marlin."

I couldn't contain myself: "Christ, what a conformist!"

Manolo gave me a surprised look. "Hey, watch it! And what have you done for the betterment of mankind lately?"

I felt an impotent rage. "Nothing . . . yet."

Roberto added, "That's what everybody says, but real revolutionaries are a different thing. They are extinct in Cuba." He gave me a scornful look. "Would you give up this fine life you lead?"

"Of course I would!" I said, excitedly. "Don't think my father was born rich. When he was young, he was just a shoemaker."

"And mine sold tobacco," Manolo said with a smile, "but I have acquired a taste for marlin fishing, and I'm not about to give it up."

Unlike Manolo, I grew more heated: "The life I lead has not sealed my eyes. This is an unjust society, and Batista has done what he has because many people are as lazy as you. You are the one who can't see straight!"

Manolo got serious: "God damn it, who do you think you are? You spend your life screwing around, and now you get all patriotic. You couldn't take candy from a baby."

"You shithead!" I shouted.

"Fag!" shot back Manolo.

"Son of a bitch!"

We began to fight until friends separated us and things quieted down.

## chapter 2

# First Revolutionary Impulses

By now it was August, and my summer vacation in Cuba was drawing to a close. I had been dividing my time between my family and my friends, but the days were flying by, and soon I would have to return to Miami.

My family lived in a district in the middle of Santa Clara, a city of more than one hundred thousand inhabitants. Our street was narrow, with raised walkways, little traffic, and tall houses with red tile roofs and colonial-style grates on the windows. All our neighbors were like family. If people became ill, there would always be someone to care for them. There were small shopkeepers, businessmen, and some university graduates. Despite the improvement in my father's fortunes, he never considered moving to a more exclusive district. He was wrapped up in his work, and it was my mother who took care of my younger sister and me.

In addition to their friendships with the neighbors, my parents occasionally got together with other Jewish families of the city. There could not have been more than fifty families who met at a small synagogue near our house for religious observances and social events like weddings and bar mitzvahs. At home and in the synagogue, we all spoke only Yiddish. Everywhere else, we spoke Spanish. My parents were not orthodox Jews, but our home did have the flavor of Yiddish Eastern European culture. My mother made the traditional Jewish dishes I loved—knedlach, kreplach, herring—and on Passover we would import my favorite matzo from the United States for our seder.

I knew the children of the families we saw at the synagogue, but really my friends were my Christian neighbors of the district or from school. I never felt the slightest discrimination for being Jewish; rather, I was a curiosity.

My contact with the people of the non-Jewish world made me more and more like them. I was interested not in the Jewish hero Theodore Herzl but in José Martí, the great patriotic Cuban who had led the fight against Spain and whose thoughts still guide us today.

My father, however, never really identified as I did with Cuba. For him, the motherland was Israel, and after the founding of the Jewish state in 1948, I remember visiting him at his office many times when he would be giving money to various Zionist organizers who would come to him for donations.

As an employer, my father always tried to be just and fair, but he didn't think that the big problems of poverty and injustice in Cuba had anything to do with him. He was a businessman, not a politician or revolutionary.

Guillermo Rodríguez—Guillermito—was one of my better friends. He and his sister Martha had been my companions in my senior year of high school. After graduating, they had both left to study at the University of Havana, he in medicine and she in pharmacology. They were both influenced by their father, a distinguished doctor in Santa Clara.

From my conversations with Guillermito that summer of 1952, I discovered that he thought just as I did: that we had to rebel against Batista and fight on behalf of the poor classes in our country. Through Guillermito I learned that the first insurrectionary movements had already been organized that year, and that he had joined the National Revolutionary Movement (Movimiento Nacional Revolucionaria, or MNR), led by the university professor Rafael García Barcena. García Barcena had fought against the dictator Gerardo Machado as a student and was known as the Professor, in part to disguise his identity for security reasons. Guillermito and I agreed to go together to Havana so I could also join the MNR.

We were climbing the gigantic staircase to the University of Havana that hot August night. Soon I would be returning to Miami. I did not want to leave without strengthening relations with the nucleus of students beginning to arm themselves against Batista.

We reached the top of the stairs and turned toward the offices of the Students Federation (FEU), where I met various students who were in the MNR. When the president of the FEU arrived, we discussed the possibility of obtaining aid from the United States. We spoke quietly, with the lights turned low. The door opened and closed regularly, as small groups of men went in and out. Occasionally I heard the dull sound of gunfire. ("The future action groups are practicing," a student named Carbonell told me.)

We decided that I should speak with a few of the leaders, perhaps even meet the Professor. We went downstairs and were starting to cross the small plaza, when a car emerged from the shadows and screeched to a halt in front of us. In a moment we were surrounded by three men with machine guns. They gave us a thorough search, and the one in charge said, "What, shooting off your guns, eh? One of these days we'll come into the university and screw your heads on straight."

"Captain Castellanos, you are mistaken," said one of our group.

"Mistaken, my ass!" exploded the captain. "Keep up that shit and see what it gets you."

"Should we take them with us, Captain?" one of his henchmen asked.

"No . . . not this time. But watch out."

They got into their car, slamming the doors, and drove down the street.

We got to our own car, and as we got in, Jaime, an old friend from Santa Clara who now lived in Havana, said, "Think they followed us? Took our license number? If my father found out, he'd have a fit."

"Don't be a jerk," someone said.

"I'm not talking about me. It's my family," maintained Jaime, turning the wheel to pull out between two cars. Finally making a

sharp right, he hit the gas and almost ran into a black Buick racing past us. Somebody said, "It's Captain Castellanos!"

Guillermito disappeared down the long, dark corridor. We were in an old Havana mansion that had been turned into a clinic. A lot of these private clinics had sprung up lately. Just about everybody was going into medicine, and then they couldn't find work when they graduated. The big private clinics were run by a handful of famous doctors and were beyond the reach of most people. There were only a few public hospitals, and you could get into them only with the recommendation of some politician. So young doctors had begun to join together in small cooperative clinics.

I glanced around the dimly lit space. The living room was now a waiting room. There were benches against the walls and, in a corner, a metal desk painted white. The rest of our group hadn't arrived yet, so I passed the time by trying to read the signs on the walls. That's what I was doing when I heard Guillermito's voice behind me: "Hey, Enrique, let me introduce you to Dr. Faustino Pérez, member of the National Council of the MNR."

I turned to shake the hand of a young man of average height, with fine features and blue eyes—striking even in this dim room—which he fixed on me. He was wearing a white smock and carrying a doctor's bag. We exchanged greetings. While we talked, Faustino studied me. I must have passed the test, because he said, "There's a bright side to everything. Batista shook us all out of our haze. Of course, overthrowing Batista is only a start: we must go farther to establish the social justice Professor García Barcena describes. With the guidance of the man who has fought for his principles all these years, and with the energy of our youth, there is no doubt that we will prevail!" His voice was smooth and warm in the tepid light of that room. "Our direction is clear: no playing politics, no compromising. Only armed revolution can give us the power we want. And besides, to succeed in Cuba you need a gun in your hand. The words of Martí show us the way!" He reached into his bag, pulled out a pamphlet, and handed it to me. "I am a Martí disciple," he said.

I flipped through the book—quotes from Martí relevant to the situation confronting our country, selected by Faustino. "I will study it thoroughly," I said in parting.

The next morning, I was still in bed when the phone rang.

"Hello."

"Enrique?"

"Yes."

"Listen, it's Guillermito. The Professor is meeting us later, at his house. I'll see you at two."

"Good," I answered, and hung up.

I threw myself back into bed—I had nothing to do until afternoon. I closed my eyes. Guillermito always brought back memories of Martha.

Our senior year of high school had just started, and I got back from vacation late. Roll was called, and a new voice answered, "Present."

In the next class, she was called to the blackboard. She was very petite. Dark hair. Dark skin. Almond-shaped eyes. A delicate nose. Her lips, slightly parted, revealed her white teeth.

Pablo, sitting next to me, seemed to follow my thoughts, because he whispered, "She's the sister of the Rooster." (That's what we called Guillermito.) After that, I kept looking around for her, hoping to meet her eyes and feel the heat move through my body.

One day I suggested that we study together. She agreed. We talked while we did our homework, and got to know each other. When we discussed religion, we saw a huge abyss open between us.

We tried to convert each other, but our beliefs did not waver. Martha was a Catholic, as unbending as the nuns who trained her, with all the intransigence of Sunday masses and the mysticism of religious retreats. I had been an atheist since I was fifteen. But I had been brought up in a Jewish home and small Jewish community. My family was not orthodox, but we did observe the main Jewish holidays: Passover, Rosh Hashanah, Yom Kippur.

Before my thirteenth birthday, I began preparing for my bar mitzvah. Then I would be considered a man in the synagogue, with full religious rights; according to Jewish tradition, you have to be at least thirteen to read the Torah, the book of God.

Directing my study was an old Viennese cantor who had lost his voice and now ran the synagogue in Santa Clara. We had no rabbi, just the cantor, whom we called the Maestro. He was a good man, both intelligent and more cultured than the families of Russian and Polish Jews who left the ghetto to set sail for America.

I completed the training and went through my Bar Mitzvah as was expected of me, reading the Torah and Haftorah. The only present I remember or have kept from this occasion was the first five books of the old Testament in Hebrew, with the date of my bar mitzvah printed in golden letters on the front cover.

During my lessons with the Maestro, I asked him my first questions about the logic of religion, and he answered with more sophisticated arguments than did my father and his friends, who simply took refuge in some Biblical quote. Nevertheless, the Maestro did not manage to quiet my doubts, and when I began to study biology and physics, I broke with my parents' religion and became an atheist. That precipitated a long quest through history and philosophy books, studying bourgeois thinkers. I was looking for something to believe in, but each time I thought I had settled on the ideal doctrine, I would find some new theory.

It was during this period that I met Martha. I tried my best to prove that her faith was wrong. But it was useless, and I liked her too much to start a love affair with no future. At that point it seemed impossible that a Jew and a Catholic could have a long-lasting intimate relationship. She graduated that year and left to study in Havana. Mutual friends told me about her without my asking.

Guillermito arrived at two. We caught the crowded minibus on the corner. We could barely stand up, clinging to the bars along the ceiling. We got off two blocks from our destination. There was a blonde girl playing on the sidewalk in front of the house. "That's the Professor's daughter," Guillermito told me. When we reached her he said, "Hey, tell your father the police want to see him." She disappeared into the house, and we went to the door.

A young woman came out, her worried expression changing into a smile when she saw Guillermito. "How nice . . . You must be the Rooster! Come in."

We walked in. A medium-sized man, somewhat older, came out and offered his hand. A vigorous shake conveyed enthusiasm, self-confidence. This was the famous Professor, Rafael García Barcena. He joked with Guillermito, then turned to me: "Everyone has told me about you. We think you can be useful to the Movement. First, by mobilizing public opinion against the Batista dictatorship among students and in the Cuban colony in Miami. And second, by trying to obtain supplies for armed warfare. Our strategy calls for the overthrow of Batista by a force made up of young revolutionary army officers and students."

He stared fixedly at me through the lenses of his glasses, as if measuring the effect his words were having. He was placing a great deal of confidence in me to tell me all this. He continued, "When the time is ripe, a combined force, the new military plus the students, will capture the bastions of the dictatorship. We will purify the army, remaking it into a revolutionary force, and then establish a government that will sweep away all the crimes of the past and set up a regime of social justice. It will be a society not of proletarians but of proprietors."

His eyes burned with the same spark I had seen in Faustino's. He wanted me to tell him my own ideas, but after hearing his words, I had nothing to add.

We drank coffee while the Professor and Guillermito talked about the university. I thought about what I had just heard. Among all the many revolutionary groups during this period, García Barcena was the only one to organize for an armed revolt. That's what attracted me about him, as well as his ideas about changing society. He was not a Marxist; far from it: his motto was "instead of all proletarians, we should all be owners. Everyone should own, rather than no one should own." But at that time, before Fidel, he had the most credibility, because my friends and I had by this time concluded that the struggle could be effective only if it was armed.

After a while, other people were waiting to see García Barcena, so we left.

## chapter 3

# Student in the United States

It was election time back at the University of Miami that autumn of 1952. We decided to join together with several fraternities to form a new all-university student party. It was suggested that one of our members run for an executive position. I was the logical candidate, because in addition to being a member of the fraternity, I was president of the Foreign Students Club. So I was nominated for the position of treasurer of the new combined student organization.

Soon there were Spanish posters all over the university. Conga players, with their tumbadoras, began to show up at meetings.

Our party's presidential candidate was a law student named John Buchanan. I discovered that he had been to Latin America and spoke a little Spanish. We became friends. He was exceptionally intelligent and really cut out for politics. He knew everybody. He handled the campaign expertly.

Under his able direction, we easily won the election. That triumph brought new honors. Soon I belonged to more than fifteen organizations and naturally spent less time studying.

Through my new relations both inside and outside the university, I tried to carry out the goals the National Revolutionary Movement (MNR) had set for me. It wasn't easy.

We used to go to a restaurant called the Minerva. The jukebox had plenty of Spanish records, and the food was good.

After the fall of his government, Prío moved to Miami. Some of his security men ate at the Minerva, and I soon decided to make use of this corrupt and defeated exile group to contact their arms salesmen.

Dealing with Prío's men disgusted me, however, and I soon realized it was going to go nowhere. Anything associated with Prío was filthy. They obviously wanted to bring politics into their offers of aid, and when they told me, "We mentioned you to the president"—as they still referred to Prío—"and he really wants to meet you," I put an end to these troubling negotiations, as I knew that nothing would ever come from their insincere efforts.

It was the day of an open house at the Buchanans' new mansion. This beautiful residence sat atop a hill on a smooth rise of lawn. It was a pale rose color with white moldings and a tile roof; it had huge windows with colored glass that softened the Florida sunlight and kept the air-conditioned rooms cool. Stylish furniture rested on thick carpets; modern paintings with tropical motifs decorated the walls.

John took us to see the library. The Buchanans were hardly upstarts. In fact, they were an old New England family that had moved to Florida, a family with a history and enough of a past to have accumulated a library.

John had carefully selected the group of students invited to his house that day. Many were Latin American, because the Buchanans moved in the best circles of the Latin colony, and they had interests in common. The Urdaneta sisters, whose father did business with the elder Buchanan, were present, of course.

While we walked through the new gardens, filled with rare Latin American plants, someone suggested a ball game. We divided into teams, one American, the other Latin. We won, the girls looking on. Back in the huge living room, the sweaty players were met by cool air and cold daiquiris.

From the middle of a group, Buchanan's father shouted, "No complaining now, Enrique—I hear the Latin American team won."

John had told his father about my activities at the university, and we also had had a few discussions about relations between the United

States and Latin America. They liked me and welcomed me, imagining no doubt that over the years I would evolve from an angry young man, idealistic and nationalistic, and become more pragmatic, prominent in business and politics, a person worth cultivating.

Amid general laughter, I replied, "See, we're not so bad."

"I never said you were bad, simply young and rebellious; when you give up revolutions and start some serious work, you will be a significant force."

Everyone agreed, but I felt deeply pained by his scorn. I said, "We do not make revolutions because we like to make them but because when all the other routes have been exhausted, there is no choice but force. Besides, you call everything a revolution here in the U.S.A., even the slightest change. When it's a true revolution, one is enough."

This time there were no smiles, and Buchanan asked, "And what would you consider a real revolution?"

"A true revolution would not benefit just a few, but all the people. It would establish a society based on equal rights; one where men would be brothers, not beasts preying on each other; where the government would protect the national interest, not sell it to the highest bidder, even a foreign one."

One of Buchanan's friends spoke up: "That is what we have in the United States!"

And I took advantage of this to add, "Then what we want is not bad."

Buchanan felt he had been misrepresented. "No one said that what you want is bad, but you have to make it happen, and it doesn't seem that you are, to judge from what I read in the newspaper every day."

"That's true, but what do you expect? We have to fight at home and abroad," I said.

"Oh, I see, Enrique," said John's father, "it's all our fault."

"Not all, Mr. Buchanan, but some, yes. There are plenty of examples to prove it; Cuba is just the most recent case."

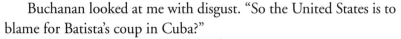

Buchanan looked at me with disgust. "So the United States is to blame for Batista's coup in Cuba?"

"In large part, yes. Without encouragement from you Americans, the pro-Batista elements would not have dared to act against the will of the people; they couldn't have been sure their government would be recognized in a few days if they hadn't had promises beforehand."

Buchanan's friends did not think this was fair. Eduardo Andrade, an Ecuadorian student, felt he should come to the aid of the North Americans: "Come on, Enrique, that's not true; the government of my country was elected by the people."

"Really, Eduardo, do not be so naive; your government has about as much popular support as Batista's; it is just not quite so obvious in your case."

John Buchanan spoke for the first time: "Let it go, Eduardo; you know Enrique always has to win."

Everyone laughed, and I took the opportunity to slip out. I got a fresh daiquiri, lit a cigarette, and went into the library to look at the books. In the living room, someone put on a record, and couples started dancing.

After a while, John came in. "What happened to you? I've been looking all over. Are you still upset by the conversation?"

"I certainly am. They are completely misinformed and stubborn in their prejudice. And even worse, they don't know it."

"Look, I don't want argue, but there is one thing they are right about. The United States has to extend its economic borders. To do so it must treat other people with respect, just as the top leadership does in this country with its own people—that is, improving their living conditions, integrating them into society economically while directing and organizing them. Anything else would be playing into the hands of the Communists."

I said to him, "That may sound more attractive to you, but it doesn't make the future you offer our people any brighter."

"You are just an idealist, Enrique."

"It has not always been this bad, even in Cuba."

"No," he agreed. "A reactionary military man takes power against the will of the people, and we are such fools that we support him against the more progressive elements. What have we gained in return? The hatred of everyone. If we had been faithful to our national system, we would have done just the opposite."

I decided to test him: "And how faithful are you to your ideals?"

"I have my principles."

"Would those principles include, for example, helping us obtain arms to overthrow Batista?"

John looked surprised. "Are you serious?"

"I have never been more serious."

"Trust me," he said decisively, "and you will find out."

We were changing classes. Jorge Rodríguez shouted over to me, "Coming over tonight?"

"Yes," I yelled back.

I went to Jorge's house most Friday nights. It was boxing night on television. Lolita, Jorge's wife, stocked up on cold beer and pork chicharrones, put the kids to bed early, and the three of us would sit down to watch the fights and talk about the past week, what was going on at home, at school, in politics.

Jorge and Lolita were Puerto Rican. Lolita worked as a secretary in a company that had something to do with Latin American farm products, and Jorge was studying engineering at the university; he had a scholarship through the GI Bill and a part-time job as a draftsman besides.

Lolita set down the cold beer and put clean ashtrays and plates of chicharrones and olives on the table between us. The small screen displayed the latest Chevrolet.

"If we could scrape up a few extra dollars we could afford a new car," said Jorge, his eyes on the TV. "Ours needs paint, and pretty soon repairs will cost more than a new one."

"That's true," agreed Lolita. "You should see the convertible the Garcías got!"

They launched into a careful analysis of the family budget, trying to find the money.

"I would make ten dollars more every week if I went in an hour early every day," Jorge said.

"And I could teach Spanish at night," added Lolita.

The sound of the theme song drew our eyes back to the television: the boxing match was starting. I stretched out in my easy chair and put my feet up on the end table; Lolita and Jorge did the same.

Between rounds, while the announcers talked to the boxers, Lolita went to the kitchen for more food. I asked Jorge, "Have you heard anything?"

"You mean about the boat?"

"Right."

"I spoke with the man, and he agrees in principle. He wants to talk to you. He says that if our project is serious, he won't care about money; he is a revolutionary."

"Jorge, are you sure about him?"

"Completely. We spent two years together on a PT boat in the Pacific. The war lets you really get to know a man."

I finished my beer. "Have you seen the boat?"

"Yes, I saw it. It is military surplus but still in good shape. It has just been sailing around Florida, but could make it to Cuba easily, taking over five hundred tons of supplies."

"Can we go look at it tomorrow night?"

"Sure," Jorge agreed.

We heard the gong announcing the first round of the main event.

"Lolita, the beer, the fight's starting!" yelled Jorge.

"Still awake?" asked John, coming into my room.

"Yes, I'm reading."

"What?"

"*Parallel Lives,* by Plutarch."

"What, looking for inspiration?"

I sat up in bed. "It's always good to know the past; it teaches good lessons, don't you agree?"

"Yes," said John. "Sometimes history just seems to be repeating itself, but with different characters."

John took off his jacket and reclined on the bed. He took off his tie and said with a smile, "I have good news . . ." I jumped up. John continued, "You can have the weapons you want."

"How?"

"By paying for them, naturally," he said, turning serious. "They're businessmen."

"Who are?" I asked.

"Some people in the army. The equipment has been retired, but not destroyed. As you can imagine, the whole business is top secret."

"And what are the conditions of payment?"

"Cash on delivery."

I accepted the cigarette he offered.

"Look," I said, "We don't have enough money to arm the men we have. Ask your friends this question: Do they want to sell us a few guns now at cash prices or sell at a discount enough guns to ensure our success, payable when the revolution has triumphed?"

John answered, "I think I know what they will answer, but I will pass along your proposal anyway. I don't like this kind of thing, but I will do it for you." (I never heard from him about it again.)

"Another thing," I said. "Our new student association has an invitation from the Catholic University of Chile to participate in an international student art festival this summer. Don't you think I would be a fine representative for our group? Seriously, I think it would be good experience for me."

"Sounds great," said John. "I'll back you."

Mary Ann was in her last year of law school. She was an unusual American. Like me, she read philosophy looking for the truth. We discussed it during meetings of the university literary society, to which we both belonged.

"Enrique, have you seen the latest philosophical study? *The History of Philosophy,* it's called, and it's sure to be a best-seller."

"What's so good about it?"

"The author has selected twenty philosophers whose work, he says, represents the history of philosophical thought, from the Jews to the modern era, progressing through the Greeks and the Germans. It summarizes the work of each philosopher in a few pages, distilling it with brilliant clarity."

I read the book. Marx was one of the philosophers. Ricardo, my friend from primary school, now a militant Communist, sometimes spoke about Marx, but I found him incomprehensible. Now I understood the essence of Marxism, which impressed me with its logic, although I wouldn't have counted on its success.

I bought a condensed version of *Das Kapital.* I made my way through it on my own, as through a stormy sea, never finding a clear course. I will have to apply myself, I thought.

Then Mary Ann guided me to the next book: *Three Who Made a Revolution,* by Bertram D. Wolfe. It was the history of the Russian revolution through the biographies of Lenin, Trotsky, and Stalin— the best thing I had read in long time! It recounted the most incredible history from a human viewpoint so that the epic adventure seemed normal and natural.

I was no longer the same person; I had been transformed. I had previously appreciated Marxist ideas, but they seemed utopian, not a practical approach, as they seemed to require a fundamental change in the nature of man. But when I read this book about how it had actually been done, when I began to appreciate the human stories of Trotsky (with whom I particularly sympathized from the very beginning) and Lenin, I felt that these were recognizable people, that this had really happened, and that, yes, revolution was possible, it was realistic, and we could do it in Cuba.

## chapter 4

# Journey to Latin America

Three weeks later, I was on an airplane bound for Panama, the first stop on my trip to the international student festival in Chile. The route took us over Cuba, so I stared out the window and saw, far below, the lights of a fair-sized city. I leaned toward the person sitting next to me and asked, "Are you sleeping, Rolando?"

"No."

"You know, I think we just flew over my hometown, Santa Clara; according to the map, it is more or less on the route from Miami to Panama."

Rolando looked out the window. "I can't see a thing," he said.

We were quiet. I was cold. I reached for the blanket and bundled up in it.

I had communicated with the MNR in Cuba about my trip to Chile, and they had approved my mission of clandestine education, activity, and interaction. My cover was that of a representative of the university student association. We were a delegation of two, taking advantage of the fact that Rolando Torres was returning home for a vacation.

At last I would see Latin America! That dream overcame my anxiety. I would represent my student association, but I also had another, more secret agenda: I wanted to know more about South America. We revolutionary young people always had in mind that we were part of a larger nation, as Bolívar and Martí had said. So this festival was also an opportunity to express our revolutionary points of view to the students and other people who would be there from the rest of Latin America—without of course revealing that I was playing a personal role in the fighting or that I was an underground conspirator.

When I woke up, the airplane was landing at the Tocumen airport in Panama City.

We went out to see the city. The narrow, crooked streets and the low houses with thick walls reminded me of pirate films. That Panama was one of the crossroads of the world was obvious from the windows of the stores, where things from all over the world were for sale. As the morning advanced, the heat grew more suffocating, our clothes stickier.

One day we took the train to Colón, another city in Panama along the route to Chile. Docked at the wharf was the ship that would take us to Valparaiso. We spent the rest of the day arranging our passage, and that night, after our first meal on board, we went sightseeing with some young people. The streets were quite similar to those of Old Panama, with a similarly astounding variety of shops displaying the merchandise of the world. There was one bar after another. The blaring of the jukeboxes blended into a single huge noise. The men walking those streets spoke every language. Sometimes we passed a couple. Occasionally someone would approach us with a proposal.

We entered a bar with a long counter that had fifteen or twenty women seated along it; the men would come up and ask them to dance. We drank and got to know our new friends from the ship. Later some of us started dancing. There was a small, dark, rather plump woman who was not dancing much, so I asked her.

"Thanks," she said, and hung onto me. I smelled cheap perfume mixed with sweat.

"This just isn't my night," she began.

"Why?" I asked.

"I don't know. Well, it must be my color. And you know what? Sometimes I'm the most popular."

"How come?"

"Well, when a Norwegian boat is in, they're looking for blacks. You like blacks?"

"I like you. You were alone, and you looked sad."

She laughed for the first time. She said, "You seem nice."

"Aren't all men?" I asked, teasing her.

"No, they're beasts!" And she grew serious again.

We went back to the bar and had a drink. She raised her eyes from the glass. She asked me, "Should we go?"

"Yes, let's go."

We walked through dark side streets. It had rained, and we dodged around puddles. We got to a door, she opened it, and we went in.

"Wait here," she whispered. She moved through the darkness and lit a small lamp; the dim light revealed the room: a bed, a wardrobe, a table with two chairs, and a gas burner.

She caught my look. "It's not much."

"So what," I answered.

She came toward me.

Later, when I was on top of her, she said in my ear, "You're a good person, you know."

"But how do you know? You hardly know me!"

"I just know. I have learned about men, to defend myself from them. I am like a wild animal."

"Still, you seem to like men."

She gave me a cunning look. "That's why I said I am like an animal."

"No, you are a woman . . . one who needs affection."

She was thoughtful for a moment and then said, "Yes, I am."

She told me about herself. Later, we smoked in silence. The first light of day appeared through a crack in the door. I sat up in the bed. "I have to get going."

She appealed to me. "Don't go away. Stay a few days. Are you a sailor?"

"Yes," I lied.

"Stay. I'll take care of you."

"No, I can't. It's impossible. I'll come back soon and look for you."

Sadness returned to her face. She watched me dressing, and I felt guilty.

"Don't look at me like that," I said, and sat down on the edge of the bed. I stroked her face, while her tears wet my hands. My fingers were very white against her skin. I pulled my hand away and went out to the street without another look. It was a new day.

∾  ∾  ∾

I stared out the porthole, expecting to see a clear blue sky furrowed by white clouds, and instead saw a dark gray mass sliding by, almost touching the ship. We were going through the Panama Canal.

Days went by. Soon we had passed Buenaventura on the Colombian coast, with its ugly parks and stores, its whorehouses with doors and windows wide open and prostitutes sitting around inside, conveniently displayed for clients in the street.

And we left Lima behind, where for the first time I became aware of the Indian, small, coarse, sallow, manning the army in his cloth uniform or pushing a cart through the streets or leaning against a pillar for hours, thinking—what?

Valparaiso. The journalists were waiting for us. Yes, we were attending the festival. No, we had never been to Chile before. Yes, we bring greetings.

Rolando's family came on board. Middle class. Nice people who had been simple and were becoming more complicated. Eliana, the younger sister, was a student. Rose, the older one, had not come along; she was waiting at home. (Later I learned she was married to a truck driver.) The mother, a thickset woman, stayed in the background. Alberto, the older, political son, the pride of the family, was out of the country. Don Alberto, the father, was an imposing figure: tall, burly, gray haired, with complexion and features revealing a mixture of Spanish and Indian. He was semiliterate but carried himself proudly.

The next days were full of long, formal meals. Every night we had visitors. The girls brought guitars and we danced the *cueca*. We joked about whose songs we were singing; to my surprise, some familiar songs turned out to be Chilean. Each afternoon we went out for a snack with the young people. There was a lot of political and literary activity. Most of the people we met were Christian Socialists, and I began to hear about the Chilean phalange and its leader Frei. Many wrote poetry that they read in the evening at Don Alberto's house, which was becoming known as a literary salon, making him even more proud. Rolando was in love with a blonde who didn't return his feelings, while I spent my time with my new friends.

We went to Santiago for the start of the festival. President Ibáñez came to the opening ceremony, and the Minister of Education spoke in his name. When I entered the meeting, the Communist students there tried to leave because they thought I was someone who had sold his soul to the American imperialists. Of course I did not reveal to them or anyone else my role as a member of the MNR.

One interesting fellow was Sergio Mercado. He came from the interior and was attending the University of Chile to become a teacher. He was a student type I had often read about in Spanish novels. He was of medium height, well put together, with a wide forehead and black hair beginning to gray, a pleasant voice, and an easy manner. He dressed with casual elegance, his clothes carefully pressed beneath his mattress, as he was always short of cash. Sometimes when he ducked his head in a nervous gesture you could see that his neck was none too clean.

Sergio had an active love life, which I read about in his many poems. I suspected that he made love to "the girls" partly to gather material. Teaching would be his livelihood, but poetry was his reason to live. I became familiar with his room and its crumpled white sheets, the small, round table with its wine-stained cloth, the solitary chair. There was a window leading to a balcony, but a thick, faded curtain kept out most of the light.

Sergio and I became inseparable. We attended the main festival events and the rest of the time led a true Bohemian life. Every night we went out to eat, always a different place, always plenty of good wine. We would drift toward the literary shoals that formed toward dawn in the cafés along the Alameda, where Sergio was well known. Young people of every political creed met there to discuss art and literature.

It was during those dawn talks that I discovered the poets Pablo Neruda, Andrés Eloy Blanco, and our own Nicolás Guillén. It was a young labor leader who declared, "So Cuban," repeating, "So Cuban." And he recited these lines from Guillén:

*On the Sea of the Antilles*
*drifts a ship that's made of paper . . .*

I assented, catching the Cuban flavor of those verses in that cold Santiago dawn. Back at my hotel, Sergio was talking about something, but running through my mind was

*On the Sea of the Antilles*
*drifts a ship that's made of paper . . .*

Yes, that was Cuba exactly: a paper boat sailing aimlessly.

The student leaders of the Catholic University arranged an interview for me with members of the Federation of Chilean Students, which represented all universities and political groups. At the start of the meeting, the Communist members refused to enter the room. Finally they were persuaded. As at the opening ceremonies, they considered me some kind of colonial capitalist from a corrupt North American university, but I pretended not to notice the incident.

I made a few introductory remarks, and soon we were discussing various topics. We spoke of U.S. life, of U.S. activities in Latin America, of the need to unite our people. And we spoke of Cuba and the fight against Batista. A year later I learned that one of those present denounced my opinions as subversive to the U.S. student association I represented. But I am sure that the Communist students attending, though they probably changed their minds about my being bought and paid for by Yankee gold, did not find my political ideas so radical.

The festival ended, and we all left. I had an invitation to visit the Universidad de Concepción, so I went to that city, about two hundred miles to the south. Then I returned to Santiago to spend some time with my phalangist friends. I stayed at the Archbishopric—large windows with leaded glass, heavy carved dark wood furniture, pews I didn't use. I tried to absorb the atmosphere, to profit from my surroundings. I wanted to penetrate the Catholic world that had surrounded me since childhood, to learn what it was like inside. Was it the dark shadowy world I had always imagined? After all, these young Christian Socialists were happy and optimistic; they talked about social change. I knew priests who organized cooperatives and preached that Christ was the first Communist. We ate together at long tables, making jokes and discussing politics, drinking a lot of wine, smoking cigars and cigarettes. This trend in Chilean Catholicism intrigued me and expanded my views a little, but in the end did not win me over.

The last cables were pulled in, and the boat slowly moved away from the wharf. The thick, oily water held all manner of waste, marring the scene I engraved on my memory. People became smaller and smaller, until they were unrecognizable.

We retraced our voyage. I raised my eyes from a book to try to retain those sights. It was painful to leave those scenes behind forever. That sea, that sky, those coasts, those mountains, those ships. I had learned a lot about Chile and the other countries I had visited. In many ways they were just like Cuba. These countries had the same problems, but they had not yet arrived, as we had, at the stage where they had made the decision for armed struggle.

That is what I was thinking the dawn we arrived in Havana. From up on the deck, the cars on the Malecón, the broad boulevard along the waterfront, looked like toys. The old Morro was on the left, a familiar sight. Havana looked like a big city: modern skyscrapers, activity all around, dazzling light. My fellow travelers from other countries were impressed. They congratulated me as if Cuba were all mine. I was proud to be back.

The boat docked, and we made the long trip through customs. On all sides police in blue, with loosened ties and caps pushed back. In the cafés on the other side of the Avenida del Puerto, the whores were beginning to stir, and record players were starting up, blaring out mambos, guarachas, and boleros.

## chapter 5

# Attack on the Moncada Barracks

One afternoon that June, a few days after I returned to Cuba from Chile, Pepe Contreras, who went to school with us in Miami, invited Manolo and me to his house one afternoon to play pool. The table was in the living room, temporarily, until the new house was finished that Yoyo, Pepe's father, was building in suburban Biltmore. Yoyo was home, and when he heard us, he came downstairs in his pajama bottoms.

"Boys, let's play a game; I'll give each of you ten shots," said Yoyo, picking up the cue. We knew how good he was with a pool cue and that the advantage he was offering was not enough.

"Come on, Yoyo, pool is your vice," said Manolo.

Yoyo chalked the end of his stick. "Call it my vice if you want. I would call it my love. When I was broke, it often fed me. And where are you heading anyway, to the whorehouse? I've warned Pepe before that in the whorehouse he will find things that aren't moral."

"Like what?" asked Manolo.

"Like his father, the dumb shit."

We all cracked up. And Yoyo broke the rack with the cue ball. Manolo, irked, couldn't resist: "You're quite the fucker, pardon my saying so."

"Don't get so hot, chico," laughed Yoyo. "There's not much choice. What's more, I think that all Cubans are born fuckers, and if not"—sinking a good shot—"like the politician Chibás, I am a fucker because I have to be. It helped me to make it through hard times, and now, to become head of a firm, owner of a magnificent home in Biltmore, member of the club, and in the next election a member of Congress. Not bad for someone who started out a go-fer in a pool hall."

"Sure, Papa, but these revolutionaries don't think so," put in Pepe.

For the first time, Yoyo missed a shot. "Revolutionaries? Prío was a revolutionary, and look what he is now. Being revolutionary is for when you're not in power, when you don't have the trappings. Once you get into office, you revolutionaries become just like all the rest. Politics is like any other career, except you don't have to go to college."

Manolo was putting on Yoyo: "But Barcena seems honest."

"I'd bet my balls that group would be just like us if they were in power. To get an honest government in Cuba, you'd have to replace all the Cubans with Swiss."

Nodding to me, Pepe asked, "So, Papa, got any advice for Enrique, who sympathizes with these rebels?"

"Why bust his balls with that crap? Sure, it's OK if you're dying of hunger, but studying engineering, with a career ahead, why start playing with fire?"

The cue ball bounced off two cushions and hit the last ball, which slid smoothly across the green cloth and dropped in the pocket.

"OK, gentlemen, done," said Yoyo. "When you've had a little more practice, come back for your next class."

Still in Havana, I went into a café and sat down at a small gray marble table with my companions from the MNR: Faustino Pérez, the doctor I had met at the university that first night, and Armando Hart, a young lawyer. We ordered Coca-Cola, and when the waiter moved away, Armando took out the newspaper again. He had arranged for the famous journalist José Pardo Llada to interview him about our cause.

"This interview improves our position," Armando said.

"And proves your positioning too," added Faustino, trying to serve God and the Devil.

"But the important thing is that we're talking about the revolution," insisted Armando. "Don't forget that Pardo Llada still has a huge following, and everything he says or writes reaches thousands of people. I think this interview will be great publicity for our cause."

"I'm not so sure, chico," Faustino persisted. "Pardo Llada is a shameless phony, and it's a disgrace to have anything to do with him."

Armando laughed nervously: "Not too political, are you? Faustino, we must use every weapon available to us. What do you think, Enrique?"

"Well, I don't know much about it, but I'm inclined to agree with Faustino."

"Then you and Faustino are both naive. Our strategy calls for armed struggle, but don't forget a political base. Besides bringing the revolution into the newspapers and unmasking Pardo Llada, through this public exchange I have been able to transmit some basic concepts and provide guidance to members of the Movement and the people. And all this in such a form that the dictatorship allowed its publication, despite its content."

He began to read excerpts from the article.

"Fine, Armando," interrupted Faustino, "that's all well and good, but this is the fifth time you have read it, and besides, we're going to be late for the trial. Let's go."

We arrived at the courthouse just in time for Armando to don his lawyer's robe and go in to defend a boy from the MNR accused of distributing secret propaganda.

Faustino and I waited in the central courtyard until the trial was over. Some suspicious-looking people were moving around the building, watching everything. Some young people came up to talk to Faustino. I was worried. I glanced at Faustino to compare impressions, but he continued talking calmly.

⁓ ⁓ ⁓

When I got back to my hometown, I ran into Allán Rosell, a young doctor who was a member of the MNR and one of its leaders in Santa Clara.

"There's something happening," he said.

Suddenly everything stopped. "What . . . ?" I responded.

"I don't know much, but something is going on. Dr. Pedrosa, a military doctor, told me this morning at the hospital that there seems to be an uprising in the Oriente. If I hear anything more I'll let you know."

Just the same, I decided to spend the day at Allán's house. We went back to his place and through the door to his office. The air-conditioning felt good on this hot July day. Guillermito came in, and we waited together for news while Allán saw patients and got back on the phone to find out more about what was happening.

A few minutes later, Allán burst back into the room. "I spoke again to Pedrosa, and he told me there's been an attack on the Moncada barracks in Santiago de Cuba!"

The news fell like a bomb. Before we reacted, Allán continued, "The attack was led by Fidel Castro. It was on the 26th of July."

"Who?" I had to interrupt.

"Fidel Castro, a young lawyer who ran for representative in the party of Eduardo Chibás."

"That rings a bell."

"I know him from the university," said Guillermito. "He was a student leader."

"And what kind of man is this Fidel?" I persisted.

"A man of action. He has maintained an aggressive stance against Batista," explained Allán.

"But what a shock!" Guillermito repeated. "We knew they were training, but nothing else."

"It took place at dawn, taking advantage of Carnival. They almost captured the army barracks!" Allán related. "According to Dr. Pedrosa there are more than one hundred dead."

"And Fidel?"

"No one knows. He either escaped or died. Some of the attackers went into the hills."

"So the fight will continue. We have to do something," Luis spoke up for the first time.

"I wonder if the Professor knew anything," said Guillermito.

"I'm sure not," replied Allán. "If he had, so would we."

"But what were they after?" I wondered. "Suppose they had taken the barracks, then what? Santiago is Santiago. The problem is Havana."

"Fidel has never believed in a single strike. He always thinks in terms of a prolonged fight. Perhaps his idea was to take the Oriente and then march on Havana," speculated Guillermito.

"Still, what happened in Santiago will have big repercussions in the fight against Batista," observed Allán. "From now on, the fight will be to the death. Just watch how the struggle will intensify!"

When I went out into the cool night air, despite the calm atmosphere, I had a clear sense that something had changed.

David, an old acquaintance, had insisted on getting together. I did not have much interest in seeing him. He was from a Jewish family from Santa Clara who now owned a factory in Havana. David had abandoned his studies to work with his father. Their name was one of the most distinguished in the Jewish colony of Havana, part of the elite according to the rigid social stratification of Cuban Jews. Despite his living in Havana and our rarely seeing each other, we had maintained a distant friendship, which we revived when I returned to Cuba over my vacation.

David always insisted I go to the Jewish get-togethers, and he also wanted me to attend the family parties that were given in a different house each Saturday night in this narrow set. He knew my political ideas and argued against them. He said a Jew should never get mixed up in the internal politics of any country, illustrating this with events in Russia, Germany, and France. Our true mother country was Israel. Lately I had been trying to avoid him.

He came looking for me in his new Packard at the house of my uncle Felipe—my mother's brother, who lived in Havana, where I was visiting—and I felt there was no choice but to go out with him that morning.

"Hey, what a job I've had catching up with you," said David as he held out his hand.

"No, chico, it's just that I've been hassling with renewing my visa. In just a few days I go back to Miami."

He accelerated the car and asked, "So, how is school going?"

"If all goes well, I'll graduate in January."

"And then what?"

"Then, I don't know."

"If I were you, I'd stay there."

"That would be the most practical, but there are other considerations."

"Like your homeland, for example."

"Right. I would feel bad if I did not come home now."

"But, why you? Let somebody else do it."

"Look, David, there is one thing you have never developed—a conscience. That's what won't let me take the easy way out. Besides, so many think like you that I'm almost forced into it."

David didn't take the hint. "Be reasonable, man. Politics is just for the Cubans, not the Jews. You don't need it: you're going to be a professional with a degree from the United States. There or here, you'll find a job immediately. As far as money's concerned, your life's assured. The flip side of the coin: the risk. Since Fidel attacked the Moncada, they will pull in anyone."

We were driving through Old Havana and turned into a parking lot. David suggested we go to a store on Muralla Street. There was a party at his house that night, and he wanted to invite some friends.

Walking down the narrow sidewalk single file, I told him, "Look, David, I can't come to your house tonight."

"And why not?"

"I have a previous commitment."

"So break it."

We went into the huge, crowded fabric store. I followed David to the back, where he pushed open the door to a small air-conditioned office. David introduced me to Mr. and Mrs. Stein and their children, Ernesto and Maria.

I answered a few questions before the conversation turned to David. I looked at Maria: blonde, with thick eyebrows and dark brown eyes; a nose that was small, if a little too thin. Full lips, with tiny creases at the corners when she smiled. No individual feature was perfect, but together they made a striking impression, strong and vital. Nice size, shapely, youthful. My eyes stayed on her, forcing her to return my glance. Maria was trying to pay attention to the conversation, and she often laughed. Still, she kept looking back at me.

We left, Maria and I saying nothing, knowing that we would see each other that night. When David and I were in the street, he said, "I won't ask what you thought of Maria; that was pretty clear."

"Amazing! I thought I was being so subtle."

"Too bad you can't come tonight," said David slyly.

"You know, chico, I've changed my mind. I sure wouldn't want to hurt your feelings," and we both laughed.

## chapter 6

# Return to Cuba

It wasn't easy to complete my degree. I no longer had time for any of my other activities. I buckled down as never before and reached the finish line like an exhausted runner on his last gasp.

My father had never wanted me to be a businessman like him. He hoped I could achieve a higher status, such as by becoming a doctor, a profession held in high esteem in our society. Unfortunately, I didn't go along with his plans for me. I had always liked nature and the outdoors, and I told him I didn't want to spend my life in a closed room seeing people suffer.

As a young man I had always been interested in agriculture; I proposed that I study farming so we could buy some land and start a large enterprise. But sounding very much like Che did that rainy night in the mountains years later, my father said, "What? Rain . . . mosquitoes . . . dirt and mud? No, no, no. Look for someone else who will finance that kind of career."

I tried to think of something else. In secondary school I had always been a reader and very interested in drawing, so we reached a compromise with architectural engineering, a practical profession that was also artistic.

During the spring of my senior year, my father had some temporary economic reversals, and I had to get a job for the first time. It was only four hours in the evening at a movie theater; the rest of the time I studied. I put aside my previous life and filled the space with my desire to finish—and the letters that arrived from Maria.

When I graduated in spring 1954, I went to work with an American who had been one of my fellow students. We designed houses and shopping centers. They were small jobs that we just dashed off and made good money on. I bought a new car, rented a bachelor apartment, and created what would become a kind of cover for my double life, a way to make a living while I continued my secret work in the revolutionary underground.

I heard little from Cuba. Our organization was in an inactive period. Fidel was a prisoner whose absence was keenly felt. The old politicians looked for a negotiated solution. No one believed in Prío. García Barcena, the Professor, had formed an alliance with a group of revolutionary army officers that was brutally defeated by Batista, so the Professor's MNR had nearly faded away completely.

Months later, García Barcena arrived in Miami, exiled, and I went to see him. It was as cold inside his apartment as out in the street. The Professor was wearing an old-fashioned double-breasted suit. Esperancita, his wife, bustled around in the kitchen, and his daughter dismantled a toy in front of us. Seated on the sofa bed, we tried to fight the cold with the warmth of our words.

"I never imagined it got so cold in Miami," said the Professor.

"Sometimes there are hard frosts that kill all the plants and do millions of dollars in damage. I know because then they hire students to harvest at night, under spotlights."

"Good thing I'm not growing anything in here," joked the Professor.

"You should move. Maybe we could find an apartment with heat for the same price."

"Don't bother; winter will be over soon." Changing the subject, he asked, "Have you heard anything about the job for me at the university?"

"Yes, I went back to talk to the dean. He didn't say yes or no. I think he's stalling us. The thing is not to rock the boat. That's how they are."

"Well, don't worry about it. We'll find some way to eat, even it's only frozen vegetables."

I got serious: "You still haven't given me an answer about the guns we were offered."

"That's because things have changed. We have suffered some setbacks: people talk too much, and the police hear and act. We have decided to change our tactics. A civil group within the organization will be limited to political action, while an armed group will work with military conspirators."

"But that is dangerous for the civil force."

"There won't be any problems. These are young army men who were my students and are faithful followers."

"OK, if you say so."

"You don't sound convinced."

"Actually, I'm not."

"Don't worry. Trust me."

"All right."

Esperancita brought in Cuban coffee. The Professor continued, "Prío wants to see me."

He watched me to measure my reaction. I knew what he would do, but said anyway, "Naturally, you won't go."

"Why not? It's always good to know what others are up to."

I began to feel a certain mortification. I said, "Prío is not up to anything good. Dealing with him is demeaning to us."

"You are too absolute in your ideas," said the Professor, smiling. "In politics you have to be flexible right up to the point where you mustn't yield."

"I have a lot to learn, but some things I will never understand."

"I would agree. But don't worry, there's time for that."

I spent a lot of time with the Professor. Few people came to see him. I tried to make his stay in Miami more enjoyable. We would make short trips to the surrounding areas, or I would bring some friend to see him. Sometimes we went to a bar near his house and spent hours discussing Cuban problems and drinking beer.

One night, we were at the bar. I said, "I'll bet time seems to be moving slowly to you."

"Right, but since I started writing, it is more bearable."

"What are you writing?"

"*Rediscovering God* is what I'm calling my book."

"Do you mean the title literally?" I inquired, hoping for a no.

"Yes," he answered.

"But . . . how can you believe in God?"

"Why not? Although my God does not have specific religion. The source is the same in a church or a mosque."

"Pardon me, but to believe in God is to dwell in darkness," I persisted anxiously.

The Professor laughed heartily. "I am going to end up disappointing you."

I didn't answer. I had nothing to say. I drank in silence. The Professor felt forced to give me an explanation of his book. I listened without hearing.

Not too long afterward, Armando Hart arrived in Miami. Batista had given amnesty to all political prisoners. Fidel was free and wanted to talk to the Professor. The idea was to unite all the honest forces in the fight against Batista, and since there was no realistic political solution, the only approach should be a general strike supported by armed fighting. It was time to go home.

The Professor disappeared. I was bogged down in my reflections. My mind was filled with conflicting feelings. On one hand, I felt let down and empty and wanted to forget all about the struggle. On the other, an abstract sense of duty kept calling me to return. My moral principles kept me from remaining on the margins of what was to come. I had to keep fighting. If I quit, I would be a coward. A dangerous period was approaching in which I could be killed, but I had to face whatever would be, or my conscience would never forgive me.

One morning I got up and told myself, "Today is the day." I finished my preparations in a few hours and flew back to Cuba that afternoon.

## chapter 7

# Revolutionary Quest

I was back in Santa Clara, where I had to look for work, but I thought it was more important for me first to define my involvement in the revolutionary process.

It was now 1955. After being released from prison, Fidel had been forced to flee the country under pressure from Batista's forces and was living in Mexico, where he was organizing what would become an armed invasion. Internally in Cuba, other revolutionary forces were developing along various lines. So I needed to talk with my friends about what to do.

"We will meet at Luis's store."

"OK," Allán answered, and I hung up the phone.

I walked down Colon Street, bought a newspaper at the corner, and went into the store. Luis and his employees were waiting on some customers, and I sat down on a stool and started reading.

In a little while Allán came in, we embraced, and he sat down on the floor and started to talk: "The MNR is inactive. The Professor depends more and more on the military. He is thinking about a putsch."

"I had already noticed that when he was in Miami," I replied. "What about you? What do you have in mind?"

"I've been thinking about this for a long time. And I've concluded that armed revolt, by itself, is not the correct method. Something more is necessary: bringing the masses into the fight. And only the Communists have a lasting sense of this, I believe, and a strategy

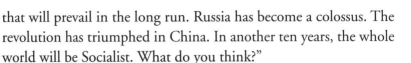

that will prevail in the long run. Russia has become a colossus. The revolution has triumphed in China. In another ten years, the whole world will be Socialist. What do you think?"

"I don't know. What you say sounds utopian to me. I have no doubt the Communists are serious, but I don't really know enough about them to judge. Are you a member?"

"No, not yet. I am talking to them, getting to know them better, reading some things. You want to meet them?"

"Why not? There's nothing to lose."

The next day I accompanied Allán to the house of a lawyer who belonged to the Communist Party. Allán introduced us, and the lawyer said, "I know your father, although I met him in rather unpleasant circumstances. I defended several workers against him."

"If he finds out I've been here, he'll whip me for keeping bad company," I joked.

We had coffee in an office filled with books. Allán said, "Enrique, like me, served in the MNR. He just returned from the United States, where he got an engineering degree. We've talked things over, and he is interested in talking to you."

I added, "That's right, but I don't actually have much to say. I would rather listen. Here's how I see things: three years of armed rebellion have not succeeded against Batista. What is wrong? It seems to me that Allán is right: we have not managed to bring the masses into the fight. But how can we do that? I would like to know the Party's views on that."

The lawyer thought a while before answering. "Our strategy in this struggle is and always will be to cultivate the masses. We Communists do not believe that a paramilitary organization is the way to go. Through our political organizing in the unions and among intellectuals, we must exert such pressure on those in power that they will be forced to allow a political solution to the present situation. One possible solution could be elections with all the parties represented. In that climate our party could be very effective and have a decisive influence, because it would show clearly that our work has never lost its perspective."

He fixed his eyes on me: now it was my turn.

"I don't believe Batista will ever willingly yield his ruling power. In any free election, the people would throw him out. I repeat, I think we must organize the masses, but for armed combat."

We had quickly reached a deadlock. The lawyer saw this and said, "Well, I don't think we have to decide everything today. Let's continue our discussions so that you can study our views more deeply. Would you like to read some of our materials?"

"Sure."

Turning to Allán, the lawyer said, "You should take him to see Dr. Menéndez."

The next day, Allán took me to see the doctor, another Communist leader and intellectual. Menéndez lived in one of those old houses so common in Santa Clara, with an entryway leading to the living room, then the little hall, and a patio full of climbing plants and flowerpots. In the back were the bedrooms, kitchen, and dining room.

The doctor received us in cloth slippers. Behind the thick lenses of his glasses, he had small pupils that indicated much reading. He spoke carefully, in a rich voice, enunciating clearly, rocking slightly in his wicker armchair. Our conversation was much like my earlier talk with the lawyer. He lent me some very worn books, which we planned to discuss when I returned them.

It was noon and very hot. My friend Joaquín Argüelles suggested, "Want to go to the Frio?"

"Let's."

The Frio was the only air-conditioned bar in Santa Clara. It was a chic place to go. We pushed the door open and felt a pleasant coolness. It was dark, and we could hear the sound of guitars. When our eyes adjusted, we went to the bar and perched on stools. Joaquín ordered a Cuba Libre and I a highball, cognac with ginger ale. We sat listening to the trio, who were playing songs by Sindo Garay.

Joaquín worked for Esso and made good money. He was a romantic. Everyone liked him for his good nature and unselfishness. We had been friends for years.

"What are you thinking about?" asked Joaquín.

"An idea I can't give up," I said. "Some action needs to be taken."

"What about the Communists?"

"Chico, it's not happening. I've been talking to them, listening to their plan, and it's too long term. Besides, the way they go about it does not fit our temperament. They're intelligent and honest people, but no matter how I look at the problem, it still seems to me that humanity is not ready for such an advanced doctrine. I hesitate to devote myself to such a distant reality, when there are less ambitious ways to improve the human condition closer at hand."

The waiter brought refills.

"The battle isn't between books, but in the street. In all of my conversations with them, two things stand out, one good and the other bad. What's good is that they understand the importance of the role of the masses. The bad thing is, they don't understand the importance of armed warfare right now."

"So . . . what we are going to do?"

"It seems to me that we have no choice but to organize our own political movement."

"Us?" exclaimed Joaquín, surprised.

"Why not? I realize that the task isn't easy. Everything depends on whether we succeed in mobilizing the people. Look, this is how I see things. Cuba is a country with great agricultural potential. Therefore, its development must begin with agriculture. That is, use the wealth from modern agriculture to develop modern industry. Now, there is a problem. And that is the way land is distributed at the moment. Less than a thousand families own nearly half the land, while hundreds of thousands live off the land without owning it. This means that agricultural profits go to a few while the vast majority of farmers can barely survive.

"What is called for? Agrarian reform. Just by distributing idle fields and improving cattle operations, to reduce the land needed, we could give about sixty acres to every farmer. Naturally, small farming is not a complete solution, since it makes it difficult to use modern methods. But we could create associations for sharing equipment and even land.

"What would be the advantage of this? Well, to increase the spending power of at least half the population. And by expanding the local market, we could greatly increase industrial production for national consumption, for a start."

"Listen, it all makes sense, what you're saying, but come on, where did you pick it up?" asked Joaquín while I took a drink and lit a cigarette.

"You can see I haven't been wasting my time. I've been reading a lot. OK, I'll go further. Our battle flag must be agrarian reform. Therefore, the first line of our movement must be the peasantry. But we must not scorn city forces, and we should try to add them to our program."

Joaquín burned with enthusiasm. "When can we start? You make me think we can really do this."

"First we must select a group of leaders. This initial nucleus will have to develop my ideas, which are still quite embryonic. When we have our program ready, we make our intention public and enlarge our ranks into a military-style organization. Now we must choose the others."

The spider was swinging gently in the breeze. The rays of afternoon sun slanting in at my window glinted off the thin web of hairs by which it was suspended. Something that my mind could not understand compelled the tiny creature to swing up and down above my head. Stretched out in bed, I spent some time watching it.

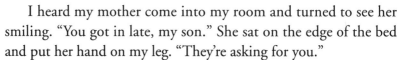

I heard my mother come into my room and turned to see her smiling. "You got in late, my son." She sat on the edge of the bed and put her hand on my leg. "They're asking for you."

"Who?" I asked.

"I don't know them, except by type. They look like revolutionaries. They are young."

"Didn't they give you their names?"

"Yes, but I did not understand too well. Enrique . . ."

"What?"

Her hand caressed my leg. "Why do you insist on getting into these things? You make me suffer so much. If they kill you, I will die! You must think about me."

"Ave Maria, again! I have already told you you're wasting your time. Forget your feelings as a mother for a moment and think about other people. The only thing you do with your sermons is torment yourself and me."

"You only talk that way because you do not have children. When you have a child then you will understand me. That's why I want you to get married, so you'll stop this intellectual stuff. Maria is a good girl, and we have known her parents since we got to Cuba. They are good people."

I went from wrath to laughter: "But look what you're saying, Mother. You're threatening me with death in the same breath you're trying to marry me off. But don't fool yourself—I don't believe I can change."

"Don't say that. I am so worried. Now, without even—"

I cut in, "No, please, Mami, don't say more, leave me alone for a while!" I rose and began to dress hurriedly.

"Where are you going?" she asked in a broken voice.

When I could speak calmly, I replied, "Somewhere where you won't bother me."

Two tears ran down her cheeks, and it felt like they burned me inside.

I had always been much closer to my mother than my father. She was a wonderful, sweet, lovely woman, whose maiden name was Ozacki, Jashe Ozacki. In Poland her beauty had been legendary. My father had ridden his bicycle from Brest, the city where he lived, twenty kilometers to Cobrin, where she lived, just to see her before they were married.

When I was one year old, my mother had a very difficult pregnancy with my sister, and for reasons that now seem strange to me, the doctors recommended that she leave Santa Clara for a while and return to her family in Poland, which she did, bringing me along.

This was in 1933, at the height of the worldwide economic depression; thus, like a lot of other struggling businessmen, my father suffered some financial problems and was consequently unable to send us the money to come back to Cuba as quickly as had been planned. So for four years my mother and sister and I lived with our family in Poland at the home of my mother's father.

My grandfather was very proud of me, his only male grandchild at that time. He took me to the synagogue and everywhere else he went. So we became very close during those four years when I was just a little boy.

Finally, my father's business recovered; he sent us the money for our journey, and we returned to Cuba. I remember when we arrived in the harbor in Havana. A little boat came out to our ship; it was crowded with people coming to greet their friends and relatives before we landed. A man was shouting to us from this little boat, and my mother said to me, "That is your father."

"No," I replied. "My father is in Poland," thinking of my grandfather. "That man is not my father."

And from that time on, I was never as close with my father as with my mother. He was a man who never showed his emotions. Like many men of his class and generation, he did not express his affections openly. It was odd, though, because he was also a man who loved to play the guitar and sing old Yiddish songs at the social club in our synagogue. He was well known for being a terrific dancer, and I remember him doing what we called the *paso doble,* or double step, at many parties and special occasions, where he appeared to be having a terrific time.

After we returned to Cuba, my mother was able to get two of her brothers out of Poland, but the rest of her family remained, and nearly all of them, including my beloved grandfather, were killed by the Nazis.

Out in the street, José Arroyo said to me, "Hey, we felt like we upset your mother."

"Don't worry, it will pass," I told him.

"My mother is the same way. All mothers are," the guy with José opined.

We went to a café across from the Parque Vidal. José said, "Here's the situation: we're spreading across the island. Our goal is to create a new Directorio Revolucionario much like the one that opposed Machado. History repeats itself. Until now, the struggle against Batista has been a failure. The reason is that one way or another, it has been controlled by politicians. The time has come for students not only to close ranks but to lead, assuming our historical role. Echevarría and his friends in the FEU have taken up the challenge, for a fight to the death. We've talked to some people here in Santa Clara. They suggested we talk to you. You must join us."

"It seems we've all been bitten by the same bug," I said with a smile. "We too are trying to organize something new, but along different lines. Ours is only in its initial phase and hardly worth talking about. But I still don't want to join some other organization.

"Faustino Pérez and Armando Hart were here the other day, and we got together at Allán Rosell's house," I went on. "They are organizing here for the 26th of July Movement, led by Fidel. I told them just what I told you. Now I am going to be honest: if I decided to join some other movement, it would be the 26th of July Movement. It has been around longer, and it already has a history. Fidel has demonstrated that he can act as well as talk, which is important in this frustrating period. Have you spoken with Fidel?"

José scratched his head. "Look, we know Fidel, and I don't think that we can work with him; we have different methods. And besides, Fidel is not from the university, and we definitely have a student movement, although we want to include all the people."

"I don't know Fidel either," I said, "but Faustino and Armando support him, and that inspires my confidence. I know them very well. And . . . well . . . time will tell."

We had a long discussion. It was past ten. The municipal band was gone, and the park was starting to empty.

We separated with a handshake.

Martha had also finished her university work and graduated as a doctor of pharmacology. She had returned to Santa Clara, and as a result of the political interests and frequent visits I shared with her brother Guillermito, she and I began to see each other again. I visited her house some afternoons. We spoke of things we had in common and avoided subjects that divided us. We began going out together on a regular basis.

One night, we went to the movies with some friends. We returned late, through empty streets. The others walked ahead, while Martha and I straggled along behind. We arrived at the door of her house; she opened it, and we went into the stairwell. The others followed at a distance and stopped at the corner, waiting for me. I could barely see Martha in the dark. I felt that this was the moment. I climbed the step separating us and when I leaned over, her mouth was waiting for me. We kissed tentatively. Her lips were moist, and

I could savor the taste of her mouth. We stared at each other in the dark. Everything was blurry, but I could imagine the look on her face. We took each other's hands. We could hear impatient steps outside. She pulled away. When she reached the first landing, she turned on the entry light. She disappeared, but I retained that image.

It was December 1955, and the year was drawing to a close. I was sitting in an armchair in the living room reading the newspaper. The sugar strike was in the news. What had started as a union dispute had grown into a powerful strike movement that threatened the political stability of the dictatorship. Every government action generated protests, but these spontaneous outbreaks had not coalesced into a winning movement. The various revolutionary groups all lent support to it, but were not strong enough to lead the strike.

A car stopped in front of the house. Through the curtain I could tell that it was Joaquín's Ford. He was agitated when he came in.

"They just captured Quintín Pino and several others from the 26th of July. They gave them a terrible beating!"

"What? Tell me what happened."

"It was just now. The people of the 26th organized a meeting in front of the park to support the strike. The police arrived and with no further ado started raining blows. Several people were wounded. They knocked Quintín—who as you know is active in the 26th Movement—to the ground and dragged him away. It was pure brutality!"

I felt awful, sitting in the peace of my home. "Joaquín, tomorrow we will join the 26th of July!"

## chapter 8

# Joining the 26th of July Movement

Gustavo Arcos led the 26th of July Movement in Las Villas. The Movement was at the height of its organizing. Gustavo and Guillermito (who had joined up early) traveled across the province trying to create a nucleus of members in each town. This was not easy; the dictatorship was becoming more repressive. Many people had been disappointed by the failure of previous efforts. The corruption, injustice, and repressive measures of the Batista regime won other members for the Movement.

I remained in Santa Clara, still not finding any professional work and beginning to despair. Nevertheless, the morning Allán Rosell and I were accepted into the Movement, we became part of the Direccion Provincial. Our first meeting was held at a villa on the edge of town, the home of Guillermito's fiancée. We had to wait while the others considered the case of a fat mulatto accused of insubordination. Finally he was given a harsh reprimand, but was also approved as head of the Movement in Sagua, as there was no one else there who could take the job.

Allán and I were then called into the meeting and introduced to the others, who already knew about us. Quintín Pino was there, unaware that his action had caused my enlistment. The first point of order that day was the organization of youth brigades. These were groups dedicated to armed action and sabotage.

Allán and I saw things differently from Gustavo, who seemed to us to view armed action in an anarchic fashion. We insisted that the armed groups had to have a military organization from the point of view of command and planning of activities. The other leaders were torn between our reasoning and Gustavo's authority.

We spent nearly ten hours arguing until late at night. Allán and I were worried that disorganized actions could result in innocent people getting hurt. We insisted that the actions be controlled and well-coordinated acts of sabotage against property, such as cutting electrical lines, burning sugarcane, and setting off incendiary bombs when there were no people around. It was important to let our fellow Cubans know that we were not against them or willing to sacrifice their lives just to further our cause. Finally, Gustavo, in desperation at our intransigence, agreed with us and invoked the military order of the organization to impose his decision.

The next day I was summoned to Quintín's house because Gustavo wanted to speak with me. When I arrived I met Allán, who had also been summoned.

"Do you know why they summoned us?" I asked Allán.

"No," he replied, "but I am sure it has to do with our attitude during the discussion yesterday."

A little later Gustavo arrived, and we closeted ourselves in a room.

"I have called you here," he said, "to notify you of the course we must follow given in the current situation. This year will be decisive in the fight against Batista. Fidel has said: 'In 1956 we will be free or we will be martyrs.' Any increase in revolutionary activity will be met by an increase in police activity. For that reason we must adopt special measures to guarantee the functioning of the Direccion Provincial. Every day it becomes more difficult for us to get together. It seems to me that we have almost reached the point of having to meet in a moving car. Since there are eight members and only six will fit in a car, two must be eliminated. Since you were the last to join, you are removed from the Direccion Provincial, effective immediately. However, there are many other important duties for you to perform, and we hope that you will accept this measure as necessary and that your enthusiasm will not diminish."

Allán and I looked at each other, not sure what to do. Allán could not contain himself: "Look, Gustavo, the reason you're giving us for your move is too preposterous. I am not a child that you can play with this way." He got up and left. Gustavo looked at the ground.

"As for me," I said, "I am afraid that you are still going to have to put up with me. Your methods are a negation of your ideas. But I will have to combat you within the Movement, becoming more militant. I will stay."

I joined the group working with funds and propaganda. There were only a few of us. We met in downtown Santa Clara in a Chinese restaurant belonging to a man named Chong. In the back room, inside a closet, was an old mimeograph machine that was almost always broken. We also operated from a pharmacy owned by Santiago Riera; there we received packages full of the manifestos that Fidel wrote in Mexico. We anxiously awaited them. Santiago would say, "Something came in" and usher us into the back where there were couches along the wall.

We savored each of Fidel's words and longed to read more. He reflected our feelings perfectly. Each manifesto was a new call to action. We left with our pants stuffed with papers, the waistbands holding them against our bodies. Later we distributed the propaganda to supporters, actually to anyone who would not denounce us. That was a good time to ask for money. They might give us a peseta, maybe a peso, no more. On one occasion, someone gave me 50 pesos—an amount that practically merited a news bulletin!

At that time, although I had already graduated, almost all of the others were students. Eventually other sorts of people began to join: some laborers, business workers, professionals right out of school. They all had one thing in common: their youth. Our elders regarded us with a certain irony, not without affection and, if they were family, with anxiety. But they all thought we were crazy idealists, chasing after some utopian dream that no serious person could support. Going along with us would be like following schoolboys.

The first months after my return were spent this way. Martha and I were talking about marriage. I had to look for work. I could not find anything in Santa Clara, so I went to Havana. I began to visit construction companies and engineering firms. I had always thought that with a degree from a U.S. university it would be easy to find a job, but to my surprise, this was not the case. Supply exceeded demand. You had to have connections or else pay off some politician to get a state contract. And then too, someone with a degree from the United States could not count on any affection from colleagues who had gone to school in Cuba.

After several weeks of interviews and frustrated hopes, I managed to find a job at Shell, thanks to the recommendation of a friend of Joaquín Argüelles. It was hardly ideal: a position as an engineer at 150 pesos a month. In those days the peso was equivalent to the dollar, so this was not a lot of money. But I had to take it until something else showed up. So I went to work for this giant English company designing buildings and gas stations, using my skills with a combination of engineering and architecture.

I worked in Havana Monday through Friday, and on weekends went to Santa Clara. I spent all my time with Martha. It was time to define our relationship. When I refused to become a Catholic, Martha insisted we be married in church anyway.

"If you don't believe in religion, what does it matter if you get married in church and then forget all about it?" she said.

"But it would not be honest to do that," I answered. "Besides, if we can't agree about this, what will we do when we have children? We'll both try to influence them, and even though we'll claim to allow them to choose their religion freely, it's obvious we will not be impartial."

"Yes, that's true; there are no half measures."

A few weeks went by. One of the times I went to Santa Clara, Martha said to me, "Enrique, I have been talking with Father Núñez, my confessor, and he feels that we have to try something new to help us get past this stalemate. Would you be willing to talk to him about our problems?"

"Why not?" I agreed. "Next week, when I come back, we'll go see him."

On Saturday afternoon we went to the Church of the Holy Shepherd. Father Núñez was waiting for us at the entrance, and he took us to a small gothic-style parlor. We sat around a small table, Martha and I on one side, the priest on the other. He was about forty, had a neatly trimmed beard, and wore glasses with thick modern frames. His gestures were eloquent; his expression, worldly. This priest rode a motorcycle and played ball with his students. Martha had made a good choice.

"Martha has told me a lot about you. I really wanted to meet you," he said.

"Thank you," I answered coolly.

"But let's get to the point. Two young people meet, fall in love, want to get married, but religion keeps them apart. How is this possible, if religion exists to unite people? You, Enrique, you say you don't believe in God, but I am sure that you actually do. You just call Him by another name. Your God and our God are the same; there is only one God. You are an engineer; you have studied science and know that order arises from chaos. How? Why? Everything has a single origin, something still governing our world. What is it? We call it God. You can call it what you want, but it is still the same. So why not call it God and worship it as we do?"

I replied, "Who can say how life began? It certainly did not happen the way the Bible says. That is like a story."

"My child, the Bible speaks in parables."

"That is not how it's taught. But we are speaking of more earthly things. How can some men hold all the truth of life and interpret it for others? I do not recognize anything in you that makes me think you are the representative of God. You are just as human as I am. It is all false: the ideas, and the institutions representing them." I spoke heatedly, perhaps even hatefully.

There was silence. Martha looked at her hands on the table. Father Núñez meditated. I stared out the open window at the leaves on the trees, which were starting to turn violet in the dusk. Our silence continued. I began to hear the sound of swallows returning to their nests.

The voice of Father Núñez brought me back to reality: "There is something that cannot be explained: you either have it or you don't, and it is faith. To have faith is to have confidence, to believe, to feel that there is something higher than us, something so great that our senses cannot begin to comprehend its magnitude. And still we know that it is there, acting. It is necessary to arrive at this faith, to feel it. For that you must be imbued with the spirit of the religion, of its beliefs, its rites. You must allow yourself to be permeated by religion to feel this faith. Some feel this faith at once, others find it gradually."

"Look," I answered. "I doubt that I will ever have faith. I think I understand what you mean by faith, and if I do, I don't want to have it. It would displace reason. It would be like . . . living in darkness." The priest made a gesture to interrupt me, but did not respond. I stopped talking, and we were silent again.

It had grown dark, and we were immersed in shadows.

"Night fell without our noticing," he said and rose to turn on the light.

"It is getting late," I said getting up. "We have to go."

"Come back next week."

"I will," I lied.

We went out and walked down the narrow sidewalks, without speaking. When we got to her house, Martha said good-bye. "See you tomorrow."

"See you tomorrow."

I returned to my house thoughtful. The next day was Sunday, and I went to see Martha early. I knocked on her door and climbed up the stairs. I looked at her face and knew her answer to my unspoken question.

We set the wedding for June 23. The preparations began. Martha came to Havana, and after much searching we found a small apartment just a half block from my job: a combination living-dining room, a bedroom, a bath, and a kitchen barely big enough for one; also, a tiny balcony facing the building opposite. The only natural thing you could see past the concrete was the sky high above. Leaning half over the balcony and way to the left, you could make out a bit of street, with automobiles whizzing by.

One day, I was walking down the street, when a car stopped at my side. It was my old acquaintance David. He called out, "Hop in, I'll drive you." I got in.

"Where are you going?" he asked me.

"Home from work," I said, so as not to commit myself.

"Why not come with me? Have dinner at my house and then we can go for a ride. What do you say?"

"Great. I'm not busy."

David told me he had gotten married. I replied that I was getting married myself.

"To whom?" he asked.

"Martha."

"The girl from Santa Clara?"

"Yes."

"I think that is a mistake."

"Why?"

"Look what you would be sacrificing. Your family will never accept your marriage. And after your initial infatuation passes you'll regret it."

"No, I am in love."

"Think it over."

"I have."

We arrived at David's apartment. It was modern and tastefully furnished. His little wife was pretty and shallow. We drank and made small talk while she prepared dinner.

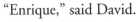

"Enrique," said David.

"Yes?"

"What do you think about inviting Maria and the four of us going to the Tropicana? Do you dare to try that?"

They kept still while I decided. Dormant feelings awoke and came to the surface. How much I would love to see Maria again! But why? It was over. I was getting married in a few weeks. I thought about my mother, who liked Maria. I still had not told my family that I was marrying Martha. I did not dare to.

"I like the idea," I said, trying to seem ironic.

David went to the phone and called Maria. "We'll come pick you up after dinner," he said, looking like a naughty boy.

When we approached the house, Maria came out to meet the car. She was wearing a pale blue dress that looked good with her hair. I got out to open the door.

"Hello," I said.

"How is everything?"

Maria did not know I was getting married. David and his wife said things to tease us, making Maria blush. It was a difficult evening that finally ended, but not until Sunday.

I did not go to Santa Clara the next weekend, in order to stay in Havana and go out with Maria. She asked if I still loved her, and I compared my feelings toward her with what I felt for Martha. Manolo called Saturday inviting me to go on a fishing trip with him. I accepted and went out fishing, without calling Maria.

The next week I went to Santa Clara. That night I was getting ready to go out, and my mother was watching me get dressed. My mother could always tell when something was going on with me. She was so sweet and sensitive. Everyone in our neighborhood loved her, not just for her beauty but for her kindness and generosity. She was always ready to help out anyone, and as we grew more wealthy she frequently gave food and clothing and money to many people in Santa Clara who were not so fortunate as we were.

But she always knew when I was up to something.

"Are you going to Martha's house?"

"Yes."

"It's not nice the way you hang around that girl."

"Why? If I like her."

"And how will all this end?"

I made up my mind: "In marriage."

"You can't be serious . . ."

"Yes, I am serious. We are planning to get married very soon."

"You can't, you can't," she wept. "You know that you can't."

"It is already decided, and the best thing would be to resign yourself."

"No, never! I would rather die."

"Don't go dying, because I am not going to give up Martha because of your bigotry."

My father, who was in the living room, heard her sobs and came in. He listened to our last words standing in the doorway.

"I cannot believe what I hear," he said. "You, my son, you cannot be capable of causing us this pain. Tell me it is just a flirtation, a silly love affair."

"No, I cannot deceive you. I have thought over the results of this act, and I am ready to face the consequences."

My father sat down on the bed with his head between his hands, and for the first time I saw him cry. I could not bear the sight of that hard man crying, and the sobs rose in my throat. All three of us wept. Finally I regained control, stood up, and left.

I did not say a thing to my parents on the night of our marriage at Martha's family home. Martha had asked only her immediate family and a few of her relatives, and as for me, I invited only Joaquín. Contradictory feelings welled up in my heart: on the one hand, great happiness to be marrying Martha; on the other hand, sadness at the absence of my parents, especially my mother, whom I loved dearly.

One day, after we had been in Havana a while, I received a call from Maria.

"Enrique, can I see you?"

"Of course, when?"

"Right away, this morning?"

"Sure. Is ten OK, in the cafeteria near Shell?"

"Yes."

I arrived before her. I sat at the counter, watching the street. Maria came in immediately, and I felt the old heat. She took the seat next to me.

"I heard you are thinking of getting married," she said, without looking at me.

"No, I am already married."

She turned her head so that I could not see her face. I did not know what to say. We took our leave with clumsy phrases. I felt like a part of me was leaving.

# The Plains

## chapter 9

# Conspiracy in Havana

I noticed people milling around. I looked up from my desk: the clerks were crowded around the time clock—it was lunch time. I stamped my card and went out. Walking the few yards to my house was enough to soak the neck of my shirt. I got out my key and opened the door. The first thing I saw was three men sitting on the living room sofa: Armando Hart, Faustino Pérez—who was now directing the 26th of July Movement in Havana—and someone I didn't know. It was Carlos Franqui, the journalist with *Carteles,* who was going to work with the 26th of July Movement as part of a plan they would soon explain to me.

Martha came in from the kitchen to talk about lunch. Were we going to eat here? As the daughter of a wealthy doctor's family in Santa Clara, Martha had never learned to cook, so when we moved to our first apartment in Havana, she nearly burned down the kitchen. She became accomplished as a cook very quickly, of course, but on this occasion there wasn't enough food in the house, so we decided to go out.

Nobody had a car, so we walked over to Club 23, which was nearby. In its dimly lit bar, the top men from the nearby offices were drinking and talking with beautiful women. We went into the dining room and sat down at an isolated table.

While they looked over the menu, I studied Franqui. He was thin, under forty. He looked like a campesino, though not completely coarse—unruly hair, sharp eyes that sometimes stared too long, bushy moustache, sallow face. He was carelessly but not poorly dressed, and his gestures were quick and abrupt, as if always cut

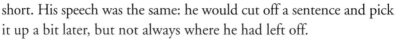

short. His speech was the same: he would cut off a sentence and pick it up a bit later, but not always where he had left off.

I tried to avoid his eyes, but he noticed that I was watching him. Not knowing what to do, he said, "So, what do you hear from Julio Iglesias?" Franqui asked me. Iglesias was the president of Shell.

"I don't know. I rarely see him, and when I do he doesn't see me."

"Iglesias is in with Batista," Franqui insisted. "He has become a millionaire so fast."

The waiter came and took our order. Faustino next said to me, "Listen, your honeymoon is over. It's not enough to let the compañeros meet at your house. You're not an active member, more of a sympathizer. You have to get into the Movement more. It's a joke the way you're always in your pajamas when anybody goes to your house."

Everyone laughed. They were teasing me because Martha and I had just been married, and we were still really on our long honeymoon after about three weeks in our new apartment. This is why I was always in my pajamas whenever anyone knocked on our door. I replied, "You're right, yes. Of course, I am ready to play a more active role. What needs to be done?"

"Here's the plan," Faustino went on. "We want to produce a newspaper. Besides helping to unify the Movement, a newspaper would allow us to make our objectives public—it would provide direction to the many people who would like to know what they can do to help. Franqui has been chosen to direct the project. He has experience, and he has some contacts who can facilitate the practical aspects. You are to work with him."

"I am at Franqui's service," I said.

Armando put in, "We need a name for the newspaper, one with some impact. It has to send a message. Faustino and I were thinking of *Aldabonazo* ("Bang"). *Aldabonazo* has an impact like Chibás had. And it would reflect our intention: it is a call."

"I don't like it," said Franqui. "It's too bound up with orthodoxy, with all that signifies. I think the name should reflect the Movement's purpose. I suggest *Revolución.*"

"I don't know. *Revolución* sounds pretty generic to me," I put in. "We should try to find something more original, completely new. I was just reading about *Iskra*—'Spark'—Lenin's newspaper. What about *Flame* or *Blaze*?"

We argued all through lunch. Finally Faustino decided on *Aldabonazo,* against the lively protests of Franqui.

That is what the first issue was called, but after that the name was changed to *Revolución,* in a unilateral decision by Franqui. (Years later, this same newspaper changed its name again, this time to *Granma,* in honor of the boat that in 1956 brought Fidel and his men back from Mexico to Cuba.)

Franqui and I soon became friends. We saw a lot of each other because of the newspaper, but also because we enjoyed each other's company. I wrote articles for the paper and worked with Franqui in printing and distribution as well as collecting the money from our sympathizers and members to pay the bills. We published a few thousand copies of each issue and distributed them very carefully hand to hand. We could never be seen distributing the paper, or we would be arrested and tortured. Some of us were, in fact, so we were very secretive about our publication and its circulation.

At this point the 26th of July Movement was organized into national, provincial, zonal, and nucleus groups in the neighborhoods. We also had various committees—for example, action, propaganda (which was how we published *Revolución*), and financial.

The financial committees recruited contributions from the members, a large group but very limited in its economic resources. Another important source of contributions was the Civic Resistance movement, the *Resistencia,* which consisted of sympathizers—professional and business people who could contribute larger amounts of money. As time went by and more wealthy people came to the conclusion that we were going to succeed, their contributions began to come in.

But this did not happen until later, and at this time we were still struggling to produce our new paper, which was passed secretly from person to person.

We had gotten a press to print the newspaper. It was stored in the garage of a private home, rented for that purpose. With great difficulty, we found a compañero to live in the house with his family. When the newspaper was printed, a car drove into the garage and was loaded behind closed doors.

One afternoon Franqui came to see me, a frown on his face. I knew something bad had happened.

"The police have picked up some people responsible for distributing the newspaper. One of them knows where it is printed. We have to move the press immediately, before they seize the house." He paused for breath, looking exhausted. "I've been to several places, but nobody wants to keep the press. I don't know what we're going to do."

We considered a few possibilities, but rejected all of them. Franqui got up and went to the door. He looked at me during one of his long pauses. Finally he said, "There is only one solution; I will keep it in my house!"

"But that's dangerous. You live in the middle of Santos Suárez."

Another pause. Then, decisively, he said, "There's no time to lose!" And he left.

We talked constantly about the need for an official program.

"Developing a program is like growing up politically," said Armando.

"A program would earn the respect of those people who doubt our maturity," I added.

"Plus, a program would show our commitment to the people," Faustino stated.

"And besides, a program would allow us to shape the ideology of members of the Movement," Franqui maintained.

We decided that we would take on the task of formulating one. When the program was ready, we would present it to Fidel—who was still in Mexico—for his approval, and make it public before he returned to Cuba. Armando would be responsible for the philosophical-political part; Franqui would cover culture and social problems, and Mario Llerena, education; I would cover agrarian reform. Faustino told us that Felipe Pazos and Regino Boti, two important economists, were preparing an economic thesis for the Movement.

With the help of Sabadí, an ex-sailor expelled for his political ideas, and Paco Chavarry and Héctor Rodríguez Llompart, two university students who belonged to the Movement, I tried to enlist a few more recognized economists in the project. But they all knew of our revolutionary fervor and refused to have anything to do with it. I decided we should attempt the task ourselves, despite our scant knowledge of economics.

We worked at my house. Armando Hart did his thinking out loud, and when he was there, none of the rest of us got anything done. He had just married Haydée Santamaría, who came along sometimes. Yeyé—as we all called Haydée—was our ideal revolutionary woman. She had been at Moncada, where her brother and his fiancée were killed. Meanwhile Llerena's work was going well, and he came over every day to read what he had written. Martha was pregnant at the time and slept through most of this activity.

Carlos Franqui, who had worked in the Communist Party, was the most advanced politically. He posed problems for us to consider. One morning, while I walked him to the corner to catch the bus, he said to me, "The ultimate aim of the revolution must be to establish a Communist society. Until we eliminate private property, we will not eliminate the evils of our current society. We must nationalize the factories and the farms, and education as well, in order to fully empower the masses. Anything less will not be a true revolution."

On that Sunday morning there was no traffic in Infanta Street. To my ears, accustomed to the din of heavy traffic, that silence was like an emptiness. Everything seemed held in suspense. A few parents were out with their children, dressed in Sunday clothes, walking to the homes of their own parents, oblivious of the changes that Franqui was proposing, which would totally upset their lives when they were accomplished.

The street was lined with tall buildings whose owners were either asleep at that early hour or else getting ready for a swim at the club. At the far end of the block were the Shell offices, where each day's work furthered the interests of its foreign investors. At the intersection of Infanta and 23rd was Ambar Motors and above it the offices of its owner, the Italian Barletta, a small state within the larger one.

All that calm, all that order, all that equilibrium, would fall to pieces if what Franqui was advocating ever became reality. The question of what might happen was food for thought. But at this point it was all just a dream. Overthrowing Batista and establishing an honest government, one that would give land to the landless and work to the poor, as well as defend our national interests—that would be enough for us. The Americans would not allow much more than that, we thought.

Meanwhile, tension was mounting. The year was almost over, and Fidel had promised to return before its end. Some compañeros had gone to Mexico to join the invading forces, Faustino among them. Armando had gone underground. Acts of sabotage increased. Anticipating future advances, revolutionary enthusiasm also intensified.

A telegram brought news: Fidel had been detained in Mexico. Weapons had been seized. Franqui was sent to Mexico—as a journalist, he could try to create support for the prisoners.

We bombarded Franqui with questions when he came back. Fidel had been freed, he told us. Franqui had spoken with him, and he shared his impressions of Fidel. What kind of man was he? What were his thoughts? What were his political ideas?

Fidel was the total revolutionary, Franqui said. He lived for revolution twenty-four hours a day. But . . . what exactly did he believe in? That had not been so clear. Fidel spoke only of the next landing in Cuba, of the uprising that would take place, of the fight, of arms. His personality was dynamic—the conversation went only where he wanted it to go. Yes, Franqui had noticed that Fidel wore a religious medal. Was Fidel religious? Neither Armando nor Franqui could answer that question.

"Maybe he wears that medal like a kind of amulet or as a memento of his family," Franqui ventured.

We agreed we had to watch this carefully.

Then Franqui said, "Since Faustino left, some of the action groups are on their own."

"It seems unavoidable," I argued. "The activists can't really know the civilian leaders."

"But they feel used. They feel that they are the ones running the risks. They refer to us, for example, as *the intellectuals.*"

"Really? But that is unfair!"

"Fair or not, that is what they say."

My voice sounded weak: "We should do something . . ."

And Franqui: "I know where to get some bombs."

"Good, let's go! Remember, the idea is to let people know that we are here and active, but not to harm them."

We caught the bus at the corner. Going down 12th Street, we saw the sea on the other side of the Malecón. The sun had just set. When we reached a building with paint peeling from the salt breeze, we went down some steps to a basement apartment. Seeing no one around, we knocked on the door. It opened to reveal Fico in his underpants. We hurried in. The air was heavy, the stone floor covered with butts. Through the cigar smoke we saw four or five young people, also in underclothes, sitting around a table covered with wires and bombs. On the bed lay dozens of bombs of all sizes.

Fico explained proudly. "These are 'elephant legs,' the kind used to blow up electric towers. And those little ones are percussives, which explode on contact." They were painted yellow and were lying on a blue blanket.

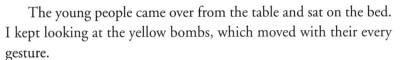

The young people came over from the table and sat on the bed. I kept looking at the yellow bombs, which moved with their every gesture.

The boys recounted their latest adventures. They went out only at night, as they were all wanted by the police. They supplied several action groups who were charged with dynamiting electric poles to cause blackouts, burning the sugarcane plantations of Batista's cohorts, and executing known police murderers, among other tasks. At this point Batista's police were killing many of our comrades, so we decided to retaliate by assassinating those identified as murderers by shooting at them as they passed in the streets in their cars.

A skinny kid with a pockmarked face told a story about someone who had made a fool of himself. During all the laughter he took one of the yellow bombs and threw it into the air. Several arms flew up to catch the bomb. The guy who caught it tossed it back, and it went back and forth.

I felt myself beginning to sweat. I looked over at Franqui, who said, "Well, Fico, we want a pair of bombs. We're going to do a little job tonight."

Back outside, where it was already dark, I took a welcome breath of fresh air. "Those assholes are crazy!"

"Those games are their safety valve," said Franqui.

The bus drove up.

"Picked a place?" asked Franqui.

"No . . . it's early, there are too many people in the street."

"We could go to a movie . . ."

"They do searches there. Maybe some store."

Two cops in uniform got on and sat down behind us.

"We'd better stop here," said Franqui quietly.

We got off at Linea and walked to the little park at Linea and E Street. We sat down on a bench.

"That garage across the street belongs to a Batista supporter," I said.

"Too many lights. We would have to drive by, throw our bombs from the car."

"Or we could plant them in the park here, except that couple has seen us. Let's hope they leave."

Franqui stood up. "We're acting suspicious. We'd better split up and plant our bombs separately."

We went in different directions. I wandered this way and that, but nowhere seemed right. My hands were ink-stained from the newspaper wrapping the bomb. The streets seemed empty; I was the only one out. Anyone who saw me would be able to identify me. Finally I found an empty spot where no one was around and set off the explosion, knocking down a telephone pole and some electrical wires.

Then I caught a bus and went home.

When our program was ready, I was selected to go to Mexico to present it to Fidel and talk it over with him. Under the pretext of attending the wedding of an old friend, a buddy from the university, I obtained a short leave of absence from my job at Shell and even a letter of recommendation for the Mexican authorities.

Nobody at Shell knew, of course, that I was leading a double life. In fact, when some of my coworkers would come up to me and innocently ask me about politics or show me a clandestine copy of *Revolución* that they had somehow acquired, I would pretend to be totally indifferent and even horrified that they should approach me with such ideas. I appeared to them at all times a very conservative and unpolitical person.

Meanwhile, the 26th of July Movement managed to scrape up the money for the trip. Somebody got me an overcoat, since it was the last week of November.

In the airport, with my briefcase full of subversive papers, I felt as though everyone were watching me. Finally I boarded the plane and began to feel calmer. In Mexico City I checked into a discreet hotel. Then I took a cab to one of the two addresses I had been given to establish contact. When we finally got there, I discovered that the people I was looking for had moved. Nobody in the neighborhood could give me any information about their whereabouts.

I began to worry: I had only one more chance to find Fidel in that immense city, where I did not know anyone. Because of the recent police actions against Cuban exiles, I took a devious route to lose a possible tail. I switched taxis several times, and once, when I got into a tourist cab, I went along to see the ruins at Teotihuacán. We drove through a desolate landscape, with adobe houses on both sides of the road. We passed Indians. I was absorbed in my thoughts and hardly noticed what I would have found interesting in other circumstances. The ruins were full of Indians selling all sorts of things. There were lots of American tourists.

We returned at dusk, and the driver suggested I stop at a brothel. When I said no, he gave me a surprised look in the car's rearview mirror. I gave him my second address, which was in El Pedregal de San Angel. With the sun gone, it got very cold. I had left my coat in the hotel, and now I was shivering. It grew late, and we still had not found the place. Street after street, named for the elements: Fire, Air, Water. My anxiety increased. The driver wanted to turn back, but I insisted that we keep on searching. Our headlights lit up the number on a stone fence. There it was. Still I could not breathe easy. The doorman made several trips back and forth and finally brought a woman with a Cuban accent, her face concealed by the darkness. I told her who I was and why I had come; at last the iron gate swung open, and I was allowed in.

Outside I couldn't see very much of the house, but inside the light revealed a luxurious room. We sat in one corner of its vast space. The woman who had received me identified herself: she was Lidia, Fidel's older sister. Soon a gorgeous woman came in; she was Orquídea Pino, a Cuban singer and the wife of the Mexican engineer Alfonso Gutiérrez, known as Fofo. Gutiérrez, who owned the house, was a supporter of the revolution.

She peppered me with questions. How was Cuba? Was there much revolutionary fervor? Would the people rise up when Fidel came back? Would we win?

My opinions disappointed her a bit. There remained much to do organizationally, I told her, and there were as yet very few arms to support Fidel's landing. Other compañeros from Cuba had been more optimistic. We talked. Then they told me about the problems Fidel experienced during the detentions. The Mexican police had seized part of the arms cache. There was still some risk of arrest. Fidel and most other members of the force were in hiding.

Another woman came in—Melba Hernández, whom I knew from Cuba. She too bombarded me with questions and emphasized the danger we were in. Then we heard the telephone ring, and Orquídea ran to answer it. Everyone was very nervous, which I attributed to their fear of a police raid. It was one of the places Fidel had lived.

I told Melba the reason for my trip, explaining that I needed to see Fidel to give him some documents and get his authorization to publish them immediately. Melba said that it was a difficult time to meet with Fidel but that she would certainly raise the subject with Gustavo Arcos when he arrived.

Gustavo showed up very late that night, along with Fofo. Again I got all the questions about Cuba. When Gustavo knew why I was there, he told me that it would be impossible to see Fidel. What's more, I should return to Cuba immediately. Fidel had to minimize his contacts to avoid another detention, which would keep him from fulfilling his promise of returning to Cuba before the year was over. It was almost December. Batista had bribed the Mexican police, who were watching the house. And to make things worse, the man who had tipped off the police about the arms was being held here. His fate was to be decided that very night.

Melba, Gustavo, and I sat around the table. The evidence seemed conclusive. Our decision: the traitor must die. But how would we dispose of the body? After considering a few ideas, Gustavo proposed, "Let's drop it from an airplane!"

"But the body will still land somewhere," I said, "and even if the face is smashed, it can be identified by fingerprints. Perhaps we could find a lake."

More discussion with no decision.

We took turns watching the prisoner, because he had already tried to jimmy a window that night. When Gustavo came on duty, I lay down on a sofa in the living room.

Fofo woke me in the morning—it was time to go. He had arranged for me to leave that same afternoon. I said good-bye to everyone. The atmosphere was tense. When we were in the car, Fofo said to me, "The lives of eighty-two men are at stake." I realized then that Fidel had already left, but I didn't say anything.

When I arrived in Havana, Aldo Santamaría was waiting at my house. He told me, "We just got the news. Fidel is on his way!"

Much later, when I spoke to Raúl Castro, Fidel's brother, in the Sierra Maestra and told him I had arrived in Mexico just as they were leaving, he said, "That's too bad. You should have come a couple of days earlier."

"Why?" I asked.

"So we could have brought you with us, on the *Granma!*" he replied. But I had missed out on that unique opportunity.

"The pressure on Fidel is terrible," said Franqui. "We have to do something here in Havana."

We had been receiving much contradictory news. At first all we heard came from the national press, which said that all the men who landed from the *Granma* had been "liquidated" right at the beginning. So we were very much concerned about our comrades and what this might mean for the revolution if it turned out to be true. Of course, our determination was to go on even if it was.

Soon after receiving the initial misinformation, we received more accurate news through our own sources that Fidel was alive and that some of our comrades had survived.

Very few of the original expeditionary group were left, though. Most of them were dead or in jail. The rebellion in Santiago de Cuba, an uprising intended to coordinate with Fidel's invasion, had been crushed too, after days of heroic fighting. Almost nothing had happened anywhere else, but Batista had launched a wave of repression that had paralyzed what was left of the Movement.

"Some sabotage, something dramatic, would raise the morale of the people," I said to a group of us from the 26th of July one night. I knew that we needed to show the world that the revolution was still strong and alive. We also wanted to distract Batista's police and armed forces from their efforts to defeat Fidel's remaining forces in the Sierra Maestra.

"The College of Belen has live phosphorus in its lab," said Paco Chavarry. "Maybe we could steal it. I know some students there."

Paco and Héctor managed to get a flask of live phosphorus. We cut it with water and divided it into small vials, which we hid in canisters of rice and sugar in Martha's kitchen.

It was the Christmas season, and the stores were full of people. Most of the people in Havana were in a holiday mood, unaware of the tragedy to come. We were going to set fire to the main stores in Havana. We chose a Saturday, the busiest day. The hour: 5:45 P.M., fifteen minutes before closing. Héctor, Paco, Franqui, Sabadí, and I headed five groups; we would hit five different stores simultaneously.

We met in our small apartment. We went over the plan of action one last time. We divided up the live phosphorus, and everyone left separately. I had to set fire to the five-and-dime. Martha insisted on coming along; she was pregnant, so we would not arouse suspicion. The store was crowded. Everyone was carrying packages. Carols were playing, and decorations were hanging from the ceiling. We walked through several departments, looking for an opportunity, but there was always someone around. I checked the clock: 5:40. We had to act. We went over to a low table holding a tall stack of bathroom rugs. Martha covered me as we pretended to choose one. I had already unscrewed the lid from the vial of live phosphorus in my

pocket, and now I slid my hand into the pile of carpets and dumped it out in a spot where it could not hurt anyone. We straightened up to walk away, both of us expecting to feel a hand on our shoulder at any moment, but no one had noticed a thing, and we made it out into the street before the flash and explosion. We stood at the corner, waiting for a bus. In a while the alarm sounded. We got on the bus in the chaos that followed.

Little by little the revolutionary current grew stronger. One day, as I was going home, I met Faustino Pérez and a young man who was very quiet and serious: Frank País, the leader of the uprising in Santiago de Cuba. Faustino was one of the men who had landed with Fidel from the *Granma* and was down from the Sierra Maestra to reorganize the Movement. Fidel—with a handful of survivors—would remain in the mountains at first, as a symbol.

## chapter 10

# The Civil Resistance Movement

Fidel was in the Sierra Maestra, and we, the underground fighters in the cities, were working to strengthen the organization, propaganda, sabotage, and fundraising in order to acquire arms for the guerillas in the Sierra.

In those early months of 1957, when I was a member of the leadership of the 26th of July in Havana, which was commanded by my friend Faustino Pérez, we began to worry that the apartment where Martha and I had lived since we were married was known by too many people as a revolutionary meeting place and that we were in danger of being denounced.

"We have to get out of here. Too many people know this house. There have been a lot of arrests lately, and the police have been using more and more savage methods to obtain confessions. The last few days they've been awful. Do you remember a young lawyer, a big fat guy, who came here with Pepe Prieto not too long ago?"

"No," Martha replied, "I can't say that I do."

"Well anyway, they took him to a police station to question him about a compañero of ours who is in jail. Ventura became suspicious and held him as well. They stopped at nothing; finally they put a metal plate over his body and hammered on it. All his ribs were broken, and he died of an internal hemorrhage."

"They are monsters."

"He had to be buried in an open casket because the corpse was so swollen the cover wouldn't close."

But Martha was remembering the past: "We've been so happy here."

"Yes, Martha, but that doesn't matter. Now we must look for another apartment."

We found one after a lengthy search; it was modern and quite a bit bigger, in the Nuevo Vedado district, a half block from my sister Silvia. It met all my conditions: it had two entrances and was on a relatively quiet street. In those days, I knew we had to have another quick way out of any house that we entered.

I went to see the manager of our building to tell him we were moving. As he prepared the papers, Mr. Fontanillas looked up at me and said, "Now I can tell you. Several of your neighbors have reported you for holding clandestine meetings in your apartment. The worst is the woman next door. Her brother is a police captain, and he comes to visit her sometimes. I tried to keep them quiet by reminding them that you are young and know a lot of people from working for Shell. I didn't say anything because I didn't want to worry you. But I made an arrangement with the doorman so that if the police ever came, he would give you some warning and the key to the service elevator." With a complicitous smile he added, "I was a revolutionary in the days of Machado."

We moved the next day. We didn't even wait for the electric company to turn on the lights. That same night Faustino came to the dark apartment to see me. As we talked, Faustino's eyes adjusted to the darkness, and he said to me, "You know something?"

"What?"

"I've been here before . . ."

"No, that can't be!"

"Yes, I'm almost sure." Faustino asked Lilliam Mesa, who had come with him, "Lilliam, doesn't this apartment look familiar?"

"Yes, I do have the feeling that I have been here before."

"I know!" said Faustino. "Pepe Llanusa used to live here; he had to move when the place 'got hot'; the police were watching it. What's more, Ventura lives around here and goes down this street every day."

Martha, who had come over, said sadly, "What are we going to do? After all our work."

I thought about making another move and decided. "We will stay here! It is what God and Fate want . . ."

Remberto Junquera was one of the most active members of the Civic Resistance in Havana. Similar to the 26th of July, this organization was started in the province of the Oriente by people unwilling to be as totally militant as the 26th of July for a variety of reasons. The Resistance mainly included professionals, women, and businessmen. Their main activities were fundraising and passing out propaganda, but they also offered their homes for meetings and as places to hide fugitives from the police.

Mario Llerena was the first director of the Civil Resistance in Havana, but he went into exile when his activities were discovered. Faustino chose me to replace him.

Paging through a telephone book, Remberto said, "We have to give you a nom de guerre. We each have one. Anything occur to you? Do you have one in mind?"

"No, none."

"There are several ways to choose a name. For example, you work for Shell. Let's see . . . here it is. Let's look at the column next to it, the same line: Angel Sierra. Fine, Enrique, as of today you are Angel Sierra for Civil Resistance work."

I liked the name; I used it till the end of the struggle, not the whole name but just the one: Sierra.

Remberto dropped me off a block from where the meeting would be held that day. I walked down the sidewalk looking for the place. It was a three-story apartment building. I did not see anything suspicious around, and I went in. Going to secret meetings was like betting on a hooded fighting cock. You never knew when the door would open to reveal the police. When they seized one of our houses, they would usually stay there for several days. As it was not always possible to warn all the compañeros that the house was now a trap, some unsuspecting person often fell into the hands of the enemy.

As I went up the stairs I felt the usual fear. By this time I had developed the instincts of a clandestine operator. I would always be looking over my shoulder and checking to see if I was followed. Finally, I knocked on the door and waited for centuries. The peephole opened, then the door. I relaxed—it was Porro. There were too many people inside. Porro's wife watched the street from behind the curtains. I waited in the study until their meeting was over. Porro was an architect, and his study was full of scale models and drawings. I was studying a drawing when Porro came in to take me to Faustino, Armando, and Yeyé. We exchanged greetings before Faustino got to the point:

"We brought you here to introduce you to Ray, an engineer. He is very important to us—he has good contacts, resources he can draw on. He has helped us in the past, but now is ready to join us. We feel that he would be most useful in the Resistance, working with you, to strengthen our work on that front."

"It seems like a good idea to me. I know who Ray is. I applied for a job from him once, and he turned me down. Now you want me to employ him. That's the revolution."

I went in to Ray. He did not remember me. We got down to business. Ray had a lot of ideas and seemed very enthusiastic. He had organized some actions on his own and was telling me how he could contribute to the Resistance when the door opened and Porro's wife appeared. She said, "There is something strange going on in the street. A surveillance car has gone around the block several times."

Everyone spoke at once. Faustino took control. We had two choices: to try to jump onto the roof of the neighboring building or to leave one by one and see what happened, since it could be a false alarm. We decided on the second alternative.

Somebody had to go first. I wanted to wait for someone else to offer, but my conscience made me volunteer. I went downstairs with my body tight, as if I were pushing against inner forces. When I got to the door, I went down the last steps, expecting to feel bullets enter my body. I strode away looking straight ahead. When I reached the corner, Remberto was not there. While I waited for the bus two blocks away, Remberto drove up and got me. He too had seen the surveillance car.

Later we learned that the alarm had been unfounded.

Carlos Franqui kept going to the window and peering through the blinds: "You know that Ventura lives around here?"

"Yes, I know. Faustino told me."

"You have to be careful. Ventura is very clever."

"Don't worry; he doesn't know me."

"If they catch me again, I will kill myself before enduring their tortures."

I wanted to change the subject: "Your wife was here yesterday with Carlitos. It's been a long time since I saw him—he's gotten big. Remember when he was a baby, what fun he was?"

"Yes, Carlitos has grown." He went again to the window. "You have no idea what they are capable of. The day of the palace attack, when I was imprisoned, they were like sheep. They said their leaders forced them to do it. They talked loud, so we would hear them. But after dark, when they realized that the attack had failed, they showed us no mercy. They took me out to the yard several times and raked their weapons over me. I wanted to die."

"And to make matters worse," I said, "you have ulcers. You have to be careful. The best thing would be for you to leave the country for a while and recover. You could come back later on. In your present condition you cannot do much, and living underground you will never get better."

"No, I am better. I don't need to go abroad; my place is here. Look, do you know the people I am staying with?"

"No, Arnold arranged the house; one of them is an old friend of his. And he discussed your health with them, and they are willing to take care of you."

"Have you seen the house? Does it have good exits? I hope that Arnold's friend is not being watched."

"Look, Carlos, the house was chosen very carefully. Arnold understands the situation. On the other hand, there aren't many options; since the palace failure, not many people will offer their house to hide a wanted man."

We heard the sound of a car pulling up. Carlos ran to the window: "There's a car in front of the building!"

I looked out. "It's ours, let's go."

We went downstairs. Franqui looked left and right. We got in the car and started off. When we got to his new apartment, I said to Franqui, "You need a name. What do you want?"

"You decide; anything is OK with me."

"We will call you Félix Capote," I said, recalling that name from somewhere.

We parked opposite the house. We crossed the street and entered an old building. We went up to the second floor and knocked on the door. It was opened immediately—they must have seen us pull up.

The young man who opened the door said, "Come in. I am Arnold Rodríguez's friend."

We walked into the room. Pointing to Franqui, I said, "This is compañero Félix Capote, who is going to stay with you."

The young man looked at us, astonished. "Something is wrong," I thought, and I asked, worried, "What's the matter?"

"Félix Capote is my name," he said.

July 1957 was drawing to an end, and the revolutionary tide was rising every day. In the Oriente, Fidel won resounding victories for the rebel forces: at La Plata, Palma Mocha, Uvero.

On July 26, to celebrate that date, attacks were made on Estrada Palma, Bueycito mines, and San Pablo de Yao. Some names of the guerrilla fighters were becoming legendary: Juan Almeida, Guillermo García, Ernesto "Che" Guevara. Now the message and triumph of the Sierra Maestra—no longer just a symbol, but a model for the way to fight tyranny—began to reach the cities and the plains.

In the cities, fighting broke out again. Hundreds of compañeros were already in prison. Cuban families trembled at the names of Batista's police henchmen like Carratalá and Ventura.

The Movement had settled on a strategy: a general strike supported by armed warfare. We were working toward that when the news arrived: "Frank País was killed in a Santiago street. The city has declared a strike."

In the days that followed, city after city joined the protest movement. Frank's body became our banner. Holguín, Camagüey, Santa Clara, and Matanzas were shut down. The spontaneous strike reached toward Havana. Only the life of the capital seemed indifferent to Frank's death.

The house was at the end of a street. I knocked, and they identified me through the blinds. Inside I saw Faustino sitting at a table with several compañeros. His face was haggard: he had been freed just a few days before, after a hunger strike in the jail. He invited me to have a seat and continued the exposition that my arrival had interrupted.

"Nobody knows better than we do ourselves that we are not ready for a general strike. The organization of our various and different groups is still quite weak, as is our control over the centers of production. Nevertheless, the death of Frank has accomplished what our organization could not: to paralyze the whole country, with the exception of Havana. If we could bring everything to a halt in Havana, too, the strike would be complete, and Batista would fall in a few hours.

"But anyone who knows the difficulties of fighting in Havana—where the government counts on all the resources of power—knows that success will not be easy. What is more, if we fail, we run the risk of losing everything that we have achieved up to now. There is the dilemma: either we let this moment, in which the people have gone ahead of us, pass, waiting until we are better prepared, or we gamble everything on the strike. I would like to hear the opinions of the compañeros on the matter."

Everyone present voted in favor of supporting the strike. Faustino continued, "All right, it's a unanimous decision. Now we must fix a date for the people to know that on that day we will support the strike with whatever arms we have."

It was felt that a minimum of three or four days was necessary to get ready. The chosen date was Monday, August 5. Nobody would return to work after the weekend. The primary goal had to be paralyzing the transport system. Faustino went on giving instructions to the different compañeros. As a member of the leadership of the 26th of July Movement in Havana (besides guiding the Civic Resistance and participating in propaganda, fundraising, and sabotage), I was also the one who was in charge of relations with the Civil Coordinating Committee, which comprised religious, intellectual, and professional groups that sought a political solution to the conflict. So Faustino said to me, "As for you, you have a lot of work ahead of you this weekend. The Civic Resistance must play an important role in making sure that nobody goes to work on Monday. That will be your slogan. But there is something else we must accomplish, given the relations that you maintain with the leaders of the civic organizations. We need them to issue a manifesto calling for Batista's resignation."

I was stunned. "Faustino, do you know what you are requesting? The civic organizations are fine when it comes to calling for harmony between all Cubans, but can you imagine the leaders of the religious associations, the cultural institutions, and the Rotary Club requesting Batista's resignation?"

Faustino's look bore into me as if he were trying to inject the possibility of the idea into my brain. Then, with a smile, he said, "I don't want to see you again until you bring me the manifesto."

"That is like a good-bye forever," I said. As I was getting ready to go, I remembered something. "Listen, Faustino, I know some people in the communications sector. Do you want to speak to them?"

Faustino said yes.

I summoned a meeting of the leaders of the Civic Resistance. I revealed the instructions received from Faustino. We agreed on the form for transmitting the strike slogan, and everybody got to work.

Later, I called up Raúl de Velasco, president of the Cuban Medical Association and chairman of Civil Coordinating Committee. I told him that it was urgent that I come to his house at once; he agreed to see me.

When I arrived at his house, a beautiful mansion in an exclusive section of Havana, Velasco was waiting uneasily for me. He was imagining something bad. When we were in his office, he asked me what was going on. I replied, "The Direccion del Movimiento has decreed a strike for this coming Monday. We need you to issue a manifesto demanding Batista's resignation."

"What? His resignation? Are you crazy? That is impossible! I am sure that nobody will agree to that."

Then I spoke like Faustino: "Now or never. There is no time to lose."

Velasco rubbed his forehead. "It's already Friday afternoon. Most people must already have left Havana. I repeat that I am sure we will not accomplish anything, but I will try to get together with the executive committee and raise the subject with them anyway."

"Look, Doctor, it's not enough to pose the problem to them. You have to make the greatest effort to obtain the manifesto. Don't forget that we consider you like one of us."

"I only want what is best for Cuba."

"And in that you can count on our support. Your participation in this matter is a guarantee for us."

"Ah . . . but unfortunately not everyone thinks that way. There are some who fight with me because they see me as a competitor. That is the case with Miró Cardona, the president of the National Association of Lawyers, for example. I can assure them that I am not motivated by any personal ambition, but if someday the best destiny of the mother country demands that I occupy some public position, I would take it as a true sacrifice, believe me!"

"No, I realize that. Although you may not know it, you are a revolutionary, and now you must act like one. We know that with your prestige and your ability we will obtain the manifesto."

"Be assured that I will do everything I can, and if we fail, it is because others were opposed."

It was not until Saturday morning that I could meet with García, the person I knew in communications. I told him, "García, the Direccion del Movimiento has commissioned me to request your support for a strike. Your control of the sector would allow us to paralyze the country's communications."

"Don't you believe it. There are others who have to join in for that goal to be realized: the telephone people. They handle part of the communication network. If they go on strike, we will also go."

"Why do you make their participation a condition of yours?"

García tried to think of some logical answer. "Their participation would be a guarantee of success."

"Could you facilitate the contact for us?"

"Of course! I personally will take you to see Vincente Rubiera, the secretary general of the telephone workers union. Call me this evening."

At home there was a message waiting for me. Dr. Velasco wanted to see me in the apartment of Dr. Pérez Fernández at two.

Pérez Fernández opened the door in person and led me to an air-conditioned office where Velasco was waiting for me. After exchanging greetings, Velasco said, "Bad news. The organization refuses to issue the manifesto. They claim that this would mean the end of their role as mediators in the national crisis. In addition, I could not get even half of the delegates to attend."

I sank into a armchair under the weight of the news. I was thinking to myself, When Frank's blood was spilt, wealthy and professional people like these doctors went away for a weekend outside Havana, but I said, "The reason you give me is not valid. The organizations have acted—or, rather, have not acted—under the influence of fear. The answer is unacceptable, and I know that Faustino will reject it."

"Those are very hard words. You must understand that the members of the civic organizations are not like the members of the 26th of July. They don't have as much to lose."

"That is true. We can be killed; you don't have to worry."

"You don't have to put it that way. We can continue trying . . ."

"I am going to see Faustino, and then I will let you know."

Faustino did not want to hear about anything other than the delivery of the manifesto. I told that to Velasco, who was trying to get the representatives of the organizations together again.

Meanwhile, García informed me that the following morning Rubiera would meet us at the Club Telefónico in Guanabo, a tourist area near Havana. That night I met in Junquera's house to check the work of the Civic Resistance. All Havana now knew that the strike would be on Monday, but not everyone was ready to run the risk of not showing up for work or not opening the doors of their business or office. Everybody was planning on our intended paralysis of the transport system as a justification not to go to work. There were few who were ready to declare themselves openly on strike. The government had threatened to dismiss all those who failed to show up for work.

The next day was Sunday. We left midmorning to go to Guanabo. The sea looked very blue, sprinkled with small spots of foam. The beach season was at its peak, and there was plenty of traffic on the highway. We arrived at the Telephone Club. In the bar, the men drank beer and played dice. Through the vast inner patio walked smart-looking women in tight-fitting trousers. The Victrola played at top volume. People talked and laughed loudly, and children were shouting.

In the back, stretched out on an extension chair, a dark-skinned man with a thin moustache offered me his hand: it was Rubiera. Four or five people surrounded him. When he saw that I was watching them, he said, "They know—you can talk freely."

I explained the need for the telephone sector to go on strike. We had to paralyze communications. A movement of hips distracted Rubiera's attention. Then, with a roguish wink, he said, "The truth is that we do not have much faith in the success of the strike. We know what is involved in organizing a strike, and in three days even God couldn't do it."

"But special conditions exist now: the death of Frank País. Many other cities across Cuba have already been on strike."

"But Havana is different. Havana is large, and it takes a lot of work to mobilize. It's not like a small town, where everybody knows everybody."

Two women in short pants walked by and waved. Rubiera continued, "Where were we? Ah, yes, I was saying, a union leader has a great responsibility to the masses he leads. I cannot commit the telephone workers. They have confidence in me. I have been their leader for many years."

"García is ready to go to strike," I said.

García clarified, with a forced smile: "Only if the telephone workers go."

"The ones who really decide about this strike are the bus drivers," said Rubiera. "If they go to strike, we also go!"

On the verge of losing patience, I said, "There will be no end to this! The bus drivers will say that the decisive thing is that the power goes out and that therefore if the electrical workers go on strike, they will join them."

Rubiera burst into laughter: "Very good! Very good! A magnificent joke!" And he turned to stare at the buttocks of a fat woman who had crouched down to pick up something that had fallen on the ground.

I realized that I was wasting my time, and I cleared a path through the crowds who were amusing themselves.

Once again I met with Velasco at Pérez Fernández's house. The atmosphere had improved. I saw that there was a solution in sight. We entered the now familiar office, and when we sat down Velasco said, "We have had to fight a great battle, but we have emerged triumphant. We have obtained the manifesto!"

Moved, I said, "This is the definitive stroke! Where is the manifesto?"

"It's being written up," stated Velasco. There was a slight change in his face.

"What is it?" I asked, getting tense.

"There is a problem. The agreement is to issue the manifesto only if the transport system is paralyzed on Monday morning. Otherwise, the representatives will not have faith in the success of the strike."

"But that is crap!"

Nobody spoke. I waited until I calmed down. Then I left and went to inform Faustino. Our compañeros in the labor movement had worked arduously during the weekend in an effort to ensure the strike. The bus drivers union was divided. Consequently, Faustino had paid special attention to the preparation of the action groups, which would have to shoot any vehicle that went out on Monday.

Late at night, I arrived at my sister's house exhausted. For safety's sake, I decided to sleep there. My activity in the past few days had been out in the open. The strike was in just one more day, and it was necessary to take all possible precautions.

Daylight, entering through the open blinds of the window, woke me up. I opened and closed my eyes until they were accustomed to the light, while my mind gradually became alert. When I realized that it was the morning of the strike, I jumped straight out of bed. Through the window, winding through the trees, I could make out stretches of 26th Street.

And I could see the buses going by. The strike had failed.

## chapter 11

# The Fight in Las Villas

I smoked one cigarette after another. The scene reminded me of comics in the papers in which expectant fathers pace the waiting room in the hospital, the floor full of cigarette butts. But that memory did not make the situation any less serious for me. It was September 9, 1957, when the memory of the failed strike was still fresh in our minds. Martha's mother tried to read, without success. We looked at each other to try to raise our spirits, but were unable to do so, and so remained silent.

Suddenly the door of the room opened, and the nurse appeared: "Congratulations! It's a boy!"

I tried to control my emotions, but the tears ran down my cheeks, and it no longer mattered to me if they saw me cry. I felt that now I could die without my existence fading from memory.

We had planned to call our firstborn son José Martí Oltuski, but after Frank was assassinated a short time ago, we decided to name him Frank País Oltuski. Frank was only a few days old when Shell transferred me to Santa Clara with a promotion to technical chief for the central provinces. My work consisted of visiting the industries in the province and advising them about using Shell products. The company had provided me with an automobile, and I could move about freely, according to my judgment.

This was perfect for my double life and clandestine activities. I had the advantage of working for a company that everyone considered Batistiano because of the agreements in place between Batista and Julio Iglesias, the president of Shell. So when I went anywhere, I identified myself as a Shell engineer and had no problems. I always took along little presents that the company distributed as propaganda. Sometimes, when the army blocked the highways with its checkpoints, I pandered to the soldiers with an almanac or a mechanical pencil and succeeded in transporting my clandestine materials without further trouble. They looked on me as one of theirs. That facilitated my work considerably.

Martha, baby Frank, and I arrived at Santa Clara a week or so after the uprising at Cienfuegos on September 5, 1957, when members of the navy who were allied with the 26th of July Movement rose up against Batista and took over their units. Ultimately they had been defeated because of a lack of support from other navy bases. I visited the leaders of the Movement in the province. There was nothing further to do. It was another attempt that had failed, but at the same time, like the strike, it taught us a great deal and smoothed the way for the future.

As the year was wrapping up, the police managed to obtain a confession from a member of the Movement exposing virtually all the leaders in the province of Las Villas. These corrupt Batista henchmen used every method of torture to obtain information: breaking bones, burning genitals—all kinds of inhuman brutality and ultimately death. In this case, someone gave them a great deal of damaging information, a large number of our members were arrested, and the Movement was suddenly without leadership.

It was January 1958 when the National Directorate of the 26th of July decided that I should assume responsibility for the entire province of Las Villas, in the center of Cuba, which included the second largest mountain range in the country, the Sierra de Escambray. Because the informer was thoroughly familiar with the organization of the Movement, I decided that we would have to reorganize with new personnel and with a new system of secrecy and security. One of the ways to accomplish this, I knew, was to be sure that nobody should know anyone else in the organization who was not a direct link in his work in the conspiracy.

As for myself, I continued to lead a double life as technical chief of Shell for central Cuba. Not even my family, except Martha, knew that I was also Sierra, the head of the 26th of July Movement in the same region. I was not a hero by any means, but in one thing I was number one, and that was in how to conduct a secret life.

Only once did I make a big mistake. Shortly after my arrival, there was an American citizen who wanted to join our guerrillas. This was before Che came down to the plains from the Sierra Maestra, so I arranged to have this American join some other armed forces who were affiliated with us that were in the Sierra de Escambray.

At that time, there was a handful of private American citizens who wanted to join us, and it was thought that it would be good to show the world that even Americans were in favor of our revolution. My mistake, though, was to meet him myself at his hotel in Santa Clara before sending him off to the mountains.

As it turned out, I was quite naive, as he must have been a double agent. Not long after we met, the Batista police announced that an American had been captured trying to escape from the Sierra de Escambray and had described to them having met with a mysterious revolutionary leader named Sierra in Santa Clara. I believe this was a completely faked arrest and that the American was a spy from the out-set. In any case, he was the only man who had ever actually met Sierra, and he gave an accurate physical description of what I looked like. He also revealed my secret name to the police; we knew this because the police spoke to many people who conveyed this news back to us. Luckily, no one ever associated me with the notorious underground leader named Sierra. At that time, I appeared to be a pillar of re-spectability with my executive position at Shell. I was a member of the Rotary Club and moved in the most exclusive and wealthy circles of Santa Clara society. Nobody would think of me as a member of a clan-destine underground movement, and my secret life went on undis-turbed, though I was careful never to make that kind of mistake again.

It was not easy to find people to fill the positions of responsibility. It was one thing to buy a bond or issue a proclamation but another to occupy a leadership position. The punishment for the former could be imprisonment, even torture, but for the latter it was death. The fight in 1958 was difficult; we had thousands of martyrs already. Many of my comrades did not appreciate the art of leading a clandestine double life and talked too much, so too many people knew exactly who they were. Through its arrests, the police had come close to breaking up the Movement. It was necessary to think twice before accepting a position.

With concerted effort we filled the various positions. From the former ranks I had picked three compañeros to act as my direct aides: Guillermito Rodríguez, my brother-in-law, and two women: Teresita Caballero and Aleida March.

Later, of course, Aleida March married Che, but at this point she was one of many young women who were so crucial to the revolution. Someday I would like to write an entire book about Cuban women, because they have played such an important role, not only during these days but in all of Cuba's history. They have always been very patriotic and have participated in very critical ways.

Until that book is written, however, let me say that these young women were students, housewives, and workers, and at this time their primary role was to accompany the men on trips and actions and to transport secret documents, money, and arms. Fortunately, in those days women in Cuba didn't wear shorts but long skirts. So they were able to make special belts under the wide dresses, with pockets to carry the newspapers, weapons, and cash. These women were very important in collecting money, transporting bullets, delivering secret messages—all sorts of things. Some of them participated in sabotage as well.

Aleida March was one of the young girls of Santa Clara who was very active in all these kinds of work, even before I arrived. Aleida was only about nineteen years old when we met and began working together. She was very bright and dedicated to our cause. She also knew everybody in all the cities and towns, so she was the ideal guide. She knew where to go and whom I should meet.

My three main compañeros knew every corner of the province. Relying greatly on their judgment, we assigned the leadership of the action sector to Victor Manuel Paneque, known as Diego, who had been "burned" (exposed) in Holguín and was now fighting underground in Santa Clara. He was an ex-soldier who had been imprisoned for disloyalty to the regime. Originally a farmer, he had little culture, but like a farmer he combined superstition, distrust, and stubbornness with a great natural spark. He was a brave man with a strong appearance that inspired confidence.

For finance we chose Joaquín Argüelles, and for civic resistance, Gómez Lubián, "Totó," a doctor who undertook the position fearlessly. His son Chiqui, then twenty-one years old, a medical student and poet, had felt a presentiment of death:

*The white lady kissed my forehead*
*with a chaste kiss, a sibling's kiss.*
*The white lady kisses the forehead*
*of those who must die early.*

On May 26, 1957, Chiqui had died in a bomb explosion.

For propaganda, we originally assigned a compañero who turned out to be more slippery than an eel whenever some risk needed to be run. Later they sent us a black man, an engineering student, who had been "burned" in Havana, and whom we called Bonifacio. We were waiting for a person in charge of labor to be assigned by the national leader responsible for this area, David Salvador ("Mario").

Previously, everybody went to Santa Clara to speak directly with the provincial coordinator for Las Villas. Now we restored an intermediate level called the *zone*. There were four: Sagua; Remedios, which included both Caibarién and Yaguajay and shared borders with Sagua; Sancti Spíritus, which included Trinidad; Cienfuegos; and the central zone, Santa Clara.

I dealt only with the heads of the zones. I was very strict that no one should know who I was. It wasn't just the police who tried to establish my identity but also members of the Movement, who were accustomed to always being "in the loop."

The guerrilla movement in the province was incipient; it was concentrated in hills of the Escambray. It was commanded by the Directorio Revolucionario. In the flatlands of the northwest, a small guerrilla group of the 26th of July operated under very difficult conditions, under the leadership of a sugar worker named Víctor Bordón.

Coordination of actions was very weak. One worked in a kind of anarchy in which everything depended on casual personal connections. The reorganization of the Movement in the province would be made on the basis of selecting the most capable people for the main responsibilities. On a secondary plane would be those who were "burned," until they were "refreshed." We would severely punish anyone who talked too much. At the same time, we had to increase the acts of sabotage and begin attacks on figures of the regime and informers, as a way of breaking the morale of the enemy. We also had to step up our work in the labor sector, improve the distribution of propaganda, and increase fundraising.

We would construct a true secret organization.

The fresh air of dawn was funneled through the half-open window of my automobile. It helped me fight off sleep. I was not sleeping much lately. Secret meetings lasted until the small hours of the morning. In addition, I had to do my regular work, visiting the industries that used our products. I could not neglect that, which was my source of income and at the same time the front that hid my clandestine activities.

My family life went on as usual, because I made great efforts to keep my double life from affecting the raising of my son and my relations with my parents, who had finally accepted the fact of my marriage to Martha. This contributed greatly to our happiness together. At the same time, neither my mother nor father had any idea that I was also Sierra, the head of the 26th of July Movement in their region.

Today I wanted to arrive early to visit sugar factories in the zone and the tannery in the town. I would have lunch in the seaside restaurant that was famous for its seafood, and then I would dedicate the rest of the day to a meeting with the leaders of the Movement.

It would be a controversial meeting. There were problems in the zone. The coordinator, whom we called the Peasant, was a brave man. Lately, faced with the ever-increasing shortage of men ready to run risks, he had taken part in most of the acts of sabotage himself. Burning the cane fields and blowing up electrical poles were part of our nationwide plan to damage the finances of the rich landowners and Batista's cronies and to cause blackouts in the cities in order to remind the population that the Movement was alive and well. But the nervous tension was almost breaking the Peasant.

In three months, Batista's local henchman, police lieutenant Masvidal had assassinated more than twenty young people, workers, and students of the town and the factories. These were people who had either been betrayed or had unconsciously revealed themselves by talking too much to too many people about their underground activities.

Even though all that was true, the Direccion Provincial of our movement could not allow Masvidal's repressive activity to paralyze our insurrectionary action. If we did permit him to intimidate us, then with one hundred Masvidals the dictatorship could eliminate the revolutionary movement entirely. So for each Batista blow, we

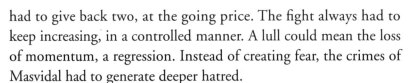

had to give back two, at the going price. The fight always had to keep increasing, in a controlled manner. A lull could mean the loss of momentum, a regression. Instead of creating fear, the crimes of Masvidal had to generate deeper hatred.

I had no doubt that the situation was difficult. The Peasant did what he could. But his attitude was a defeatist one. He saw in Masvidal an almost supernatural whip. We too had pressed him hard, and the Peasant was caught between our demands and the impossibility of taking the offensive against Masvidal.

I was ready to relieve the Peasant. It would be the best thing for him and the Movement. A new man would mobilize new resources; perhaps his own inexperience would lead him to undertake tasks that the Peasant considered impossible.

As I drove through the predawn darkness, I thought I saw a red light flashing on and off. I began to slow down. It had to be someone's hazard lights. It would be somebody who had gone off the road or been hit. Perhaps they would ask me to help, and I would have to stop and lose time. I wanted to get there early. The best thing would be to pass on by. I began to make out a vague shape. I would pretend not to have seen the signal and keep moving. It was a truck. Nevertheless, if it signaled, I would have to stop. It was a milk truck, painted yellow. More than once I had been in the situation of needing help, and then I had railed against those who passed me by. The highway was blocked: two men had stopped, and there was a bulky shape on the ground. I stopped behind the milk truck and shut off the motor.

I got out of the automobile. Both men watched me, but they did not say anything. As I approached, I saw a big man lying on the pavement, barefoot and dressed in trousers and a short-sleeved shirt. His dark socks contrasted with the white skin of his legs. His eyes were open, and the pupils reflected the lights of the truck. I realized that the man was dead.

There was something familiar in that lifeless body that caught my attention. I could not take my eyes from his face. Red lash marks covered his cheeks and forehead. In his mouth, the lips of which were very swollen, some teeth were showing and others were missing, broken off by some terrible blow.

I took a few steps and leaned against the fender of the truck. The men had been looking at me strangely. One asked, "Do you know him?"

"No," I lied, "it is the vision of the death."

"It's not pleasant."

Then the other said, "Looks like it jackknifed and turned over."

I knew the truth. This man had not died in an automobile accident. I looked up and saw the first light of dawn in the sky. Against the line of the horizon the royal palms appeared in silhouette. I became aware of the noises of awakening life.

"Who could it be?" said one of the voices.

And his name flashed into my mind: the Peasant. One of the men went on, "We sent word into town with a car that went by a little while ago."

I did not want to start a conversation, and I answered with a grunt. Seeing the dead and damaged face of the Peasant, I tried to remember what it had been like in life. I tried to imagine a heroic death, but I was assaulted with base thoughts. Now the sun began to rise. There were clouds in the sky, and the sunlight colored them.

After a while, a hearse and an automobile arrived, and several men got out. They placed the corpse on a cot; it was getting more and more swollen, and its features were becoming erased. They put it in the hearse, and the small caravan started off. I followed at a distance.

The town still slept. Empty streets. The cars stopped in front of an old building with a facade painted yellow. I entered and sat down in a chair. Disordered thoughts danced in my mind.

I saw the father of the Peasant appear, with messed-up hair and unshaven beard. Later he came back, and when he passed by my side he saw me but kept his distance and stopped in the framework of the wide front door. His silhouette stood out darkly against the clear sky. I went over without knowing what to say, and his broken voice reached me: "Why, for God's sake, why?"

The sweet scent of crushed cane wafted through the atmosphere. It was carried on the breeze, from the factories. On both sides of the highway were the fields where the machete workers looked like lobsters devouring the green cane. It was in that zone, in which the traffic of carts and cane trucks was most intense, that the highway was the most broken up. In spite of all your efforts, you could not avoid falling into one pothole or another, and you felt the crack of the car deep down in your bones.

At my side, Teresita was reading the latest issue of *La Carta Semanal* of the Partido Socialista Popular (the Popular Socialist Party, or PSP), which was the Cuban Communist Party. She read,

> The political opposition, in contrast, contributes to the confusion and obstructs the fight against the tyranny through its lack of unity and its haphazard tactics. On one hand, there are those who accept the electoral mandate of the government and refuse to make any attack on its antidemocratic character, through which guarantees and rights could be obtained that would give it the mantle of reform. On the other hand are those who refuse to participate in any type of election unless the government first resigns, so they entrust everything to armed guerrilla action, or to the counterstroke of the terrorism and putsch, or even to mere passive abstention. In still another position are those who understand that it is possible to make a genuine first step with guaranteed free elections—which would help the cause of national mobilization—and ensure that, in any case, either the reform or the overthrow of the government, if the electoral routes are completely closed, has to come through the sweeping united mobilization of the masses, as has just happened in Venezuela.

"Is that what the Communists' manifesto says?" I asked as I maneuvered to avoid a pothole, which actually was impossible. "Look at the highway! No one knows how many years it has been since it was fixed. They are stealing everything! You think that these people are going to loosen their hold in elections, because the Communists want them to? What naïveté!" (Only later did I learn that the Communist Party line had been questioned by many of its own militants.)

Teresita said, "The PSP told me they want to meet and speak with you."

"Why? In order to repeat to me what the manifesto says? No, tell them that I don't have time."

"Look, Enrique, I believe that you must see them anyway. It is always good to exchange opinions."

"All right, we will see, I'll let you know. Look here, did you find out about Bordón?"

"Yes, I was speaking with some people from Sagua. They complain that Bordón is undisciplined, that he does not explain matters to them, and that he only wants to operate independently."

"I believe that what we must do is to move Bordón toward the center of the province and put him directly under the command of the Direccion Provincial."

"That would be the best solution, but we would have to convince the people of Sagua, because they are requesting his expulsion."

"All right, convince them, and afterwards you and Diego can meet with Bordón."

It was the end of January 1958, and we were driving in our company car to a Shell meeting in Cienfuegos. I had also arranged for a secret meeting with a wealthy doctor whom we wanted to have help us organize that city, so Teresita was at my side. We crossed Palmira and kept on talking.

"And what do you think about Faustino?" asked Teresita.

"What a tragedy! To fall into the hands of Ventura!" Faustino had been arrested in Havana by Batista's chief henchman and murderer, our old nemesis police captain Ventura. So far, though, we had heard that he was still alive. Had he been just an ordinary poor worker or student he would have been shot by now, but Batista and his criminal forces were sensitive to the status of their enemies. They knew that killing people from the professional or upper classes would alienate them from popular support. So because Faustino Pérez was a highly respectable doctor, he had some chance of surviving, we hoped.

"And who has been assigned to replace him?"

"Marcelo Fernández. His nom de guerre is Zoilo."

We approached Cienfuegos.

"Teresita, are you sure that this doctor we are going to see is the man we need?"

"Sure. He is the best one still in Cienfuegos since September 5th."

"You think that he will accept the coordination of the zone?"

"I believe so. Look, turn down this street, there where that red-and-white car is parked is his office."

We parked across from the doctor's office. On the wall was a sign: "Dr. Serafín Ruiz de Zárate. Diseases of the Skin." It was nearly noon, and there was only one patient left to take care of. The receptionist announced Teresita's name and told us the doctor would see us soon. We sat down to read magazines. The last appointment went past us and out the door. Then a young, pleasant-looking man received us in an elegant office. Teresita introduced us:

"Serafín, this is compañero Sierra, whom I have already told you about."

We shook hands and sat down. I began, "Doctor, as Teresita has told you, we are reorganizing the province. We have created five zones, one of which is Cienfuegos. At the moment, this zone lacks leadership. After the uprising on September 5th, the Movement in Cienfuegos has not managed to recover. This city is too important to allow the 26th of July to be inactive any longer. We need to assign new leadership as soon as possible. Teresita and other compañeros have suggested you for coordinator of the zone. Although I don't know you, I have high respect for the judgment of those who have nominated you, so I do as well."

Ruiz de Zárate considered his words before answering: "I appreciate the confidence they place in me, but I cannot accept."

A silence followed, which I broke. "But what is the reason? We must discuss—"

"Because, to speak frankly, I am disillusioned. I believe that it is impossible to do anything other than isolated actions. There is always someone who becomes frightened; there is always someone who betrays the others. And it is only the best who act and die. The uprising of September 5th in Cienfuegos was a big experience for us here. We were deceived and left to our own chances. The dictatorship crushed the people of Cienfuegos before the whole nation, and nobody raised a finger. I was active in the 26th of July during those days and encouraged the town to fight. How can I ask them to sacrifice themselves again?"

His voice became broken. I would have preferred to remain silent, but I had to speak: "But if everyone shared your reaction, Cuba would still be a Spanish colony. The destinies of the towns are not decided in one battle, but in a longer process. In the end we will prevail."

I sank back in my seat. My own words sounded a little pompous to me.

"No, please don't insist, my decision is firm. It has been a lot of work going back to doing consultations. I am going to dedicate myself to my work and my family."

Our hopes had been dashed. Teresita addressed Ruiz de Zárate: "You really surprise me, Serafín. I was sure that you would accept. Nobody knows the people of the zone as you do, and you were always so enthusiastic. Now we will have to start over."

Serafín felt ashamed. "I'm sorry, but it is an irrevocable decision. That does not mean I will not help in whatever way I can. What I do not want is to hold a position of responsibility. There are other valuable compañeros who might accept the leadership. You can speak with Osvaldo Dorticós, for example. He is a respected man from one of the best families in Cienfuegos. He has just been named president of the National Association of Lawyers in place of Miró, who has been exiled."

"Do you know him well?" I asked.

"Quite well. He is my neighbor and in addition my personal friend."

"What do you think, Teresita?" I insisted.

"Whatever Serafín says."

"All right, let's go see him."

Serafín called a number. "Is Dr. Dorticós there? Put him on, please . . . Osvaldo? I have a matter for you. Could we see you now? All right, we'll be there."

And to us: "Dorticós will meet us in his office."

We were received by a man of medium height. He was dressed in a collar and necktie. He spoke with facility, and his diction was impeccable. I was filled with confidence. We told him the object of our visit. Dorticós was quick to answer: "I don't think that I am the man you are looking for. Naturally I am inclined to collaborate. The difficulty is the time. Due to the demands of my work, even more now that I am taking over as head of the National Association of Lawyers, I must travel frequently to Havana. This position is one of great political importance now, due to our role in the civic organizations. We have to use that position against the government and to devote all our attention to that. It seems to me that the coordinator of the Movement must always be available. You should look for another compañero who fits the bill better than I do."

An idea occurred to me: "Would you accept the leadership of the Civic Resistance?"

"You see, this is better suited to my situation. I accept." (Later, of course, Osvaldo Dorticós was to become the Minister for Law Revision in the first Council of Ministers after the revolution, and then the second president of Cuba just a short time after that.) "But now," he went on, "the important thing is to find a coordinator. Do you have any ideas, Serafín?"

"I'm thinking . . ."

"What do you think about Dr. González Abreu? He is an enthusiastic man, he has always been against Batista, and he behaved admirably on September 5th."

"I don't know what to say," said Serafín. "He seems a little ambitious. But, on the other hand, there isn't a lot to choose from."

Teresita put in: "It's not a bad idea. What Serafín says is true, but if Julito González Abreu accepts, I am sure it will strengthen the Movement in the zone. You could count what's left of it on your hand."

"OK. Give him a call, and we'll talk to him," I said.

We went to Serafín's house. It was almost two in the afternoon. While we were having a bite to eat, González Abreu arrived. He overflowed with vitality. We talked it over, and he accepted—a little too quickly for my taste. Soon, between the lot of us we convinced Serafín to accept the position of treasurer. Finally we shuffled around names for people in charge of action, propaganda, and labor.

When we proceeded up the highway to return to Santa Clara, the calm of the dusk comforted me, easing the tensions of the day.

## chapter 12

# Strike of April 9

**E**nrique!" I heard Martha say very quietly.

I shook myself awake from a deep dream. "What? What's happening?"

"Someone is knocking at the door!"

I tried to arrange my thoughts. At last I asked, "What time is it?"

"Two in the morning."

Again there was a knock.

"It must be the police! That's who comes at this hour," I said, and I looked around hoping to find an exit. Then I remembered that there was only one way out: the apartment was a mouse hole. I had said as much to Martha! But she had liked it so much! I tried to remember whether there was anything compromising in the house. No, there was nothing that I could recall.

"OK, I'm going to open the door." I got up, and Martha sat on the bed.

I ran the bolt and opened the door. Out of the darkness of the corridor a hand was extended.

"Greetings . . ."

It was Marcelo Fernández. Behind him came Frank Carbonell and Marcia, two compañeros from the Santiago de Cuba branch of the 26th of July Movement.

Martha appeared, saying, "What a shock you gave us! We thought you were the police."

We all laughed with relief. We asked about friends we had in common. They wanted to see the baby, who was sleeping. Martha and Marcia went to the kitchen and made coffee. Carbonell unloaded some things from the car. Marcelo and I stayed and talked. Marcelo had come from the Sierra.

"Tell me about it," I said.

"Everything is going well. The last details have been completed. I've brought a copy of the twenty-one-point manifesto, which outlines the final strategy of the struggle. The position of the government can no longer be sustained. In the Oriente, with the exception of the large cities, the rest of the province is in our hands. If we can expand our position to the remainder of the country, we will have triumphed. Now at some point we can decree the general strike. I will let you know by a coded message. Get a pencil and paper so I can explain the code. You will have to memorize it."

I got the pencil and paper. When I had memorized the code, we destroyed the papers. Marcelo said, "Now tell me how Las Villas is going."

"Things have improved here, though the province is nothing like the Oriente. We have filled almost all the leadership positions, and our ranks have grown. The collection has been a success: we have almost 70,000 pesos. When I got here the system was haphazard and random, but we imposed a quota system so that each of our thirty-two municipalities must provide an amount proportionate to their share of the region's entire population. The owners of the big businesses and sugar mills are also beginning to make larger donations in order to protect and ingratiate themselves with us in case we prevail. Originally the total quota was 25,000 per month, but we are increasing it now to 50,000. I was in Havana a few days ago, and I gave 20,000 in cash to Faustino, who was just released from jail thanks to his high-level connections."

"That should make him happy."

"No kidding! But there is a problem: we have no arms. Faustino has promised us some. I've promised them to the zones and they to the town; but events are unfolding very fast, and I doubt we will be prepared when the strike is called."

"You have to be optimistic. You will see that everything will work out satisfactorily. This time for sure we will not fail. And how is Diego?"

"Good. He has done great things. The situation in the province is very tense, especially in Santa Clara. As soon as we begin to bring the criminals to justice, some people are going to become very uncomfortable. The Batistianos have realized that we're not just playing at insurrection, like Prío's people. Naturally the response is terrible. Every day more compañeros turn up shot or tortured to death. Sometimes they kill innocent people. They are trying to paralyze us with terror, but the people are beginning to lose their fear."

"And how are relations with other organizations going?"

"Chico, neither good nor bad. Each one goes its own way and distrusts the others. What's certain is that it has been a failure for the Movement not to have organized a front in Escambray. That territory now belongs to the Directorio Revolucionario." (The DR was another revolutionary group that was sometimes our ally and sometimes our competitor.)

Martha and Marcia served coffee.

"Now we are trying to raise guerrillas with Bordón," I continued. "We are also fomenting guerrillas in the hills of Yaguajay. They say that the terrain is broken and ready. But really there is little we can do if we lack arms to begin with. Listen, what can you tell me about the Sierra?"

Marcelo replied, "It's formidable, chico. You can't imagine how good it seems there. There's a great spirit of battle, and enthusiasm reigns. There are already compañeros who have considerable combat experience, and some of them have proven to be real strategists. Besides, Fidel is spending a lot of time training people. What a difference between the rebel soldiers and the soldiers of the tyrant! Our men are pretty careful about the peasant population. Nobody touches anything that isn't his. Anything that is taken is paid for. Any abuse is severely punished. Thanks to this exactitude, the peasants support us without reservation. Already many compañeros have entered our ranks. There are some like Che, who are extremely industrious and have built factories, hospitals, schools."

"And how is Che? Is it true that he is a Communist?"

"Che is a great compañero. I talk to him every chance I get. He is very intelligent. He is a man of leftist ideas, but I don't think he is a Communist. Certainly he sympathizes with them and defends them. The thing is, Che doesn't know the history of Cuba. I'm sure that when he knows our country better he will change some of the beliefs he now holds."

Without our being aware of it, dawn had come.

"I'm going to sleep, even if it is only for a couple of hours."

We lay down to sleep, the women in bed and the others on the sofa or the floor. Soon I heard the rhythmic breathing of the sleepers. I stayed awake.

We were in the house of the lawyer Armando Díaz, a member of the Civic Resistance.

"They are offering 1,000 dollars," Díaz said. "They claim that's all they can give."

"Don't accept it. Not a peso under five thousand. We need money now more than ever. Have you read what happened in Miami? The American police seized several shipments of arms bound for Cuba that had been bought by compañeros of the 26th of July Movement who live in Miami. It seems it was a setup between the police and the arms dealers. As soon as the arms were received, the police showed up and seized them."

"What sons of bitches," said Diego.

"Things can't go on much longer like this. The tension is unbearable. Everyone expects the strike at any moment. Nobody is concentrating on work; on the contrary, all they do is talk about the strike. The level of enthusiasm that we have created in the nation cannot sustain itself much longer. Either it yields results soon or it will die, and the ideal moment will have passed."

"So what is the National Directorate waiting for to call the strike?" Díaz interjected.

"Arms, man, arms. And now, poof! They've all gone up in smoke. Anyway, the tactic that we planned is based on the assumption that we won't receive any aid." I turned to face Diego. "That doesn't mean that we won't try every means to obtain the arms the Auténticos have stashed at the town of Caibarién."

"The problem is that Panchito Hernández has gone to Havana to see Faustino," said Diego.

"What a pig he is; he's quite the politician," I exploded. "He disregards our authority to go to Faustino. But you know where that peasant has hidden them, don't you?"

"Yes, but he says that he won't bring the arms without authorization from Panchito."

A knock at the door interrupted us. Diego and I hid in one of the rooms. In a little while the door opened, and Díaz entered with Frank Carbonell, who said to me, "I've brought you this letter from Marcelo."

Everyone watched as I opened the envelope. The letter said, "I enclose the resolution of the national committee for the strike, as we had discussed. I assume Las Villas is organized according to the agreed-upon plans. . . .

"The situation is very favorable for us. The atmosphere has reached a climax."

Then came a series of numbers.

I deciphered the numbers: the strike would be on April 9 at 11:00 A.M. Just five days from now? That was impossible and seemed crazy to me. But the decision had been made, and there was no time to lose!

"Diego, get your hands on the arms! If the peasant won't respond to the carrot, give him the stick. But those arms have to be here by tomorrow. I'm leaving immediately to travel around the province giving final instructions."

We parked far from the appointed place and walked to the house. The living room had been converted into a tailor's workroom, and there were several people working there. Martínez and Samuel got up and came to meet us. We went into a nearby room.

"The strike is on the 9th, at 11 A.M.," I began the conversation. "We assume that at that time there will be an announcement on the radio, but even if there isn't one, the strike will still go ahead."

The eyes of Martínez and Samuel shone brightly. "And the arms?" they finally said.

"There are no arms," I said.

"Once again," Samuel began, and then fell silent.

"We gain nothing by complaining. I feel the same as you. Still, this is the order, and we have to carry it out. Anyway, we foresaw this possibility. We are going to revise once again the plan of action."

An old, dark woman, the mother of Martínez, brought coffee. She smiled at me sympathetically, without knowing that death was traveling with me. I put such thoughts out of my mind and began, "We have to fix the position of as many members of the armed forces—police, soldiers, and civil guards—as possible. We have to know where they live, what places they habitually frequent. Each compañero of the Movement has to be assigned a member of the armed forces he can attack and disarm at the moment the strike is begun, in this way obtaining all the arms we can. Next they must block the street, totally disrupting traffic. They have to turn cars over and turn the buses sideways, so that the dictator's vehicles cannot move freely. That will make the enemy move on foot, which will give more strength to us. At the same time, armed groups will take the key spots in the city, from which they will control the main access roads, so that with few arms and sniper tactics we can hold in check superior forces.

"Remember that the idea is not to fight a battle to take the city. For that we don't have enough strength. We must guard the few bullets we have to harass the enemy with the snipers. Our objective is to unroll a series of small actions in support of the strike, so that people simply can't go to work, maintaining that situation for several days. If we succeed in keeping the cities paralyzed, their economic life halted, that will be enough to topple the dictator. Are there any questions? Any doubts?"

There wasn't a single question. We shook hands and left without anything else being said. Life passed as usual in the streets. I studied the faces: nobody imagined what was coming.

There was a building in the alleyway of Los Angeles. I went up to the second floor and rang the bell. The door quickly opened to reveal the smiling face of Nico Núñez Jiménez. I followed him down the narrow passage, which was made even narrower by the full bookshelves that ran along the walls. In the little room was a stout man who looked like a dock worker, who was introduced to me as Armando Acosta, labor organizer of the PSP, the Communist party of Las Villas. His physical appearance and his open character won my attention. He was very different from other Communist intellectuals I had known. After exchanging a few sentences, we went into the dining room, where we sat around the table.

"The strike is on the 9th at 11 A.M.," I began the conversation.

"Yes, that is why we wanted to talk with you," said Acosta. "We believe that it is necessary to unite our forces in view of the strike."

"I agree. The more who are among us, the better our chances of success. Now, there remain some problems to work out; the main one is, how can we get our people in touch with each other on such short notice?"

"This is not a major problem," smiled Acosta. "We know all the leaders of the 26th in each work center. The problem is in how to integrate the directions of the strike committees."

"I don't see why we should have problems with that. Each one should simply mobilize the men in their group, and if any difficulty emerges, they can discuss it and reach an agreement. Since the objectives of both organizations are the same, there is no reason why fundamental difficulties should arise."

"We agree. And another thing: we believe that we need to release a manifesto directed at the public, calling on them to support the strike and signed by both the 26th and the PSP."

"Well, there I do not agree. I think that would be a mistake. I think that the participation of the PSP should be done discreetly without any public announcement and that it should be known only by our worker groups and their leaders. At least at this stage. To do otherwise would reduce the participation of a whole range of other people who would have an embolism seeing the name of the PSP alongside that of the 26th of July. Moreover, it would give ammunition to the enemy that they could use to attack us."

"Yes, but it wouldn't be right to continue to marginalize our organization," insisted Acosta.

"But I have not suggested that you should be marginalized. On the contrary, I have suggested that you should be included among the forces. The level of participation of each will be decided later. The important thing now is to overthrow Batista."

We established several centers of command in Santa Clara. The idea was to avoid confining the entire provincial command to a single location, because of the danger that it could be discovered, leaving the Movement without a head. But there was one fundamental aspect that we did not give the attention it merited: communications. In the clamor of the battle, our men, divided by barrios, remained cut off from each other. Also, the lack of an efficient system of communications kept us from evaluating at each stage the progression of developments and therefore the appropriate measures to take.

Barely the day before, we had succeeded in introducing into the city a few of the arms that we had obtained from the Auténticos, the Authentic Revolutionary Movement, the people who had belonged to Prío's party. As typical Cuban politicians during the period when they were in office, the Auténticos had managed to take away a great deal of money and were now very well financed, but only a minority within their party favored an armed struggle and had therefore obtained some weapons. Originally, they had smuggled these arms in to the coast north of Santa Clara but had refused to give them to us. So I had given the order to seize them, which we accomplished without any real resistance.

These arms were kept in the Luis Hernández bakery, in Santa Clara's Calle San Miguel. The weapons were being cleaned and loaded, but by the time of the strike not all of them were ready, and many could not be used as a result.

Two days before this, an unfortunate event had also occurred. According to the general plan of action, Víctor Bordón was supposed to enter Santa Clara the day of the strike. Unaware of the imminence of that date, however, he decided on his own to attack the quarters of Quemados de Guines to seize arms and artillery. The quarters could not be taken, and instead of getting more artillery Bordón used up almost all he had; he was turned aside to the Central Highway, at the level of Manacas, where he intercepted the transit and was now stalled.

The city remained calm on the morning of the strike. It seemed that activity was less than normal. Tension was running high, and the people seemed to be expecting something. At midmorning, I went by foot to the location selected for me. Everyone had precise instructions. Diego had direct control of the action. The instructions we had given for conducting the strike corresponded to the nationwide guidelines that had been drawn up, and I personally had met with each zone headquarters to explain the strategy.

I had to stay informed about the course of events, both through Diego and through a group of compañeros who had been designated as messengers, as we could not count on modern means of communication. It was hoped that I could make the necessary strategic changes and important decisions as we went along.

A few minutes after eleven, the first shots were heard. The action took place in the Condado barrio, quite near the place were I was hidden. Then we saw a black column of smoke ascend into the air. They had set fire to the San Miguel and Central Garage. We thought that the plan would unfold as we had foreseen. I was disoriented by what had occurred around me and thought that this was the general situation.

The army fell back to the quarters, because they feared a strong offensive on our part. But they greatly overestimated our forces. By 12:30 the first reports arrived that in the majority of the barrios nothing was happening. In many places there was no one in command because some of our leaders had failed to show up, so the men dispersed. With our militias failing to go out into the streets, we tried to mobilize other militias that had not yet appeared.

Unfortunately, by the time this situation came to our attention, we had already lost precious time. The city had practically been in our hands without our knowing. In reality, for two hours the city had been nobody's ground.

Because of the lack of communication between the barrios, we didn't learn quickly enough the failures that the plan was producing. By the time we reacted it was already late. The enemy had not been nailed to the cross, and when they discovered, just as we did, the reality of the situation, they took to the street in tanks. They took the offensive. We lost our initial advantage. When the army gauged our weakness, they lost their fear. Then they gathered in Condado with the goal of eliminating the focus of resistance.

By the afternoon, when the last flames were dying out, we received word from Sagua la Grande saying that the city was taken and requesting assistance. Those were the bitterest hours: to know that Sagua had been taken and to be able to do nothing to help them. They were hours of impotence, of questioning. What to do? Nothing!

The next month, I received the following letter from Sagua la Grande:

*Sr. Coordinator*
*Santa Clara*

*Señor:*

*Having received on the 8th of April the orders of the general strike from the Direccion Provincial, we had to arrange a meeting between the Coordinator and the followers, planning and ordering every detail and seeing them carried out, as well as determining the objectives and assigning the men for them.*

*When 11:00 A.M. of the 9th of April arrived, our men threw themselves upon their assigned objectives, and at 11:30 A.M., work had been paralyzed as all businesses and industry had been shut down.*

*The action groups were very active. Group C penetrated the train yard, disarming the soldiers who guarded the Cuban Electric Company plants, proceeding immediately to burn them; one of the two that provided service was rendered unusable.*

*Immediately this group moved to the offices of the train lines, where they met up with Group D to aid and reinforce them. Between the two of them they set fire to two cars and threw a locomotive on the platform; then they poked holes in the gasoline reserves tank and tried to ignite it, but the petroleum would not burn. An extinguisher was also destroyed. Quickly they moved on to the railroad maintenance shops and burned them down completely.*

*From there they passed on to the lumberyard owned by señor Francisco Linares, which was also burned until it was completely destroyed. They also destroyed a furniture factory belonging to a man named Acosta. Of the compañeros who participated in these works, three were killed and two were injured. Later, we were unable to rescue the wounded compañeros, and they were taken at 4:30 P.M. by three infantry units of Regiment 3. Together the rest of the groups took the building of La Villa de Paris, and held it all afternoon and night; they had to evacuate it on the following day with the aid of Group A, which had taken the Union Hotel.*

*The A group, at 11:00 A.M. of the 9th, proceeded to set fire to the pipes that fed the El Infierno distillery, rendering them inoperable. They immediately moved on to the Isabela aqueduct and destroyed the pump house with a wrecker, damaging some of the pipe with well-placed* "elephant" explosives. This group moved on to the house of señor Alberto Beguiristaín, where they requisitioned a number of arms, later used to take the Hotel Union building, which was held until the next day, when they went to the aid of the evacuation of the La Villa de Paris building.

Group B, through information obtained from compañeros who worked at these jobs, knew that at the appointed hour some compañeros designated by the Worker's Bureau would shut down work and attack the only soldier who was there at the time, since the rest were eating. They killed him and abruptly left the Central Highway, without completing the ordered sabotage. They were pursued by a soldier and a civilian, having killed a bus driver in their flight. Compañero Lieutenant Julio Vega of the militia completed the part of the job assigned to him but then abandoned his companions and failed to report to his superiors, in effect deserting. The others joined those who had taken the Jesuit School building.

Group E proceeded to blow up the two sections of the aqueduct of Sagua at 11:00 A.M., failing as a result of their inexperience with explosives. Afterward, they joined the groups that had taken the school.

Group F couldn't achieve its task of taking the subplants out of commission because of a lack of demolitions, so with the other groups they took the Telegraph Hotel and Agencia Comerciales, S.A.

Group G, under the personal command of compañero Samuel, took the Jesuit School building, quickly posting snipers. By noon they were receiving fire from an army truck, which finally had to retreat. Later, the building was practically surrounded since the army established itself in Rincón Martiano, the Unidad Judicial, the Resulta Roadway, and the Reparta Oña. During the night of the 9th, we had to withstand fire a number of times, as the troops tried to advance on us; they were repulsed by our own counteradvances, which took place at Reparta Oña, on the Santa Teresita creche, by the banks of the river, and behind the Municipal Medical School. By the La Pastora farm, an advance took place during the day as the radio broadcast a call to the people to fight, highlighting the role of fighting by the public sector.

Group H, called the knife group, proceeded to slice the tires of vehicles that were in the street during the strike. Throughout the day of the 9th, special groups were assigned to requisitions, and they obtained some results, although we almost completely used up our ammunition.

*The Sitiecito group burned the railroad station and an automobile that arrived just then from Santo Domingo. Following the order of sabotage, the next act was to ignite forty million pounds of sugar at Corazón de Jesús.*

*On the 10th, at 8:00 A.M., a group of vessels with 150 sailors reached the port of Isabela de Sagua. Taking into consideration that in the rest of the island the Movement had not had good luck, and that the head of the army had announced they were going to bombard the buildings we had taken, we got together and fully discussed our situation—we decided to evacuate and try to reach some of the coastal mountains. The order was given to abandon the buildings. The people quickly evacuated, with the forces that had arrived from Santa Clara hot on our heels. We went along the other side of the river, exchanging some fire with the army. The men who had joined together at the Jesuit School abandoned it and joined those who were just crossing the river, forming columns of guerrillas on both sides of the neighboring road in order to move more rapidly. At this time, a small plane backing up the army showed up and began throwing hand grenades—many of which failed to explode—but the plane had to retreat upward because of the fire that three compañeros peppered it with, two with Springfields and one with a .44.*

*Having gone several miles in this fashion, we ran into two B-26 bombers. Fortunately, we had reached Monte Lucas. The airplanes began to bomb the mountain, and then to machine-gun it. We lost two casualties to the bombing. Then the infantry appeared, thinking that as a result of the air attack everything was ready for them. They got into jeeps and trucks and were met with renewed shooting. A short skirmish took place in which we took six casualties; the army took two casualties, and one of their lieutenants was seriously wounded in the mouth. The superiority of the army in arms was once again demonstrated. After that, they didn't try to advance up the mountain but began to machine-gun it, while our men divided up into groups of ten or twelve to better escape attack from the airplane, which kept after them through the night. Later we learned that compañero Antonio Chávez had been shot in the back when he tried to return to Sagua without his having done anything at all suspicious, and they even took a ring and a chain of gold off his body. This was done with all the dead compañeros.*

*That night the groups did not sleep but walked all night to flee the area, since it was easy to block the way along the Uvero road, the nearby road that led to the Frenes salt farm, the river, and the sea, which had already been taken by the Marines. As a result of this, there was no escape for any of us, since the difference in men and above all in arms and munitions was overwhelming.*

*In the two following days, the groups were dissolved, some of them returning to Sagua and the rest to other places where they had family or friends.*

*To conclude, it has been decided that next time if we do not receive arms, we will refuse to fight. Better that way!*

*Samuel*
Captain of the Militia

*Martínez*
Coordinator of the Zone of Sagua

## chapter 13

# The Sierra
## Assumes Command

A few days after the strike, we met in the house of one of the compañeros to assess what had occurred and determine the next steps to take. We were four men shut in a house full of cigar smoke. Through the window we could see the road, where few vehicles were moving.

"We've been isolated. No one wants even to see our faces," said Orlando Bosch.

"Tell me about it! I've knocked myself out to find a place to hide," said Diego.

"The failure of the strike has dealt a terrible blow to the Movement. Every time we have a setback like this, people begin to have doubts that we will ultimately succeed, and it becomes harder to sustain the level of support and financial donations that we had achieved. It's going to take a lot of work to recover from this," I said. "We have to determine where we made mistakes and take steps to correct them. But I know we can restore the enthusiasm. We have to launch more actions immediately, to prove that we haven't given up and are still strong."

"The problem is that without arms we can't fight," argued Diego.

"Arms are important, but that is not the only thing," I said. "Look at Sagua." I took the papers out of my bag. "I want to read you some paragraphs from the last circular of the National Directorate. They list as reasons for the failure of the strike lack of organization, the surprise form in which the strike was called, the scarcity of arms, the passive role given to the workers, and the difficulty of communications." I read aloud:

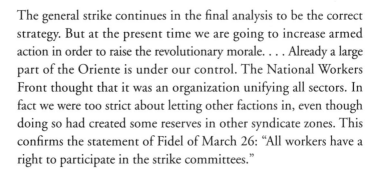

The general strike continues in the final analysis to be the correct strategy. But at the present time we are going to increase armed action in order to raise the revolutionary morale. . . . Already a large part of the Oriente is under our control. The National Workers Front thought that it was an organization unifying all sectors. In fact we were too strict about letting other factions in, even though doing so had created some reserves in other syndicate zones. This confirms the statement of Fidel of March 26: "All workers have a right to participate in the strike committees."

"Then they talk about unity." I continued reading:

The National Directorate is prepared to hold talks in Cuba with the leaders of any opposing organization to coordinate specific plans and to produce concrete actions leading to the overthrow of the tyranny.

"Then comes a report of radical reorganization. An executive committee has been created by the National Directorate in the Sierra, and the militias have been placed under the command of the rebel army."

"Power is being concentrated in the Sierra," commented Bosch.

"Yes. The failure of the strike is the failure of the plains," I said. I read the conclusion of the circular.

Having succeeded in crushing the strike movement, the regime will now attempt to do the same to the rebel forces. At this time thousands of soldiers are gathering in Manzanillo, Bayamo, Santiago de Cuba, Guantánamo, and other locations, with the objective of loosing a large-scale offensive. We must all make the greatest possible effort to obtain arms, equipment, medicine, and clothing for the combatants. The watchword is "Everyone must turn back the military offensive of the tyranny!"

Weighed down with worry, nobody said a word. I resumed the thread of the conversation: "What Fidel and Raúl accomplished in the Oriente shows that the guerrillas can be more than a symbol. While the strike failed in the cities, its sole successes were the result of military action. This indicates that it is possible to create a revolutionary army that is more powerful than Batista's. We have to change our tactic in the sense of emphasizing the fight in the hills. Las Villas has great possibilities. If we develop the fronts of Escambray and Yaguajay, they can reach the point of joining together and cutting the province in two. Then we will really put the dictator in a tough position. What's more, we can ask that they give us a commander of experience. Perhaps Raúl himself, or Almeida."

"That would be a thunderbolt!" Bosch exclaimed enthusiastically.

"What do you think, Diego?" I asked.

"I don't see any other way. The army is already pursuing Bordón; they are getting close. I think we have to move Bordón to Escambray and fortify it with the arms that we can gather in the cities and the front at Yaguajay."

"What you are saying is not going to be an easy task. How will you do it?" I asked.

"As a guerrilla organization it can't be done. We have to split up in groups, dressed like civilians. We will go by car to Cienfuegos and there take to the hills."

Guillermito intervened: "On the other hand, there is the task of reorganizing the Movement. We have to cleanse everything that failed. Although right now fear is provoking a real self-cleansing. We have to find new people. We practically have to start over."

"The hard core remains," I reminded him. "What we have to do is regain the confidence of the masses and sustain their support. Now we have to aid Fidel with whatever resources we have, but once the danger is past we can try to convince the National Directorate that all the money recovered in Las Villas should be dedicated to sustaining our own front of combat."

I said to Bosch, "Your assignment is to work with the Caibarién fishermen to prepare the conditions for an arms drop. For my part, after we have reorganized the Movement, I am thinking of making

a trip to Miami. I know some people there. I'm sure we can get some arms."

"I don't know if it was Fidel or someone else who said that each failure along the way is a stone on the road to final success," said Guillermito.

Outside the window everything was black.

"All right, let's do it!"

We left one by one. On the street, we could see the government surveillance cars patrolling.

Neno brought me a letter. It read:

> *Friend Neno*
>
> *Best wishes that when you receive these lines you will be well. I am well Neno. This is to tell you that I am waiting word of you because I think that you can easily forgets us because all of you live so comfortable and sleep on a fine pillow, whenever it suits you and even in Santa Clara so Diego will let me into the Sierra Maestre because I am the man that you need there in the hills. I don't like this business because you have given me men without clothes or belts or shoes, and so this I cannot accept.*
>
> *I am going to where Diego is so that you or some other leader comes here. I want he to take me to the Sierra Maestre because that is where the real reblushnaries are with beards and not just tongue-wagging and faith in God.*
>
> *That's it then,*
> *Captain Regino Machado*

I gave the letter back to Neno. I said, "Take it to Diego and have him go see Regino. Tell him I'll expect him in the clinic Sunday morning at ten, so he can inform me."

When I came to meet Diego that Sunday, Neno led me through empty examining rooms. We entered the operating room by the side door. There was little light.

"Make yourself comfortable," said Neno. "As soon as Diego gets here I will bring him in."

I sat on a metal stool that reminded me of the ones in my design studio. Memories of the university surged up in me. Several faces passed through my mind. My thoughts wandered, without settling on anything in particular. In the middle of the room were the operating tables; above them, enormous lights. At one time I had thought of studying medicine, but the idea of human suffering had made me give it up. I couldn't watch people suffer. I thought about Regino Machado, a worker in a tannery in Santa Clara. We had made him head of the Yaguajay front. Diego said he was good. Regino in his letter said that we lived in luxury, that we slept on fine pillows. It was true. Is that what workers like Regino Machado thought of us?

I thought of what the hills would be like during the rains. The mud. Wet clothes sticking to the body and producing such a disagreeable sensation. And when it's time for sleep? Everything is wet. And when you have to go to the bathroom? Everything is wet. But there are people who are used to that. It's all a question of what you are used to. If someday I have to go to the hills, I will get used to it too. Likewise the workers are used to living the way that they do. But not entirely, since they want to improve their living conditions. I would like them to live better. For Regino Machado the hills aren't so hard: as a worker, he is used to that.

And me? I think that I would get used to it. I would resist. But Regino Machado is there, and I am here, and I feel a vague sensation of guilt. But I am not going to throw up my arms. The danger is greater here than there. I am defenseless, stuck in this operating room, which is clean and dry but in the middle of Santa Clara. Regino's men travel in the rain: they don't have nylon to cover themselves with; their feet sink in the mud and their shoes get stuck, or maybe they are even barefoot. I couldn't go barefoot. I've never been able to . . . No, others are the guilty ones. I am the brother of Regino Machado. I fight by his side for the same ideals.

"Are you dreaming?" I heard the voice of Diego.

"No, I'm thinking nonsense. How has it gone for you?"

"Not too smoothly. Regino is moving around. The army is on the offensive, and they want to wipe out that unit."

"Will Regino resist?"

"I told him that considering his weakness the best thing would be to keep moving constantly."

"Is he very bad?" I read from a paper: "Thirty-three men. They are short eighteen uniforms and five pairs of boots. They have sixteen air guns, five rifles, a carbine, and the rest are revolvers. There are almost no bullets." I said to Diego, "Did you discuss the letter with Regino?"

"Yes."

"Can you give him anything?"

"Sure, empty words."

Guillermito was now in Miami. For more than five years he had been one of the leaders of the revolutionary movement in Las Villas. First in the MNR, then in the 26th of July. His situation had become intolerable. The police were looking for him, and he was very well known. He had planned to go to the hills.

We thought that he would be more useful in Miami, as a delegate for the acquisition of arms. We had an agreement: nobody could leave the country without authorization from the Movement. The battle had to be undertaken from within, and one could leave only on a revolutionary mission. Even so, Guillermito did not wish to go. We managed to convince him on the condition that he would return on one of the first ships.

Now we were joining him on a trip to buy arms. I had told Shell that Martha and I had to go to an important family party in Miami;

we left Frank with the family and took the next plane. We spent some time flying over the keys south of Florida. The sea has distinct colors, according to the depth. It goes from an almost black-blue to a milky yellow, passing through a fine green. Then you return to terra firma, although it is marshy. And then the Everglades, with its pines like those of Pinar del Rio. You see more and more houses and roads where tiny cars are moving around. Finally you are above Miami, and the plane descends in a wide arc.

Once again I saw the familiar sight of the American immigration functionaries in their clean khaki uniforms. From the pages of my passport they discovered that I had been a student in the United States.

"Where did you study?"

"Here in Miami," I answered.

"So you're a hometown boy," and he looked at me like one of his own.

We stayed in a hotel on the beach. It was summer, and there were other Cubans on vacation everywhere. Martha and I got back together with Guillermito, and we went to have breakfast at a restaurant in north Miami Beach. From there we called Yeyé (Haydée Santamaría), who was now directing the Movement in exile. We were just finishing breakfast when Yeyé joined us. It had been a long time since we had seen each other. She was well. Her look, with the clothes she was wearing, made her appear to be an American. We laughed about how skinny she had been when she married Armando Hart and how we used to make a point of how we had to fatten her up.

She took us to her house. When we went in, we met Miró Cardona and José Llanusa. We talked, and then Yeyé, Guillermito, Llanusa, and I went to one of the rooms.

I explained the plans to intensify the guerrilla fighting in Las Villas. We already had Bordón in Escambray, Regino Machado in Yaguajay, and Julito Chaviano with a new guerrilla group that was operating on the central coast. We didn't have any arms. Nonetheless, conditions for introducing them were good in the north of the province. We were counting on the aid of a group of Caibarién fishermen.

"This is the idea," I said. "You let us know the day and time when the ship with the arms will be at the latitude of Cayo Anguila in the Bahamas. One of our fishing ships will be waiting at that place. The arms will be loaded onto it, and our ship will deposit them in Cayo Lucas in the north of Yaguajay. After that they will be taken by boat to the coast, where they will refresh the guerrillas. If we are careful, we can use this route more than once."

"To us it seems easier to fly them in," said Yeyé. "We already have several planes."

"The problem with the air route," I answered, "is that I don't think we are consolidated enough to construct a line and defend it. Possibly in the territory where the Directorio Revolucionario is operating we could do something."

"We'll have to see," said Llanusa. "Here in Miami our relations with them haven't been good. They don't recognize the revolutionary authority of Fidel."

"In Cuba," I said, "there was a division among them. Eloy Gutiérrez Menoyo has separated from the Directorio and has started what he calls the Second Front of Escambray. Menoyo has sent us a message that he wants to talk with us. What do you think?"

"We have to talk with everybody," said Yeyé. "This is the moment of decision."

I made a gesture of uncertainty. "The problem is that the Second Front has accepted a group of people who we rejected, such as Nazario Sargent and Conrado Rodríguez, who are political operators."

"In any case, I think you should talk with Menoyo," Yeyé repeated. "At least we can establish a common action. We can work together, while remaining separate."

Yeyé summarized the situation. The revolutionary movement was again gaining momentum. The rebel army had repulsed the Batistianos and was now on the offensive. It had gone beyond a guerrilla war to a war of positions. With the increase in rebel territory, a government in arms would next be established, on Cuban soil, and international recognition would be requested. As for Las Villas, Yeyé would deliver to us all the arms we could handle. Guillermito was placed in charge of preparing the first shipment.

We left Yeyé's house euphoric.

We looked up John Buchanan and went with him to eat in one of those restaurants on the beach with low lights and thick rugs. The ambience was exquisite. The Cuban tourists never got to that place. John knew the maitre d' by name.

As we drank our martinis, we recalled our time at the university. Then there was an agreeable silence. We tried vaguely to bring back other memories. John found the thought he was looking for, because he said, "I'm on the go, old man."

"What do you mean?"

"I'm being put up for councilman on the beach in the next elections."

"You're kidding."

"It's true. And I am a member of the Democratic Party of the county."

"That sounds important. How did you manage that?"

"It was easy." There was a smile in his eyes. "I've made connections since we were at the university. In the elections of 1954 I influenced all my friends to vote for the Democrats.

"I used to speak a lot in my role as student leader. That led me to my first law firm position. Now I'm a junior partner in one of the most important firms. They're the ones who financed my campaign."

"And what caused you to change?"

"The tacit understanding that I will faithfully respect the interests of those who financed me."

The look on my face surprised him.

"I seem cynical to you? There is nothing of that sort, for the simple reason that the interests of which I spoke coincide perfectly with those of my country, and of myself, of course. There is no inconsistency."

The food was brought.

"I'll give you a tip—our foreign policies will be much more progressive than the Republicans'," continued John. "You will be the beneficiaries."

"Thank you in advance," I said.

"Don't be proud, Enrique."

"Jerk!" I said to myself as I felt myself flushing.

John read my expression. "Excuse me. I didn't mean to offend you."

"Forget it."

Nothing much else occurred to us to say. Of course I never said anything of my real reason for being in Florida.

I was back in Cuba after having spent a week in Miami when I received orders to approach the Directorio and other groups that were active in the mountains, in accordance with the directive to unify the revolutionary forces opposing Batista.

We decided to begin with the mountains at Escambray, which abutted the region of Cienfuegos. Nico Frías, the office partner of Osvaldo Dorticós, had a farm between the mountains and the sea. The farm lay on both sides of the Southern Bypass, the road that went from Cienfuegos to Trinidad. In the southern portion of the farm was Playa Inglés, which had yellow sand and was practically covered with riparian grapes. In the part of the farm north of the road, the foothills of the Escambray began.

It was early on Sunday. There were few people in the street, and our cars were making good time. Soon we were on the highway. We went along Central Soledad. We caught our first glimpses of the very calm sea on our right. On the left were the purple mountains. When we arrived at the farm, the lawyer Frías was waiting for us. We got out boxes filled with drinks and ice. The pig was already trimmed and cleaned so that it was white and gleaming. Firewood was arranged in an open pit in the ground. The roast began.

Frías made signs for me to follow him. Behind some brush ran an arroyo. There, stretched out on a rock, was a bearded man, with a rifle between his knees. Upon seeing us, he went on guard, but his features relaxed when he recognized Frías, who was returning to the group. Serafín Ruiz de Zárate, Osvaldo Dorticós, and our respective spouses and children were at the beach, having the picnic that was to serve as a cover for my activities.

I followed the bearded man. We climbed a path between two trees. We walked in silence, attentive to the sounds all around us. The man stopped and asked me, "Do you want to rest?"

"No!" I answered from pride.

We continued our hike. I began to pant, and the sound of my breathing kept me from hearing the surrounding sounds very well. We passed through a hedge by a wide abandoned road.

"We wait!" ordered the bearded man.

We waited beneath a gigantic carob tree. I leaned against the trunk and looked behind me. Below—far below—appeared the sea. I tried to locate Playa Inglés, but vegetation covered everything. In a narrow strip by the coast the sea was green; the bottom was sandy. Beyond that the sea was an intense blue, spattered with small white patches, a sign that the wind was beginning to blow.

"This was a state road that once joined Cienfuegos and Trinidad," I heard the voice of the bearded man behind me say.

I answered, "Is it still used?"

"Yes, but not much. Only by some countrypeople who live around here."

On the other side of the road some shrubs were shaking, and out of them emerged several armed, bearded men. One stepped forward and embraced me, patting me on the back vigorously.

"Don't you recognize me?" he asked.

"To tell the truth, no."

"Look carefully."

I tried to picture him without the beard. "Armandito Fleites!"

"How's it going, brother? Ha ha ha!"

More back slapping. He introduced me to the others, and after I assured them that I was rested we continued the hike.

We kept going up. From time to time I looked down behind me to fix the landscape in my memory. After several stages of climbing, we could no longer make out the sea; then, a little higher, hidden in a thick mass of trees, we saw several houses.

"It is there," Fleites told me.

Seeing our objective gave me new strength. But the path rose and fell tortuously, and again I felt we would never arrive. There were bearded men everywhere, along with civilian country folk with their wives and children. From the largest house a group came out and headed toward us.

"It's Eloy!" said Fleites, referring to Gutiérrez Menoyo.

We introduced ourselves. More back slapping. One of the principal figures was William Morgan, an American who said he had joined the guerrillas because Batista had killed a friend of his.

We entered the hut, where a large table had been set on the earth floor. A dozen of us sat around it: Gutiérrez Menoyo, Fleites, Morgan, and the rest of the military staff. The food was abundant and well prepared: hot salsa, cassava picante. Through the doors and open windows appeared the faces of the local children. I thought that the breakfast had been very carefully prepared. As we ate we exchanged stories. In them the men of Menoyo performed epic deeds. Coffee was served, and they even passed around smokes.

Once the table had been cleared, we sat back in our chairs and got down to the subject that brought us together. Armandito Fleites, representing the civil leadership: fighting in the Escambray should be considered a unified revolutionary front, rather than the particular offensive of any one organization; therefore he urged the 26th of July to team up with the military staff of Gutiérrez Menoyo. On the national level, they recognized the revolutionary authority of

Fidel, and on the civil level they were ready to collaborate closely with the 26th of July, though without joining our ranks. As for Faure's group, there were problems. They refused to recognize the military authority of Menoyo, even though he had effectively founded the front of Escambray, according to Fleites.

"Still, we will have to talk with them," I said.

"That would be a waste of time," insisted Fleites. "We have exhausted every possibility."

"Anyway, they're nothing," Morgan put in. "If you like, I'll go tomorrow and wipe them out myself."

"No, no, calm down. That's not the way it is," I said. The reason for the lack of unity in Escambray was obvious. Well then, what should we do? Clearly the most important thing was the support of Menoyo. His group seemed to be the most powerful, and it operated in an area that is fundamentally dependent on Cienfuegos. Precisely where we were the strongest. From there we could easily supply Bordón. What is more, Bordón could take advantage of Menoyo's general staff, to influence the future course of developments. Without a doubt, our influence would be greater with Menoyo than with Faure. What they had told me in Miami made that clear. This was definitely a temporary situation, which would be resolved favorably for us when a comandante with prestige arrived from the Sierra and our own army of the 26th of July would then be converted into the largest and most veteran group in Escambray. Then the danger that Las Villas would fall into the hands of an organization other than ours would disappear.

Fleites was used to speaking. He made a long recounting of the benefits of the Second Front of Escambray. The comandantes and captains of Gutiérrez Menoyo listened enthralled to the dramatized story of their own deeds. It was getting late, and I had to leave. We had to enter Cienfuegos in the morning, with the change of guards.

Menoyo noticed my uneasiness, because he decided to interrupt Fleites. We completed the details of our agreement, which was sealed with Fleites's sonorous pats on the back of everyone present.

I was already dressing when Martha came in to tell me that a message from Bosch was waiting for me.

In the course of the daily struggle, it had been weeks since I had thought of him. Now that thought returned forcefully.

Orlando Bosch had tried for several months to join the 26th of July. I had been opposed. Bosch practiced medicine in Santa Clara. He had been a friend of Guillermito at the university and through him insisted that we accept him into the organization. I had never known him, but I remembered that some friends of mine had spoken of him, when he was a student leader, as a political operator with links to the underworld. They said that he had used his position as a university student leader to win favors from Prío. When the others were simple students, Bosch already owned two automobiles.

Faced with the insistence of Bosch and Guillermito, I finally decided to talk to him and explain to him openly the reasons for his rejection. We met in Guillermito's house. I cut to the gist:

"In view of your insistence, we have decided to give you an explanation. We have the impression that your past is cloudy. It is said that several times you betrayed the student protest movement to accept favors from Prío. That you were an underworld element. That the only thing that motivated you was ambition." I looked at Bosch as I spoke, to judge the effect of my words. But I couldn't read his eyes. "These are widely shared opinions. Something must have happened. I don't have any basis for a personal opinion."

Bosch took the floor, his glasses slipping down his thin nose. He said, "Everything that they have told you about me is false. I have nothing to be ashamed of. It's all loose talk. Give me concrete examples. Fidel was a friend of mine at the university—ask him about me.

If I've been guilty of anything that stains the revolution, shoot me. But meanwhile let me work for it. When I graduated from medical school, I promised my mother never to get involved in politics, but I can think of nothing else. I try to concentrate on my work, to work myself to exhaustion. But all around me people are doing things, and I feel like a coward. I want to fight for my country. Can you deny a man the right to fight for what he considers his duty? There is nothing concrete against me. Give me the humblest responsibility, and if some day I am discovered to have dishonored the revolution, I will pay with my life."

As time passed, I did not find anything to hold against him. Bosch worked with enthusiasm and gained my trust. In time, he became one of my chief aides. But his nervous nature reopened an old ulcer. With an internal hemorrhage, he had to be taken to Havana. After he was admitted, a guide from Escambray was detained in Santa Clara; this guide subsequently denounced Bosch, among others. Ventura personally took him out of the hospital. An all-out effort by the medical school managed to save his life. We authorized his exile to Miami.

As for our activities in Miami, we were unlucky. In the first shipment of arms that Guillermito sent from Miami, the ship was surprised by a storm and sank to the depths of the Bahamas. Everyone was on the point of drowning and had to be pulled out of the sea.

I finished dressing and went down to the room. A young woman stood up and handed me a letter:

> *Dear compañero Sierra:*
> *I began these lines recalling the saying that God drenches but doesn't drown, so I am hopeful. The pilot who raised the shipwrecked vessel was a Cuban youth named Romero. The uncle and father of this boy have a cargo ship of several thousand tons that makes trips to Miami, Baracoa, and South America. When these men found out what had*

*happened to their nephew and son, they came to see me, late at night, two days ago. After a lot of conversation and some patriotic comments of mine, the man stood up and said to me: "I have never been mixed up in revolutionary activities, because my ship is worth a lot of money, which provides for ten Cuban families, but I think that the moment has come when we each must throw in a grain of sand to bury the tyrant. Therefore, I put my ship at your disposition for this trip."*

*Imagine how I felt at that. There's no rub here, Sierra, because this is a commercial transatlantic ship, piloted by real sea wolves. After that meeting I went to see Yeyé, who was very happy and told me that in this trip we would be carrying several 30- and 50-caliber Browning automatic rifles and Thomson machine guns and 30,000 rounds, which, of course, we will have to protect carefully. All this equipment is here in Miami. She is in the best position to continue cooperating with us because she has been following our efforts and interests. The men who will be coming in the ship from there will have to bring iron-cutters, since the equipment will be inside barrels of gasoline.*

*The ship leaves here between the 5th and the 10th of November. So the people there will have to be ready. What is really important is to make sure there is no problem with the facilities there. Here there is no problem.*

*As for Guillermito and company, I will tell you that those fellows are now in Nassau, and we are expecting them here soon. Yeyé helped us, including with money, for we have to pay out money, even to the immigration people. Answer me soon. Send someone or come yourself. If this ship leaves, as we are sure it will, make sure we have the 10,000 pesos promised to continue buying equipment.*

*Last night I met again with the captain of the ship. We drank coffee, discussed patriotic themes, etc., and the matter was confirmed. Of my health I will tell you that although we are working as hard here as you are there, I am feeling good. Send me a good long letter.*

*An embrace,*
*Orlando*

# Photographs

Bar mitzvah boy, age 13, in 1943.

Oltuski at age two with his beloved mother, Jashe, in 1932.

Bar mitzvah dinner for the Santa Clara, Cuba, Jewish community, 1943. Oltuski at the rear with father Bernardo, left, sister Sylvia, fourth from right, and mother, fifth from right.

174

Enrique's father,
Bernardo Oltuski,
c. 1945.

Oltuski with his father, c. 1946.

Sweethearts: Enrique and Martha
in 1955 when he was 16 and she 15.

175

Santa Clara High
School, class of
1948. Enrique is
in front, Martha
is in the second
row far right, and
Martha's brother
Guillermito is in
the middle of
the third row
from top.

Student card,
University of Miami, 1949.

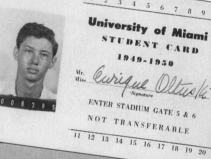

With friends on
Miami Beach,
1950.

Frat party, c. 1951.

Sister Sylvia's wedding to her husband Samuel in 1955.
Father Bernardo is just to the left of the bride, Enrique
to the right of the groom.

With Che Guevara in the mountains, 1958.

Assuming his new position as Minister of Communications, the youngest member of the first revolutionary cabinet, January 12, 1959.

178

On the beach with
Martha and first son,
Frank, 1959.

Enrique, Martha, and Frank lived in an apartment on the ground
floor of this house on 23rd Street in the Havana Wood district of
New Vedado. It was here on the morning of February 13, 1959, that
Fidel Castro agreed for the first time to become Prime Minister of
Cuba (photo taken in October 2001).

179

An important moment: signing the intervention order of the telephone company then owned by ITT, October, 1960. The American manager at Oltuski's left is smiling here but left Cuba shortly thereafter.

With Fidel during the intervention of the telephone company in 1959.

Speaking on television in his role as Minister of Communications in 1959.

OLTUSKI

Che becoming president of the National Bank in 1959.
Oltuski is in right rear. Then President Osvaldo Dorticos
is to the left of Che, Faustino Perez is on his right, and
Osmani Cienfuegos is at far left.

Oltuski on his weekly
TV show with Juan
Almeida, who fought
with Fidel at the
Moncada barracks,
came with him on the
*Granma* from Mexico,
was a leader of the
guerilla troops, and
is now vice president
of Cuba.

181

Attending the first summer Carnival, 1959.
*Left to right:* President Osvaldo Dorticos, Prime Minister
Fidel Castro, Dorticos's wife, and Enrique (then 28).
Martha is in the second row between Dorticos and Fidel.

With Jean-Paul Sartre (second from left) and Simone de Beauvoir (far right) during their first trip to Cuba in 1959. On the far left is Jose Naranjo, the Minister of the Interior, and third from the right is Regino Boti, Minister of the Economy.

With Raul Castro, far right, around 1960.

The four children of Martha and Enrique in the mid-1960s: Carlos, Frank, Haydee, and Sylvia.

With Fidel after the session of the National Assembly in 2000.

184

Enrique Oltuski at La Terraza in October 2001.

With Fidel after saying goodbye to the president of Haiti in 2001.

# The Sierra

## chapter 14

# Che in Las Villas

*Sierra Maestra, September 20, 1958*
*Compañeros Sierra and Diego:*
*Because of the extraordinary workload of recent weeks, I neglected to officially communicate to you the sending of troops to Las Villas and the designation of compañero E. Guevara as comandante of the forces of the 26th of July there.*

*I suppose nonetheless that Zoilo has kept you fully informed of our plans. I think that the position of the Movement will improve markedly. Support from our organization for the campaigning troops will be a decisive factor. We hope that a chain of success awaits you all. We are ready to keep sending reinforcements. Las Villas is of great importance to our strategic plans. It is worth all our efforts.*
*Fraternally,*
*Fidel Castro*

I went back and forth several times along the highway, but there was nobody at the meeting place. I had to see Che at all costs—something had gone wrong. Nobody was waiting at the designated crossroads. I couldn't turn back. I decided to continue traveling to Trinidad and try to get up to the hills from there.

In Trinidad, I looked up Carlos Trelles. Neither dull nor lazy, Trelles obtained two good horses and offered his services as guide. With the pretext of a visit to a farm on the outskirts of town, we started off. The horses went at a pace, and we talked. Soon we exhausted our subjects and continued in silence.

We didn't meet anybody on the road, and night had begun to fall by the time we reached Condado. This was a village with houses along both sides of a narrow street. We rode down the middle of the street. The horses' hooves resounded with a sound that I would have liked to be quieter. The doors and windows of most of the houses were closed as if they were empty. According to our most recent information, Condado was in rebel territory, but one never knew. Many families had fled, fearing a possible bombardment.

On a porch, three men were talking; they turned to watch us pass, and we greeted them with a wave of the hand. Afterward we met two or three more groups of men, who watched us with curiosity. Finally we reached the end of town and turned around.

We went back down the road and brought our horses to a halt in front of the first group who had greeted us. Trelles got down to talk with the men while I kept watch mounted on my horse.

One of the men gestured toward a gasoline pump by the opposite sidewalk. Half hidden in the shadows of the overhang was a rebel we hadn't seen before. Trelles crossed the street, and I got down from my horse and followed him.

Trelles spoke: "We want to see Che, but we've lost contact. Can you assign someone to take us to him?"

The man regarded us distrustfully, without answering a word.

I said, "Look, I am Sierra, the provincial coordinator of the 26th of July. I have a meeting with Che. I know you're uneasy. But why not take us to him? We'll go unarmed. If we try any tricks, it will be like putting our heads in the lion's mouth."

His eyes scrutinized us. We had presented a grave dilemma. "Wait here," he said, and he disappeared into a house. In a little while we heard the sound of a horse galloping away from us. Then the man reappeared and insisted that we wait.

Time went by. The rosy tones of the setting sun appeared in the sky. Trelles looked at me uneasily.

"Let's wait a little longer," I said, "and if nobody comes, we'll go on our way." We heard the sound of a motor.

"It's our jeep!" said the rebel.

A slight rise prevented us from seeing the road. The sound came nearer. We began to make out a cloud of rising smoke, and then the jeep quickly appeared. It braked in front of us. Several rebels had come, but nobody got out.

"But of course this is Sierra!" said the one who appeared to be the boss, and he got out of the jeep. Then the obligatory question: "Don't you recognize me?"

"No . . ."

"I am Nieves, from the 26th of July militia. Now I am with the Directorio . . . When I came up, there was nobody here from the 26th."

"Yes, I remember," I lied. "What luck you were here. You know we're looking for Che?"

"So I'm told. It's been two days since I've seen him, but we know more or less where he's gone. Get in. We can get most of the way there in the jeep."

Night fell. The driver went very fast. The road headed straight up the mountainside. There were too many people in the jeep, and each pothole carried the danger of falling out, or worse yet, hurling us over a cliff.

It was the dead of night by the time we caught up with Che's rear guard. In the jeep's headlights we saw the first men of the Sierra Maestra. They were different from those of Escambray: scruffy beards, worn-out clothes and shoes, hair very long and disheveled. They spoke with an eastern accent. They were graceful and handled their arms with ease, as if the weapons were part of themselves.

We had to leave the jeep; the road had become too rough. We continued on foot. It had rained, and our shoes sank in the mud. We met more and more of Che's troops. Nieves and his men watched them respectfully. We could see the lights of several houses. A post blocked our way. We identified ourselves, and one of the men went to the houses and then returned. They let us pass. In what was the center of a group of huts, in the dark of night, there was a fire; around it were several men.

We went over to them. I had in mind an image of Che that I had seen in magazines. None of those faces was his. But there was a moderately robust man, just a little shorter than I was, who wore a beret on his very long hair. His beard was not very thick. He wore a black cloak with his shirt open. The flames of the bonfire, together with the moustache that ran down along the sides of his mouth, gave him a Chinese look. It was Che, but I thought of Genghis Khan. This is how it must have been back then. Shadows from the firelight danced in his face, giving him constantly shifting, fantastic expressions.

He fixed me with a look.

"I am Sierra," I said.

He simply smiled in answer, as we shook hands. Many people had gathered around him, speaking to him. They did not seem inclined to let me disturb them. I stood to one side. Still more people came, and the scene became even more confused. I went to urinate and then sat on a rock. There was tremendous confusion, with all sorts of people coming and going. Then Nieves came over and told me that Che was waiting for me. I followed him to a room in one of the huts. Che was sitting on a stool in a corner, eating.

"Are you hungry?" he asked me.

"Not very."

"It doesn't matter. The guerrilla fighter has to eat whenever there is food, because he never knows when he will see it again."

I took a piece of meat and began to chew, without enthusiasm. When we were done eating we went outside and sat on some logs that had been set on the ground. Che offered me tobacco, and we smoked. Then he said, "I have already met two of the Provincial Directors."

"And what is your impression of them?"

"The black fellow in charge of propaganda seems good. The worker . . . he doesn't seem like a worker to me."

"But he is. He worked in Rayonera Matanzas."

"Even so."

There was a pause, and then: "I have met with the people of the Directorate. They made a favorable impression on me. It seems to me you managed the Escambray matter very poorly."

I felt a hole in the pit of my stomach: "It's very easy to make that judgment now, but things weren't so clear a few months ago." I told him the story of our relations with Escambray. "At the time, as we saw it, it was best to ally ourselves with Menoyo. Once we had an agreement, difficulties began. The first problem was when they published some declarations attacking the Directorate and gave out the impression that we shared their view. We had to disavow them in our underground publication. Then, when Bordón began to get stronger, they started to worry. At first they took supplies destined for Bordón, but in the end they surprised and disarmed him. And that's how we ended up in hot water with both God and the Devil."

"I'm done with him," said Che. "Menoyo didn't want to talk with us."

A thin rebel came over; his long beard glowed in the firelight.

"Comandante Ramiro Valdés, my second; compañero Sierra," Che introduced us.

Ramiro stretched out on the ground and rested his head against one of the logs. "What a difference from Camagüey!" he commented, making himself comfortable. Che smiled.

I took the occasion to ask, "What do you think of the things we have sent you?"

Che answered, "Up to this point we have received little aid from the Movement. The ones who have done a lot for us are the Partido Socialista Popular."

"The PSP?"

"Yes, they sent us a shipment of clothes and shoes that have come in very handy."

"When?"

"Two days ago."

"Shit on the PSP! That shipment was sent by us. We had been lugging it around ever since you passed through Camagüey. Those clothes and shoes didn't come from the PSP."

Two rebels arrived to consult about something. When they left, Che picked up the conversation: "In the coming days we will establish our permanent camp. Once the men have rested, the action will begin. We have to get some ammunition; we have almost none."

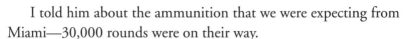

I told him about the ammunition that we were expecting from Miami—30,000 rounds were on their way.

"Seeing is believing," said Ramiro.

"Yes, we will see," I said. "The bad part is that then you'll say they were sent by the PSP."

Everyone laughed, and we felt closer.

I told them, "The arms will come in through the north, through the region of Camilo Cienfuegos. This weekend I'll go and see him."

"When we find that we have extended and consolidated our territory," continued Che, "we will implement agrarian reform, dividing the land among those who work it. What do you think about agrarian reform?"

"It is essential," I answered. Che's eyes brightened. "Without agrarian reform economic progress is impossible."

"Nor social progress," interrupted Che.

"Nor social, of course. I wrote a statement on agrarian reform for the Movement's program document."

"Really? And what did it say?"

"All idle land should be given to the peasants, and heavy taxes should be imposed on the large estate holders so that the land can be bought from them with their own money. Then the land would be sold to the peasants at cost, with easy terms of payment and credit for production."

"But that is a reactionary position!" Che boiled with indignation. "How can we keep the land from the people who work it? You are just like all the other people of the plains."

I got angry in turn. "And what do you want, asshole? To make a gift of it?! So that they can destroy it, like in Mexico? A man has to feel that what he owns cost him something."

"You jerk, look at you!" cried Che, and the veins swelled in his neck.

We argued tirelessly. Ramiro went off to go to sleep. A cold wind began to blow that gave me chills.

"Besides," I added, "you have to disguise things. You can't believe that the Americans are going to just cross their arms when they see us do it so blatantly. You have to play with their heads."

"So you're one of those who believe that we can make revolution behind the backs of the Americans. How full of crap you are! To make revolution we have to fight imperialism to the death, from the first moment. A real revolution cannot be disguised."

We went on talking and arguing for hours. Except for the sentries, everyone was asleep. The dawn was biting cold. My teeth chattered. I could hardly hold Che's tobacco in the ends of my fingers. A light fog drifted in.

Che looked at his watch. "Let's go to sleep."

We went to one of the huts. They had saved two beds for us in one of the rooms. Still we kept talking, until we heard the sound of people moving around and raising a ruckus.

"What happened?" I asked.

"A stray shot," said Che.

We went outside. Indeed, a shot had escaped from a shotgun, sending pellets in every direction. Several people were wounded. By the bright light of the headlights, the doctors were extracting the ammunition. There was one rebel who was holding his genitals with his hands and complaining bitterly.

Finally it was his turn: the man began to cry as he lowered his pants. "I'm wounded in the balls, Doctor," he moaned.

The doctor poked around in the man's testicles and then extracted something with his clamp, while the rebel let out a heart-rending shout.

"Here's the cause of your grief." He extended the clamp to him.

"The bastard!" said the rebel. "It's a tick!"

Everyone died of laughter, and Che had a coughing fit.

When we went back to lie down, the fog had gotten brighter.

We were in one of the houses that we kept in Santa Clara for secret meetings. Diego watched me with a remorseful expression.

"No way will we do as Che wants," I said. To attack the bank in Sancti Spíritus is madness. That would turn many people against us who now support us. Besides, it's unnecessary. We have more money now than ever. Almost 50,000 pesos. We will send him a good part of it, so he can see. I'm sure that Fidel will not approve this action. Don't worry; we will write to Che right now explaining our reasons."

At the end of several days, Che's answer arrived:

> *Santa Lucía, November 3, 1958*
>
> *Dear Sierra:*
>
> *I have just received your letter with great surprise, because I see that after passing through the filter of the plains, what is said differs from what was discussed and approved here. You tell me in the post-script that Diego agrees with you, whereas here he agreed with me. It may be that Diego doesn't express himself well, or simply that he doesn't have an opinion on the fundamental issues of the revolution.*
>
> *You say that Fidel did not do this even when there was nothing to eat. That is true, but when you have nothing to eat you also lack the strength to perform an action of this kind. When we ask for assistance from the classes whose interests could suffer from the uprising, we get evasive responses and in the end betrayal, as occurred with the rice dealers in the recent offensive.*
>
> *According to the person who brought me your letter, the directors of the towns are threatening to resign. It's fine with me if they do. What's more, I ask them to do so now, because we cannot permit an extended boycott to delay a revolution as beneficial as this one.*
>
> *I see the sad necessity of reminding you that I have been named commander in chief precisely to provide a unified command to the Movement and to make things better. By God, we couldn't make the attack on Fomento as we had planned. At the time of the shooting, there were a ridiculous amount of Molotov cocktails, there was no military man to see that assigned tasks were performed, and they left at the wrong time. Resign or don't resign, I will make a clean sweep, with the authority invested in me, of all the wavering people in the towns outside the Sierra. I didn't think I would end up being boycotted by my own*

*compañeros. Now I realize that the old hostilities we thought we had gone beyond resurge with the word "plains," and leaders who are out of touch with the feelings of the masses cast their opinions on this. I could ask why no peasant has disagreed with our position that the land belongs to those who work it? And yes, of course landowners disagree. Doesn't the fact that the fighting forces agree with the assault on the banks have to do with their not having a penny between them? Didn't it ever occur to you to consider the economic roots of their situation with respect to the most arbitrary of financial institutions? Those who make money by dealing with the money of others, by speculating with it, have no right to special consideration. The miserable sum they offer is what they make in a day of exploitation, while the suffering people are bled dry in both the Sierra and the plains, and every day they suffer the treason of their false managers.*

*You place full responsibility for the destruction of the organization on me. I accept that responsibility in the spirit of revolution, and I am ready to give an account of my conduct before any revolutionary tribunal, the moment the National Directorate of the Movement calls for it. I will give an accounting of every last centavo given to the combatants of the Sierra or that were obtained by them in any way. But I need an accounting from you of the 50,000 pesos you have announced, since I must tell you that by resolution of Fidel, in a letter that I will show you when you come here, the treasury of the Second Front of Escambray is to be kept here.*

*You ask for a receipt with my signature, something we are not accustomed to doing between compañeros. I am absolutely responsible for my actions, and my word is worth more than all the signatures in the world. If I demand someone's signature, it is because I am not convinced of his honesty. It hadn't occurred to me to ask this of you, although it was demanded a hundred times from Gutiérrez Menoyo.*

*I finish with a revolutionary greeting and wait here with Diego,*
*Che*

At this point I realized that it was crucial to get Che as much money as we could so he would not pursue any further his ideas about our robbing banks. Since I was unable to go myself at that moment, I sent Aleida March to deliver the cash. This was the very first time that Aleida met Che, whom she would eventually marry.

After first turning back and then defeating Batista's troops in the Sierra Maestra in the summer of 1958, Fidel had sent two columns toward the west of the country. The column led by Che occupied the mountains of Escambray in our province of Las Villas in order to divide Cuba in two. The column led by Camilo Cienfuegos, another of our victorious commanders of the Sierra Maestra, had to pass through Las Villas and continue its march to the mountains of the province of Pinar del Rio, in the extreme west of Cuba on the other side of Havana.

Taking advantage of Camilo's making a stop in the north of our province, I had promised to see him with the hope that the additional arms that were finally coming from Miami would also serve to supply his troops.

Night was slowly falling on the little store on the outskirts of Yaguajay. I was going to meet Camilo. I waited in the shadows, until a man came and told me to follow him at a distance.

We entered an alley that led off into the darkness. The ground was slippery from recent rains. After walking a while, the man signaled to me, and crawling under the wires we entered the cane plantation.

Hidden in the canes was a hut whose door opened in response to the password. By candlelight I was introduced to the guide. We put on heavy boots and took up our arms. We set off again through the canes, leading the horses by their bridles.

At last we left the cane plantation and mounted the horses. Behind us were the lights of Yaguajay, and in front of us the dark mass of the hills was approaching. Soon we heard the first shots.

"Are those ours?" I asked the guide.

"Perhaps," he responded. "Maybe the guards are shooting from nervousness. In any case, don't worry, friend; if one has your number on it, not even the strongest hide can stop it."

We reached the first heights and began to descend again through a fine rain. The horses slipped in the mud, and low branches scratched our bodies. Through twisting paths and dense vegetation, we came to the first guard. We gave the password and went on. We were drawing near the camp. Our excitement was mounting with each step of the horses. Finally we were reaching Camilo.

It was raining heavily when we arrived at the meeting place. William Gálvez greeted us without getting out of his hammock. He was sick with a fever. He lifted his head to tell us that Camilo had to leave suddenly to see the gunsmith, who had been wounded. We went on to the new location. The rain was beginning to let up, reducing the darkness a little. The first stars appeared and also distant lights that I thought might be those of Caibarién. For a long time we went on, smoking in silence.

"There is the hut," said the guide.

We went to it and tied up the horses. Some men were sleeping in hammocks, others kept guard. We presented ourselves at the door and went in to see Camilo. By the faint light of a candle he appeared, sitting with another man. On the table, a portable radio was broadcasting Radio Rebelde, the station that Che had set up from the Sierra Maestra. Camilo was wearing a Batista army cap, and he was stroking his beard thoughtfully. He took no notice of our presence. I cast my glance around the humble room with its earthen floor and made out the family of the house. In the darkness of the corner they adored Camilo. The flickering light of the candle drew strange patterns on his face. It was all like in a painting.

At last he got up and came over to us. We introduced ourselves and shook hands. We sat on the ground outside by the door. We talked for a long time—about the struggle, about the coming months, about the campesinos, about agrarian reform. About Che. During the nights in the Sierra, Che read Neruda to them.

I told Camilo about the ammunition that would be arriving soon.

"That dog has bitten me before," he smiled.

"This time is different," I said, thinking that his confidence depended on that.

We left off coordinating everything having to do with the arrival of the ammunition.

Time passed more quickly than ever. Inexplicably, it was time to go.

Three of us were going by horseback to one of my regular meetings with Che: Marcelo, the guide, and me. We had climbed to Caballete de Casa, where Che was camped, but we didn't see him: he had gone to El Pedrero, where the army was making movements suggesting a new offensive.

The afternoon passed as we made our way along the dusty road. In camp we had been issued work clothes and wide palm hats to protect us from the daytime sun. We had encountered several groups that had arrived from El Pedrero. As they went by they warned us, "Watch out for the small plane! It's shooting."

From then on we were vigilant: we kept a lookout for trees with thick trunks, the best refuge in case of attack. But time went by, and the plane did not appear. The sun had gone behind hills on our right, and the light was fleeting. Quiet overtook us. All we could hear was the dry clack of hooves in the dust. We went on lost in thought, and now nobody was keeping watch.

Suddenly I heard the voice of the guide: "Airplaaaaaane!

Get down! Blood suddenly pumped hard through my veins. I lifted my head and studied the sky: on the right, from behind the hills, the little plane was approaching. We looked all around, seeking trees that could protect us. But these were pasture lands—there was not even a single tree that offered a sufficiently thick trunk. On both sides of the road ran rows of wheat—young plants with stalks like twigs. In the distance we could see a small mountain. I estimated the distance: it was impossible to reach it in time. Besides, there was always the possibility—remote—that they would take us for peaceful farmers, and if we took off at a gallop it would reveal who we were.

I decided to get down from the horse and sit in a ditch. The plane was coming directly at us. I could clearly see the machine gun mounted in one of its windows, aiming at us. I turned over on my stomach, put my elbows on my knees, and held my head in my hands. I expected at any time to feel the impact in my back. The bullets would press through my body and exit on the other side. In the position I was in, they would pass through my legs too.

I was going to die. At last the moment I had feared and imagined so many times had arrived. What would it be like? Would everything go black all of a sudden, or a little at a time? To my surprise, I felt calm facing imminent death. I was going to die without accomplishing so many of the things I wanted to do, without seeing so many things I wanted to see. The image of my son came to my mind. His first birthday had been a few days ago. I saw his pink face. The blond hair on his head. The reason for my fight. An eternity passed; a few seconds passed.

"It's going! It's going!" cried the guide.

I looked up to see the airplane inexplicably moving away. I got on my horse, and we began to race toward the distant mountain. But the airplane did not return.

We reached El Pedrero by night. There was a faint light in one of the houses, and we went in. It was a vast structure of rubble and roof tiles. On one side were the writing desks. By the teacher's table a young rebel, lieutenant Orlando Pantoja, was sitting. Che had left and would be back soon. On the table, a platter contained green meat.

"It's beef with salsa," said Orlando. "Help yourself."

We each took a mouthful. When I tasted it my stomach turned—it had gone bad. Hiding the fact, I went to the door and threw away my piece.

Che arrived in the middle of the night. We were lying on the floor of the school, sleeping. We greeted each other, and Che said, "We have had the first skirmishes. Without a doubt they are getting ready to make a foray into this area. Now we miss the arms that Sierra promised."

As we talked, he took pieces of meat in his dirty fingers. Judging by the pleasure he took in eating, he found them excellent. He finished eating, and we went outside. We sat on the side of the road, Marcelo, Che, and I. Che passed around smokes. They were coarse, surely made in the area by some peasant. I breathed in the strong and bitter smoke: I felt warmth in my body, and a slight nausea. By my side Che smoked and coughed, with a wet cough as if everything were wet inside. He smelled bad, like old sweat. It was a penetrating smell, and I fought it back with tobacco smoke.

Our conversation was rough, but we did not fight much that night. Perhaps Che was tired. Perhaps it was the strong, bitter tobacco that made him drowsy. Che and Marcelo had some verbal exchanges. Among other things, they discussed the program document of the 26th of July. Che promised to write something. I was leaving early for the Sierra Maestra, and we discussed how to handle things while I was gone.

When we got back, Marcelo asked me, "What did you think?"

"Despite everything, you can't help admiring him. He knows what he wants better than we do. It's all he lives for. You know? I thought I was a complete revolutionary . . . until I met Che. Compared to him, I am just an apprentice. I am still bound to so many things that he has liberated himself from."

"We must leave now for the Sierra," said Marcelo, "to attend the meeting that Fidel has called with all the leaders of the 26th of July Movement in the country. This meeting will determine the final strategy in the struggle to defeat Batista."

We were quiet. After a while I said to Marcelo, "When I return from the Sierra I will join up with Che."

## chapter 15

# The Sierra Maestra

The voice of Fidel was borne on the waves of Radio Rebelde, filling the small room, which was shut up tight as a drum:

"Yesterday at 9 P.M., after ten days of intense combat, our forces penetrated into Guisa; the battle took place within sight of Bayamo, where the dictatorship has its command center and the bulk of its forces.

"The action at Guisa began on November 20, when our forces intercepted an enemy patrol that made the trip from Guisa to Bayamo on a daily basis. The patrol was turned back, and that same day the first enemy reinforcements arrived. At 4:00 P.M. a T-17 thirty-ton tank was destroyed by a powerful mine: the impact of the explosion made the tank, thrown several meters through the air, fall forward with its wheels up and its cab smashed in on the pavement of the road. Hours before that, a truck full of soldiers had been blown up by another mine. At 6:00 P.M. the reinforcements withdrew.

"On the following day, the enemy advanced, supported by tanks, to penetrate into Guisa, leaving a reinforcement in the local garrison.

"On the 22nd, our troops, exhausted from two days of fighting, took up positions on the road from Bayamo to Guisa.

"On the 23rd, an enemy troop tried to advance along the road from Corojo and was repulsed. On the 25th, an infantry battalion, led by two T-17 tanks, advanced along the Bayamo-Guisa road, guarding a convoy of fourteen trucks.

"At two kilometers from this point, the rebel troops fired on the convoy, cutting off its retreat, while a mine paralyzed the lead tank.

"Then began one of the most violent combats that has taken place in the Sierra Maestra. Inside the Guisa garrison, the complete battalion that came in reinforcement, along with two T-17 tanks, was now within the rebel lines. At 6:00 P.M., the enemy had to abandon all its trucks, using them as a barricade tightly encircling the two tanks. At 10:00 P.M., while a battery of mortars attacked them, rebel recruits, armed with picks and shovels, opened a ditch in the road next to the tank that had been destroyed on the 20th, so that between the tank and the ditch, the other two T-17 tanks within the lines were prevented from escaping.

"They remained isolated, without food or water, until the morning of the 27th when, in another attempt to break the line, two battalions of reinforcements brought from Bayamo advanced with Sherman tanks to the site of the action. Throughout the day of the 27th the reinforcements were fought. At 6:00 P.M., the enemy artillery began a retreat under cover of the Sherman tanks, which succeeded in freeing one of the T-17 tanks that were inside the lines; on the field, full of dead soldiers, an enormous quantity of arms was left behind, including 35,000 bullets, 14 trucks, 200 knapsacks, and a T-17 tank in perfect condition, along with abundant 37-millimeter cannon shot. The action wasn't over—a rebel column intercepted the enemy in retreat along the Central Highway and caused it new casualties, obtaining more ammunition and arms.

"On the 28th, two rebel squads, led by the captured tank, advanced toward Guisa. At 2:30 A.M. on the 29th, the rebels took up positions, and the tank managed to place itself facing the Guisa army quarters. The enemy, entrenched in numerous buildings, gave intense fire. The tank's cannon had already fired fifty shots when two bazooka shots from the enemy killed its engine, but the tank's cannon continued firing until its ammunition was exhausted and the men inside lowered the cannon tube. Then occurred an act of unparalleled heroism: rebel Lieutenant Leopoldo Cintras Frías, who was operating the tank's machine gun, removed it from the tank, and despite being wounded, crawled under intense crossfire and managed to carry away the heavy weapon.

"Meanwhile, that same day, four enemy battalions advanced from separate points: along the road from Bayamo to Guisa, along the road from Bayamo to Corojo, and along the one from Santa Rita to Guisa.

"All of the enemy forces from Bayamo, Manzanillo, Yara, Estrada Palma, and Baire were mobilized to smash us. The column that advanced along the road from Corojo was repulsed after two hours of combat. The advance of the battalions that came along the road from Bayamo to Guisa was halted, and they encamped two kilometers from Guisa; those that advanced along the road from Corralillo were also turned back.

"The battalions that encamped two kilometers from Guisa tried to advance during the entire day of the 30th; at 4:00 P.M., while our forces were fighting them, the Guisa garrison abandoned the town in hasty flight, leaving behind abundant arms and armaments. At 9:00 P.M., our vanguard entered the town of Guisa. Enemy supplies seized included a T-17 tank—captured, lost, and recaptured; 94 weapons (guns and machine guns, Springfield and Garand); 12 60-millimeter mortars; 1 91-millimeter mortar; a bazooka; 7 30-caliber tripod machine guns; 50,000 bullets; 130 Garand grenades; 70 howitzers of 60- and 81-millimeter mortar; 20 bazooka rockets; 200 knapsacks, 160 uniforms, 14 transport trucks; food; and medicine.

"The army took two hundred losses, counting casualties and wounded. We took eight compañeros who died heroically in action, and seven wounded.

"A squadron of women, the "Mariana Grajales," fought valiantly during the ten days of action.

"Guisa, twelve kilometers from the military port of Bayamo, is now free Cuban territory."

Santiago de Cuba was surrounded by the rebel army. The army of the tyranny tried to break the blockade. One attempt after another was quashed by the men of the rebel columns. The only means of access to the city was from the air.

Our plane landed at the airport. As soon as we got out of the plane we were immediately struck by the air of great tension. Martha and I passed the police checkpoint and took a taxi into the city. As usual, I had told Shell I was on a family visit to Santiago with my wife. We stayed at the Casa Granda Hotel. At dinnertime we observed the effects of the blockade: already there was little to eat.

Early the next day I went to the Banco Continental. The manager, Fernando Vecino, had come to Santa Clara to make a contribution to us in the name of the owner of the bank, Julian Zulueta. Vecino had a son who was captain of the rebel army.

I went into the small office, where Vecino embraced me affectionately. "I can imagine what brings you here."

"I have come for a meeting in the Sierra. I need for you to put me in contact with the leadership."

"This very day. Where are you staying?"

"At the Casa Granda. I came with my wife."

"First of all, you have to get out of there. Your visit to Santiago must go unnoticed. Why not come to my house?"

"No, absolutely not; that would make too much trouble for you. Martha can go back to Santa Clara as soon as I leave."

"I won't accept any discussion. You come with us, and when you go, Martha will remain in my house until you come back."

We went to Vecino's house. We had to wait for two days until everything was ready for my departure. That afternoon, a car took me to a house by the bay while Martha waited for me at Vecino's. Another couple would be going with us. When night fell, we went on foot to the wharf, and there we took a small boat. We saw several navy boats anchored in the bay. We went around the obstacles until we berthed on the other side, in the docks of a club.

There we waited for a long time. The place was deserted. Batista's men did not go to that part of the bay. Finally we were found and taken to a group of houses that constituted the rebel vanguard. They were in the hands of the *escopetero,* or shotgun men, those who did not have a real rifle but only old shotguns, who were not regular members of the guerrilla army but supporters in the plains around the mountains. We changed our clothes, dressing in gray (there was no khaki green), pants and shirt, and boots, and we carried a hammock and knapsack. We got in a jeep and started off in the dark.

We went along the coast road with several rebel jeeps and trucks that were on their way to the Texaco refinery to load up with gasoline. A dray tank was clogged, and it was blocking the road. We got out to push it aside. We failed to move it. Soon a truck came and moved it with a cable. We were covered with mud, but it didn't matter—we could continue our trip.

That night we slept in a real rebel camp. There I met Captain Fernandín Vecino, the son of our friend, who was recovering from wounds suffered in an ambush near Santiago. We observed great activity, with many people coming and going, jeeps arriving and leaving. The outposts constantly harassed the enemy, as soon as they showed their heads. Everything indicated that we were on the verge of success. Fernandín and I talked until we were overcome with fatigue.

At dawn we again set off. This time we were in a truck that was carrying tanks of gasoline. We were introduced to the driver; they called him Crazy Horse. I soon understood the reason for the nickname: he drove that steep stone road as if it were the Central Highway. The coast road crossed broken ground and passed over sands, small brooks that fell from the mountains, and doglegs. Some parts were flooded, because in places in the mountain it had rained, and the streams had become stormy torrents.

At noon we reached a point that was a mandatory stop in Crazy Horse's itinerary: a small village of fishermen beside the sea. There lived people more miserable than I had ever seen. The men, the women, the children, the dogs, the hens—all were the skinniest I had ever observed. They invited us to lunch with a graciousness that I found moving. I declined: to accept would have been like robbing them. But Crazy Horse would not listen to my objections, so we stayed there.

They brought me a broad plate of rice and yucca. I noticed that everyone ate standing up, but I sat on the ground. They all ate with their fingers, and I looked around hoping to find someone who would realize I was looking for silverware, but nobody paid any attention to me. Soon there was a big commotion near me, and my plate of food flew into the air. The hungry hens quickly devoured the rice. Everyone laughed, and they brought me a second plate, which this time I ate standing up.

In the afternoon we arrived at Aserradero, where we loaded up with food and then turned north and began to climb the mountains. The truck bounced over the stones. I stood up and, holding onto the railing, watched the barrels that threatened to crush me. At times the truck teetered toward the precipice, and my body tensed as I got ready to jump if the truck went over. My arms ached from holding on, but the cold air kept me alert.

It was very late when we reached a clearing. There were several houses, and one was quite large: it was the general store for the region. The proprietor rose. The shelves were almost empty, because nothing had come in since the rebels had surrounded Santiago. We bought tins of sausages and ate them cold with crackers. Afterward I put my knapsack on the floor of the entryway and lay down to sleep. I kept waking up from the cold. One time when I opened my eyes, dawn was breaking. Crazy Horse was already moving around. We washed up. A daylong trip to the other side of the mountains awaited us. I remembered Che's advice and ate all the sausages I could. We started off.

The sun was burning off the morning fog, and mountain peaks covered with vegetation began to appear. Here and there, clearings in the mountain could be seen, with a hut and a cultivated field. At times looking down from the truck I could see a narrow valley far below. In the center of the valley were some open land, several huts, a concrete platform, and a coffee dryer. Sometimes clouds between the peaks hid the landscape, but they moved on.

When we encountered other jeeps and trucks, Crazy Horse made incredible maneuvers in the narrow road. Then I would fix my gaze in the distance. The information system was curious. People coming and going would stop for a few minutes to tell each other what they knew. We knew that after Guisa there must have been other battles and that now there was fighting in Maffo, where the army was holed up.

At noon, the intense sun told me it was time to descend. We were close to La Lata, where Almeida's general staff was located. By midafternoon we arrived. That was the end of the line for Crazy Horse. From there we would go on in another vehicle. We had become friends, and we parted with sorrow. We contented ourselves with saying that he would come to Santa Clara after the triumph of the revolution. We went on to the command center; Almeida was not there but I received a surprise: I ran into Melba Hernández.

Melba was head of the revolutionary justice tribunals in the region. The territory controlled by Almeida's column was broad, and it was necessary to establish civil administration. She told me that other provincial coordinators had already passed through there and that at the first opportunity she would find a jeep to take me to see Fidel.

I spent the rest of the day with Melba. She introduced me to several officers of the Batista army who had crossed over to our side. Fidel had always made it a policy to treat his prisoners well: they received medical attention before anyone else, were fed well, were never tortured or abused in any way, and were usually quickly released. This policy created a tremendous amount of good will and also recruited more fighters for our side.

These former enemies were allowed to carry weapons but were exempted from fighting against their former companions. They said that they were ashamed to have fought against the rebel army, that Batista had deceived them and had even told them that if they fell into our hands they would be shot. They only wanted to be given the opportunity to redeem themselves. The war was reaching its end.

They could testify that the army was demoralized. Why should they fight, they said, if it meant fighting against the people?

The atmosphere in La Lata was of great euphoria. People from neighboring towns came to ingratiate themselves with the new authorities. The old people, who had fought and suffered, said, "So begins the give and take."

The next day Melba obtained a jeep. We kept going down the whole way. Another night fell, and with it came the cold. We had entered an area where the enemy was also active. The proximity of danger made us nervous. We reached a crossroads where there was a rubblework house.

"Now we will find out what awaits us," said the driver, getting out of the jeep. He disappeared into the darkness behind the house. Soon he returned. He said, "How strange! No one was there."

We continued in silence, very worried. After a time the driver stopped the jeep and killed the lights. "We'd better continue on foot, just in case."

We walked just a few hundred meters and reached a wide road: we were at the Central Highway! The driver came back and said, "Not only don't we know the latest whereabouts of the enemy, but it is inadvisable to travel along the Central Highway without a guide, since it could be mined."

We saw the lights of an approaching vehicle. What to do? The driver made up his mind and stopped in the middle of the road and began to wave his arms. We huddled behind a row of pines. The vehicle stopped—it was a jeep. Our driver talked with the people in it, and then the jeep continued along the road. The driver came over to us. He told us, "There's no problem; the road is clear. Fidel is at the Baire army quarters."

My heart made a leap: at last I was going to meet Fidel! We got in the jeep and took the road to the left. I was going to meet Fidel! We would talk for a long time. I had so many things to tell him! I had so many ideas. I would bring him the good news that the arms had arrived, and on time! We had brought them! I would also have to talk with him about Che.

Now we were inside the town of Baire. We stopped in front of the army quarters. A rebel soldier guarded the entrance. We got out. From sheer emotion, I had no feeling in my legs. Fidel wasn't there; he had left a short time before. This was typical of the confusion and constantly changing fast pace that Fidel always maintained, but I felt an emptiness inside myself. The rebel didn't know where Fidel had gone. I told him who I was, that I had come to the meeting of the National Directorate, that Fidel surely was expecting me. Then the man told us the way.

We took the jeep into the very center of the camp. It had begun to get windy. A short, robust man emerged from the shadows and came toward me. He was dressed like a rebel but didn't have a beard.

"Luis Buch!" I exclaimed.

"Enrique! How are you, Brother?"

We embraced. Luis had arrived by plane from Venezuela, with Manuel Urrutia, the provisional president-designate.

"And Fidel?" I asked.

"He just went to bed."

"You had better take me to him; I'm sure he wants to see me."

Luis looked at me strangely. Then he said, "I think it would be better to wait until tomorrow. He is very tired." The tone of his voice left no room for discussion. "Come visit him tomorrow, and you will see him then."

He took me to a little terrace at the foot of a hill. By lantern light I could see many hammocks hanging from trees. He helped me to rig mine. It began to rain. I took off my muddy boots and got in the hammock. It was cold, and I covered myself with a blanket. Over a rope above the hammock, Luis threw up a nylon tarp, camp style.

"See you tomorrow," he said in parting.

"See you tomorrow."

I lay in the hammock conscious of being near to Fidel. I fell asleep to the sound of the rain beating against the nylon.

When I woke up it was not yet dawn. It was very humid, and I felt uncomfortable. I tossed in the hammock, trying to find a more comfortable position, without success. After a while, I began to make out trees, and then through the leaves came the first rays of the sun. I pulled back the nylon and sat in the hammock. I was putting on my boots when Luis arrived.

"What?" I asked anxiously.

"He still hasn't gotten up. We have time for breakfast."

We went into a house where they were distributing tins of condensed milk. Luis mixed his with pure water, but I drank it thick from the tin. We got some biscuits. Luis talked to me about Venezuela, about his airplane trip bringing Urrutia to the Sierra. Now the whole camp was up. I was impatient—I was afraid that Fidel would get involved with matters that would keep me from talking to him. Luis didn't seem to notice my impatience, and he kept on talking.

"Luis . . . would he be up yet?"

"Maybe. Let's go see."

He started walking, and I followed. We followed a trail that rose gently up the mountain. In a clearing, beneath tall trees for a roof, a hammock was suspended. Facing away from us, a man dressed in a thick green sweater was nodding. To his right, sitting on stones, was a foreign-looking woman who was taking pictures. Opposite him, facing us, a thin rebel with commander's stars on his shoulders was bent over in contemplation. And in the center of the clearing was an adolescent with the look of an *escopetero*.

"So you stole a gun," I heard the voice say.

I thought it was Fidel.

"That is not the kind of man that we want in our rebel army."

I turned to the left until I was facing him.

"What have you done to deserve a gun?"

I sat on a thick log. Soon I was aware of the rhythm of my breathing.

"That gun cost someone's blood."

He was very young and strong. I observed an athlete's build beneath the sweater, and he had curly chestnut-colored hair, almost blond.

"You are an *escopetero.*"

His beard, the same color as his hair, could not hide his young boy's face.

"What makes *escopeteros* rob the rebels' arms?"

He had brown eyes.

"Ah . . . You question my words? Fine, let's hear what you have to say."

He rocked with rapid movements. The woman with the camera twisted to capture his gestures. The boy spoke with a trembling voice: "It's not true that I stole the gun, Comandante. There were so many guns scattered around the field of battle that I didn't think it would matter to anyone if I kept one. I've been grown up for a long time, Comandante. And the life of an *escopetero* isn't easy. I'm always being given guard duty. I wanted to fight. My dream was to have a rifle. After they burned our house, we all went off, and I am the only one who doesn't have a gun. Just this old shotgun. I feel like I'm not a man."

The youth lowered his gaze and stared at the ground. There was a silence. Fidel rocked more rapidly than ever.

What do you think, Efigenio?" he said, directing himself to the rebel with the commander's stars.

But before Efigenio could answer, he said, "OK, keep the gun: we will see what use you make of it."

The eyes of the boy teared up. He wanted to say something but was unable. He raised a dirty sleeve to his eyes, turned around, and ran off. The foreign woman was now writing rapidly.

Luis Buch went forward and said, "Fidel, I would like to present compañero Sierra, coordinator of Las Villas. I thought that you would like to talk with him."

I took a few steps toward Fidel, who extended his hand. To my surprise, his hand was smooth. "How goes Las Villas?"

"Good, Fidel."

A group of officers arrived from Maffo.

"How's it going?" asked Fidel, turning to them.

The officials began to brief him. I sought Luis with a glance: he had withdrawn to one side. I was alone facing Fidel. I stood there for a while, hoping that he would notice me, but he kept talking to the officials. Then I walked over to where Luis was standing and once again tried to wait patiently.

Some of the other delegates and I were stretched out on the grass.

"We've been here two weeks, and nothing," said Albertico.

"Caballeros, I have the impression that they've consigned us to the shithouse," put in Paco.

"Señores, that's not how it is. Fidel is very busy—don't forget they're preparing the assault on Santiago," argued Marcelo.

The last lights of day faded into night. The headlights of jeeps and trucks came on. Motors revved, and the column began to move: the camp advanced in the direction of Santiago.

The great magnesium mine of Charco Redondo had been liberated, and the rebel army set up some facilities in the village. Radio Rebelde operated from the top of a hill. It was in a large wooden house, where the equipment took up just two of the rooms. Elsewhere in the house lived the transmitter personnel and a few of the rest of us. I preferred to hang my hammock in the entryway; though it was colder, the air was fresher—inside, the toilets were plugged up, and there was filth everywhere.

By now almost everyone had arrived for the meeting with Fidel. The goal of the meeting was to decide on a final battle strategy. I had met some old friends whom I hadn't seen in a long time: Carlos Franqui, Faustino Pérez, Aldo Santamaría. We spent long hours talking about what should be our next steps. We told stories of our times together. We told each other about mutual friends who had fallen. We went together to eat at the house of some peasant friend or else in the town boardinghouse, when they were serving something good.

In the evening we listened to the Radio Rebelde broadcast. Some of us wrote reports and editorials for the radio. Afterward we would talk some more until it was time to turn in on our hammocks. The battle of Maffo continued, and fighting was also going on in other parts of the province. Fidel and the commanders of the rebel columns were preparing for what would be the final battle: the attack on Santiago de Cuba. The fall of the regime was imminent, and we burned with the desire to return to our respective regions.

Luis Buch invited us to visit with Urrutia, who back in 1953 had been the only judge in the courtroom who had not denounced Fidel after the attack on Moncada, refusing to condemn him on the grounds that it was a patriotic duty to rebel against Batista. Because of that, and without knowing much about his true personality or abilities, some compañeros had nominated Urrutia as the best choice to preside over the new government in arms that would be taking charge after the triumph of the revolution.

Carlos, Faustino, and several coordinators went with us. Urrutia lived with his wife in a little white house not far from our camp. He was a middle-aged man. His tiny eyes peered from behind spectacles. He looked like a professor. Words did not come to him easily. His wife was a lovely, small woman who never left his side. I thought he needed her deeply, or else was jealous.

Franqui asked him some questions, to get him started on a topic: "And what do you think should be the punishment for those who supported Batista?"

"Shoot them all! They deserve no less."

We looked at each other. Someone said, "But there are thousands of them, President."

"So what! Thousands also died defending the revolution."

"But, President, it is just to shoot those who committed crimes. But the others . . . they should be punished with jail, if they stole, and they should be barred from public office if they have been active politically."

"Look, young man, anyone who has not had the civic responsibility to confront tyranny in one way or another does not deserve to live on this earth."

Again we looked at each other. The conversation fell apart after that. We soon left and went outside.

"What an asshole! Where did we get this guy from?"

"Gentlemen, I hope I'm wrong, but this character seems loony!"

"Luis, you know him: What do you think? Are we wrong?"

"No, your impression is right."

"So then?"

"We'll have to send him packing."

"Son of a bitch!"

Marcelo warned us: in his camp in Rinconada, Fidel was waiting for the meeting.

"At last Catana is stopped!" This was a Cuban vernacular way of saying that something long overdue had finally occurred.

"Run . . . liberals of Perico!" Another obscure joke with references in Cuban culture that are impossible to explain.

We joked as we got in the jeep.

"I can't remember anymore why I came to the Sierra."

We reached Rinconada. In a level spot by some rocks, Fidel was waiting for us. So was his brother Raúl, and the rest: the members of the national leadership, the national section heads, the provincial coordinators, and the military leaders.

Fidel explained the situation: the military collapse of the dictatorship was approaching. There was the danger of a false coup to co-opt the revolution; we would have to be on guard.

We discussed the takeover by the 26th of July. Only in this way could the success of the revolution be assured. Some put forward our reservations about the apparent ineptitude of Urrutia. Fidel exclaimed, "We are fools! We've made a revolution to put power in the hands of an Urrutia!"

And Raúl, raising his ammo clip in his hand: "That's why I will never let go of this iron!"

The meeting ended in a complex mixture of worry and euphoria.

Fidel took me aside and told me then, "You must leave immediately. The news from Las Villas is good. Che and Camilo have practically taken the province. Your presence there could be very useful."

Raúl came over.

"How are you getting along with Che?" Fidel asked me.

"At first there was some friction, but at the moment we are getting along well."

"And what do you think of Che?"

"Great guy. He has his ideas and I have mine, but there are more things that unite us than that divide us."

I was on my way out of the Sierra, heading back toward where I had left Martha days before. From the road, through the cold of the night, we could hear the sounds of the fighting in Maffo.

"The guards are resisting, eh?"

"Yes."

"They're firing at us!" cried the driver, and he ducked down. The jeep, out of control, went into the ditch, and we almost turned over.

"Asshole, what a pussy you are, faggot."

"What do you want? I couldn't help it."

We continued with someone else at the wheel. The previous driver justified himself: "Whenever they hear a motor, they fire in this direction."

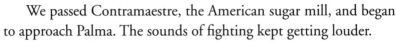

We passed Contramaestre, the American sugar mill, and began to approach Palma. The sounds of fighting kept getting louder.

"Listen, a thirty!"

"No, that's a fifty."

"It's a mortar!"

"If we take Palma, the road to Santiago will be open."

We began to meet rebel soldiers, some of them wounded.

"The barracks has fallen!" one shouted to us.

We went toward the barracks. On the other side of the river they were fighting in the middle of Palma. There were many people; a lot of vehicles were moving around. I managed to get through to the place where Fidel was directing the operations: he kept in his head the position of every man, every weapon. He gave orders, wrote notes. By his side, his secretary Celia Sánchez assisted him. The enemy resistance in Palma began to crack. Fidel went outside, and we all followed him. One stray bullet after another fell around us. Celia took Fidel's sleeve, but he paid no attention and kept talking to some rebel officers.

When he was ready to go, Fidel noticed me.

"And what are you doing here? I thought you were on the road to Las Villas. Come with me."

I followed him, and we got in a car. He said to me, "You have to leave at once. You must carry my urgent instructions to Che and Camilo."

They turned on the car light so that Fidel could write. He gave me a paper, which I tucked away.

"You are carrying to the rebel forces of Las Villas the order to divide into two forces for the push to Havana: Camilo must occupy the Columbia military headquarters and Che the Cabaña military headquarters. Tomorrow I am meeting with General Cantillo, Batista's chief of staff. He will probably deliver the province of the Oriente to me. In that case, I will take a plane to Santa Clara and assume personal control of the troops."

The car had left the road and was going along a very poor earthen track. We bottomed out, and the car stopped.

"It's fucked," said someone, and we got out.

"All right. You go on," Fidel told me, and he started down the road in the darkness of night, followed by Celia, while I remained alone, not knowing where I was.

After a while I heard voices coming along the road, which turned out to be a group returning to Santiago, whom I joined.

It was the dead of night, and fortunately not even the lights of stars could be seen in the sky. We spent quite some time walking. I diverted myself by smoking.

"Put out your cigarettes!" said the guide, "we are approaching the enemy."

Now we went on in silence, single file. After a while, the one in front said something to the one behind him, and so the message was passed along: "We're going to pass between two machine-gun posts. When the guide signals, we will crawl along the ground."

A little after that the man in front of me got down on the ground, and I did the same. We crawled along with extreme caution. We could hear clearly the conversations of enemy soldiers: "I won't put up with much more of this tussle. I joined the army to become an officer and live well, not to lose my skin."

And another voice: "We haven't been to Santiago in ten days. All I think about is my mulatta, Caballeros, and how I'd like to be on top of her!"

The man in front of me let out a laugh. I hit the ground, fearing the worst. "Son of a bitch!" I said to him in my mind. Nothing happened, and we kept going. My hands and knees began to bleed. A low branch pierced me with thorns. I tried to avoid them but couldn't see in the dark. The man behind me urged me to hurry up.

We reached a stream, crossed over, and then continued on foot. Dawn was breaking when we reached a luxurious residence in a suburb on the outskirts of Santiago. It was the house of a doctor. We

had breakfast, and the doctor took me in his car to the home of Vecino, where Martha was waiting.

On December 30, 1958, all flights to Santa Clara had been canceled. Che was at the edge of the city. Vecino arranged passage for us to Havana. We left the same day. In Havana there was great tension. There were no direct flights from Havana to Santa Clara, so we had to settle for flying to Cienfuegos.

In Cienfuegos there was almost nobody left from the leadership. Serafín had gone to join Che. Manolo Toyo, head of propaganda, had joined Bordón. Dorticós—who, after April 9, in the face of the cowardice of González Abreu, had assumed the leadership of the Movement in the region—was discovered by the police and had to leave the country. We stayed in the home of Manolo's in-laws. It was already the 31st, and we couldn't find any way out of that town. Che was attacking Santa Clara.

"The Miami radio stations are saying that Batista's planes are bombing the city," said the lady of the house.

Martha began to cry.

"What will happen to Frank?" she wailed, thinking of the baby.

"I'm sure nothing has happened to him." I tried to undo the old woman's damage.

Finally we were able to hire a driver, a Movement fighter who offered to take us as close as possible to Santa Clara. We would leave the next day, January 1, very early in the morning.

I hardly slept. We had delayed too long in reaching Santa Clara. The message that I carried was vital for the next turn of events. We finished breakfast, and as we were arranging our things in the vehicle, Manolo's wife came shouting, "The Miami stations are saying that Batista has fled!"

"And Cuban stations?"

"They're not saying anything."

"Then the news could be false."

Martha and I got into the car and left. Leaving Cienfuegos, we passed the army barracks; the soldiers were sitting on the sidewalk.

"That is strange!" said the driver.

We went past Palmira. Shortly afterward, a wide gully dug in the road blocked our way. We got out of the vehicle and continued on foot. Martha was pregnant with our second child, but she walked lightly.

In huts along both sides of the road, the first flags of the 26th of July appeared. Radios, turned all the way up, carried the notes of the national anthem to us. People coming out of the houses were waving flags, entering the road, and forming a column that was marching northward. We were just another couple in that mass of humanity.

Under a bright sun in a very blue sky, the black-and-red flags of the 26th of July made a dramatic contrast, shining in the light in the middle of the road.

# After the
# Plains and
# the Sierra

## chapter 16

# Batista Flees

January 1, 1959. Ten in the morning. In the Cuban winter, the sun at that hour already hung heavy in the sky. We spent a long time marching along the road north toward Santa Clara. The multitude kept swelling. I don't know how, but everyone seemed to know the 26th of July hymn, or many of them did, and the vibrant notes made us march with renewed brio.

From the houses along the road, more people joined us who had heard the radio. From the Dominican Republic came confirmation of the arrival of Batista there. With him had fled the principal figures of the regime. In Havana, talk was of a provisional government, presided over by the senior member of the Supreme Court, a certain Carlos Manuel Piedra. In that way, the holdovers from the Batista regime sought to usurp the power of the revolution. I had to get to Che as soon as possible.

That march by foot was desperately slow. Finally, from a distance, we made out the chimney of a distant factory. We redoubled our steps.

Now we could see the grand entrance. In an arch that rested on two stone columns, we could read: Hormiguero Sugar Mill. A great confusion reigned. People were coming and going. They were talking, they were singing. The news was spreading.

The first constituted authority appeared in the person of a clean-shaven young man who carried an ancient gun. I had been scanning the crowd in search of a familiar face, so I approached him as soon as I spotted him. I identified myself with my nom de guerre, Sierra. I raised the issue of obtaining a vehicle. People began to gather around us. A mustached man, who had been hanging by my side for some time, offered to take us to Ranchuelo, which was only about thirty minutes from Santa Clara itself. I didn't like the looks of the man, but I accepted. We got in a ramshackle old vehicle and took off, but first several young people of adventurous spirit decided to accompany us, to see what was going on in Ranchuelo.

The road was terrible. The potholes had joined together to form a single pothole, which was really the rockbed beneath the road. But this time, with the lurching of the vehicle, only a vague feeling of responsibility kept me from letting out a cry of impotence.

It seemed that time refused to pass. I wanted to will the vehicle forward. Again people were walking along the road, which indicated that we were approaching Ranchuelo. We drove around the crowds until we got into town, where the mob was too thick for us to continue except on foot. In the street, people—especially girls—were teasing and laughing with the rebels.

The revolutionary authorities had set themselves up in the best premises in town. This time I didn't have to identify myself, and after effusive expressions of joy, they began to talk to me in a new tone of voice, consistent with the new responsibilities we were assuming.

"Sit down, Sierra, sit down," the head of the town's 26th of July said to me. "It's as if you have fallen from the sky. Who would have thought that you would be here today!"

"Fine, but just for a moment. I have to leave at once for Santa Clara—I am carrying an urgent message for Che!"

"Understood, Sierra, understood. But before you go you have to help me resolve a serious problem that has arisen," insisted the head of the Movement.

"I'm sorry, but I can't lose a minute. How can I get to Santa Clara?"

"You can't go by the Central Highway. La Esperanza is still in the hands of the army, and in Santa Clara, according to the latest reports, they are still fighting."

Everyone around us began to talk at the same time, making suggestions. Finally the head of the 26th said, "Here's the answer. We will lend you a jeep, and by taking the sugarcane roads of the Pastora Sugar Mill you can reach Santa Clara through side routes."

"Magnificent," I said, and I got up.

"Sierra, you can't go like this. I have to inform you. . . ." Everyone around us sat back down.

"We have assumed civil control. As the top authority of the Movement, I have assumed the role of mayor. I wasn't looking for the job but . . . it is a time of sacrifices."

I made an impatient gesture.

"You have to hear this, Sierra. Dieguito Trinidad (head of the large industry that the town depended on for a living) refuses to recognize our authority. He knows that with us in control, power will escape from his hands, and to defend his interests he has convinced one of his lackeys—who used to be director of the Movement until he was expelled for political intrigues—to proclaim himself mayor. He has converted the club that Dieguito built into the seat of the city council, and he is trying to win over the people of the 26th. Dieguito claims he is a friend of Fidel."

I replied, "The only authority that we recognize is yours. In any case, I will be back in a few days." And I walked off. They all followed me, gratefully.

The jeep was waiting for us. Two armed rebels went with us. The driver of the vehicle and the young people who had come with us wanted to go with me. I refused.

We cut a path through the multitudes who filled the streets, and soon we were out in the country. The jeep went along the dirt road, between the canes that were waiting for the coming harvest, raising a cloud of dust that, when we slowed down, surrounded us, enveloped us, turning our hair and eyelids white.

At the sound of the jeep, the people who lived in those remote places appeared at doors and windows, and when they recognized the rebels they came running behind us.

We reached Santa Clara without major problems. The army had locked itself in the barracks, and the city was in the hands of the rebels. We asked around until we found that Che had established his headquarters in the public works building on Camajuaní Road.

As the jeep went past, people cautiously appeared but did not come outside. Despite the prevailing calm, the Battle of Santa Clara still had not officially ended.

I was wondering if we would have trouble getting to Che, but when the jeep stopped in front of the public works building, I was met by many familiar faces. As they escorted me to a small office that Che had converted into his headquarters, they peppered me with questions. We went to the door, knocked, and entered.

Behind a large bureau, Che was standing facing me. One arm was in a plaster cast that hung from a black rag around his neck. With a wave of his hand he indicated that I should wait while he gave instructions to a young rebel who, lacking a beard, had let his hair grow out.

The room was small and completely closed. I began to feel hot. I pulled out Fidel's message from the lining of my trousers: it was the order to advance to Havana. At last the rebel left, and I handed the paper to Che.

When he finished reading, he turned to the window and looked outside. "Yes, I already knew. We are leaving in a few hours."

"But . . . how did you know?"

"We managed to make contact with Fidel by radio. Cantillo did not deliver the Oriente."

I was filled with a sensation of frustration. Che seemed to recognize it because he changed the subject. "We are negotiating with the army. Except for those to be turned over as criminals, I am inclined to let the rest go free, after disarming them, of course. I think that they will accept; they are demoralized—"

"And Camilo?"

"As soon as he arrives we will leave together." Che became serious: "I have already designated a governor for the province: Calixto Morales."

234

I knew Calixto as a man belonging to Che's column who had come with him from the *Granma*. He was not familiar with Santa Clara or the plains. In the towns and regions that the rebel army had conquered, it had been the custom that it was the head of the civil Movement and not a member of the army who exercised revolutionary power. I had thought that I would be the governor of the province, considering my role as provincial coordinator of the 26th of July. But I realized that I hadn't been there when Che took the city, and there was still some political distrust that Che felt for us, the representatives of the plains. I said nothing.

Che smoked the rest of his tobacco and looked at me coolly. I saw in his eyes that he clearly read my thoughts. But he also said no more, as if we had reached an agreement not to go into that problem until a more propitious moment.

The negotiators arrived. They announced that the Batista army had accepted the terms and surrendered. Jubilation was on every face. Everyone had a thousand stories to tell. Time and again they retold the same deeds, as if there were new angles still to be covered.

News that the army of the dictatorship had surrendered spread through the city, and thousands of people converged on our building. They knew that Che was there, and nobody wanted to miss the chance to see him. It was necessary to post guards at the entrances to prevent that mass of humanity from overwhelming us.

Upstairs a provisional jail was set up for the criminals of the repressive forces who one by one were being located and captured by the public.

The situation remained unstable. In Havana, a spurious government had tried to consolidate power. In a speech to the people, Fidel had decreed a general strike. His 26th of July Movement would only recognize one government: that of Urrutia.

Che was busy preparing his departure. The new governor was interviewed by a group of journalists who had come from Havana. While Che was occupied, some members of the Direccion Provincial attended to the first problems that the change in power had raised for the new political organization. We formed a group at the foot of the long stairway that led to the floor where the criminals were being kept prisoner. Above, a rebel guard kept watch. Opposite us, behind a glass door, could be seen the faces of the murderers' families: mothers, wives, and children. They had gathered there to beg clemency. The revolutionary tribunals were already under way, and the first criminals had been shot.

The wailing of the women reached us, and they pounded their knuckles on the glass trying to get our attention. Soon cries could be heard from above: one of the murderers had pushed a rebel soldier and sent him down the stairs head first.

The vision of that scene shut everyone's mouth, and the repeated sound of his head striking each step on the way down could be heard clearly. The body reached the bottom and was crushed against the wall with a final blow that was no longer dry.

The soldier's brains were spattered on the walls, and a pool of blood began to form almost at our feet. The hysterical shouts of the women on the other side of the door broke the silence, bringing us back to reality. The corpse was taken away, and soon somebody showed up with water buckets and swilled down the floor. I watched the water run toward the drains, where particles of brain and clots of blood remained suspended.

I was talking with Che when one of his men came and whispered something into his ear. He raised his head and looked toward the other end of the hall. I followed his glance and saw two men leaning against the wall, waiting. They were wearing sports clothes. Their spotless clothing and shaved, unfamiliar faces made me think that they had come from Havana. Che gave me a rather guilty look, went with them to the small room that served as his office, and closed the door. I was sure then that those men were Communists from the Partido Socialista Popular (PSP).

Night fell. The Communists had left as mysteriously as they had arrived. There were few people left in the public works building. Many days' fatigue had overtaken them, and they had gone to their homes or were lying on the ground or on the sandbags by the barricades.

In the large room everyone slept except Camilo, who had arrived shortly before, and Che and me. Camilo spent his considerable charm relating the humorous aspects of his recent adventures. We were stretched out on the ground, leaning against the bags in the dim light that entered through the windows from the lampposts.

Someone showed up with a basket full of apples and then we realized that it was New Year's, and despite the differences between us I felt good with those men. Noises were growing outside the building; some rebels came and told us they were ready. We got up and went outside. The night was cool. The noise of the motors and the shining of the lights got everyone's attention. At that hour there were few of the curious observing us.

Some of the families of the murderers slept against the walls.

We shook hands, and Che's caravan started off. When the red lights of the last car disappeared at the end of the street, I raised my eyes and looked at the night sky. The stars were shining brightly, with gay sparkles, the way the stars of the New Year shine, apparently indifferent to what was going on down below.

## chapter 17

# Fidel Marches on Havana

From the very beginning, I had never told my parents about my dedication to the revolution or my position in the 26th of July Movement. My mother was so close to me and so sensitive, she could sense something was going on and implied to me many times that she knew I was involved. She would say how much she worried about me and how she feared that I would be killed. But she had never questioned me or pressed me about what was going on or what specifically was my involvement.

My father I never told what I did, nor did he ever have the slightest inkling until January 2, 1959. On that day I was busy reorganizing the Movement and taking care of the day-to-day operations of the government. All of Batista's government workers had fled. Calixta Garcia was the official governor now, but he did not know the area and was not directly involved in the details of the transference and organization of power or the daily operations of our municipalities.

When Che left he had taken quite a bit of our gasoline supplies with him for the journey, so only a limited amount remained; in the confusion of the times, we needed to be very careful about monitoring and rationing out what we had. So before leaving, Che had appointed me as the only man who could give a private person a permit to purchase a certain quantity of gasoline.

Now my father, as a businessman with many factories, stores, and warehouses around the country, was in great need of gasoline. My father was the kind of man who could go through the eye of a needle, as we say in Spanish, to get what he needed. So he came to our headquarters in earnest pursuit of the fuel he needed in order to continue his business. And it was there among the huge, noisy crowd

of people who were thronging our municipal headquarters that second day of January that we suddenly saw each other for the first time in many days.

"What are you doing here?" I asked him.

"I'm looking for someone by the name of Sierra. He's the one who gives out permits to buy gas. And what are you doing here?"

I could not help but smile at him as I said, "I am Sierra."

So this is how he found out. It must have come as quite a surprise, I'm sure, though as usual I don't remember him having a very emotional reaction. And of course, I was very strict about my responsibilities at that time and did not give him the permit he requested that day, as we had other more important requirements for our gasoline supplies.

Since my return from the Sierra Maestra, we had been staying in Martha's parents' house. They lived in a modern villa at the entrance of Santa Clara, in the residential community off the Central Highway. During the battle of Santa Clara, Martha's parents and our boy Frank had been forced to crouch and run to avoid the bullets flying overhead, as part of the action had taken place near their home. But they had survived safely, and now we were all together again.

I was hardly ever there, unfortunately, because I spent whole days in meetings with the local representatives of the 26th of July, or I went on short trips to neighboring towns. I got up early, had breakfast, and left. I didn't get back until dawn.

I never saw Frank, my son of a year and a half, awake. When I got back during the night, I turned on a light to look at him while he was sleeping. Martha would tell me about his activities during the day: some new word he had learned, some ceramic he had broken, a new tooth in his mouth.

One night a few days later, I heard Martha talking and opened my eyes. It was still dark. "What's going on?" I asked worriedly, and

I realized I was in bed. It was January 6, 1959, the Dia de Reyes. The reactionary sectors and the U.S. Embassy were trying to deny the triumph of the revolution. Fidel had called a general strike and was marching to Havana at the front of a guerrilla column. Che and Camilo had been in the capital since January 2.

"Mama says that Marcelo Fernández has just arrived. He's in the hall," explained Martha.

"Well, this Marcelo never changes. He always shows up at dawn."

I put on my shoes and went down the stairs to the floor below. Marcelo greeted me with an embrace.

"What a pleasant surprise," I said.

"The surprise is what's coming up the road."

"What?"

"Fidel."

"Yes?"

"I've gone a little ahead to make preparations. Fidel is coming at the head of a long caravan on the way to Havana. He will be here in an hour. He is very tired and will make a stopover in Santa Clara. I thought this house would be the best place. It's outside the city and at the same time has facilities. What do you think?"

"Say no more. That was a good idea. Let me wake people up so they can get dressed and get ready."

I called Martha, who ran excitedly to call her parents. Soon there was intense activity. The smell of coffee reached us, and we couldn't wait for them to come get us to drink it in the kitchen. Afterward I dressed, and Marcelo took the occasion to clean up. Then we sat down to wait for the arrival of Fidel. The Christmas tree was lit, and its colored lights shown on the toys we had bought for Frank.

The sun came up. There was a rosy light. The road by which Fidel would arrive could be made out through the trees.

"How are things going here?" Marcelo asked.

"They're going well, man. We control nearly the whole province, and now we are reorganizing the Movement. We already have our own place. I hope Fidel will visit it."

"We'll see. And has economic life been reestablished?"

"Pretty well. Every day we face new problems, but more are being solved successfully than not. We have an unwritten understanding with Calixto that he takes care of public relations and we work with the so-called lively classes to reestablish the economic life of the province, as well as working on reorganizing the town governments and appointing new leaders."

"With Calixto? What Calixto?"

"Oh! You don't know?" I looked straight at Marcelo.

"No, I don't know a thing. Tell me, what's going on?" Marcelo looked away from me, intuiting that something was wrong.

"Well . . .," I ordered my thoughts. "When I arrived in Santa Clara that first day I was told that Che had named Calixto Morales governor of the province."

Marcelo interrupted me.

"What? And what did you say?"

"Me . . . nothing. What could I do? To have protested would have made it look like I wanted the job, that I was fighting for position."

"But Fidel issued a disposition in which he stated that it is the provincial coordinator who will have this role. Maybe Che didn't know that?"

"I don't know. In any case, let's move on. Certainly I was in the Sierra and not here, or maybe it's the old lack of trust Che feels for the people of the plains."

"We can't accept this. We have to present this problem to Fidel," Marcelo concluded, visibly upset.

We were quiet. Life began to stir outside without our being aware of it. An indefinite time passed. I began to be caught up in vague dreaming when Marcelo suddenly jumped up: "There they are!"

We went out to the road. The first cars were practically in front of us. From one of them Fidel jumped out, with Celia Sánchez behind him. We went in the house while the guards took positions and closed the entrances. Fidel looked tired, but he greeted us all warmly and went upstairs, where he, Celia, Marcelo, and I sat down.

They had not had breakfast yet. While Martha and her mother served us, Fidel related his eventful journey of the past few days. Events were moving with giant steps. Fidel would be in Havana in a couple of days.

"How are things going here?" Fidel asked.

I looked at Marcelo and said, "Well . . . I think well. The province is getting back to normal."

I briefly explained what we had been doing. Fidel followed my words with rapt attention, until I was finished.

"Fidel is very tired," said Celia. "He needs a bath and afterward to rest a little. To sleep, if possible."

Then Marcelo spoke up. "Look, Fidel, there is something you should know. Che has named Calixto Morales governor of the province."

Fidel turned around and sat back down in the armchair.

Marcelo continued, "We have to resolve this situation. This job belongs to the Movement coordinator. You made that resolution yourself."

"Yes, yes, we will see . . . ," Fidel turned to say as he stood back up.

"Marcelo has talked to me about summoning the town today, in front of the park," I said. "What time do you think is best?"

"Noon," said Fidel, and he walked off, guided by my mother-in-law, to the bathroom, followed by Celia.

Marcelo and I remained alone, without speaking. Finally Marcelo said to me, "The members of the Direccion Provincial should meet with Fidel to exchange information and receive instructions, as we are doing in all the provinces. We have to get everyone together. Then we have to find an appropriate place to meet. Do you have any thoughts?"

"It seems to me the best place would be a house like this, but near the road to Havana. We could have lunch together after the town meeting in the park and take the occasion to talk. From there Fidel can continue on to Havana."

"Magnificent," Marcelo said approvingly. "Let's go!"

I went down to give pertinent instructions, and then I realized that the house was completely surrounded by people. Through the wide glass windows we could see hundreds, almost thousands of the curious. The guards fought to hold back the multitude from entering the house. Through the windows Joaquín Argüelles, Guillermito Rodríguez, Osvaldo Fernández López, Totó Gómez Lubián, and several more members of the leadership signaled to me. I managed to get them in and explained to them what we had to do. Everyone left to fulfill his assignment.

When I went back upstairs, Fidel had bathed and was lying in bed resting. He saw me and called me over. Although he had been awake for many days, he couldn't get to sleep. He questioned me closely about the townspeople. What were they thinking? What were they saying about the revolution? Had we acted justly during the purifications? Were all the revolutionary forces cooperating? I told him yes to all that, that we had created a kind of council in which everyone participated so that we reached agreement on decisions.

As we were talking, one of the guards came up and said, "There's someone named Bosch outside who insists on coming in."

"Who?" said Fidel. "Bosch?"

"Yes," I answered. "Orlando Bosch is a doctor who says he was a friend of yours in the university and who collaborated with the Movement."

"That is not true. He was not my friend but a crook and a political wheeler-dealer when he was student leader at the university. Get rid of him."

Celia appeared and said that the journalist Carlos Lechuga had arrived from Havana to interview Fidel. Fidel called for him. After the necessary greetings, Fidel had Lechuga sit on the edge of the bed, and instead of being interviewed, he interviewed Lechuga, an old acquaintance who had always supported the revolution. How was Havana? What were the people saying? What had the government done?

Lechuga said that everything was waiting for the arrival of Fidel. That there was some confusion. That Fidel would have to personally bring leadership to the people.

"It's necessary that the people not only hear you but also see you. People are eager for you."

"We have made arrangements for a television broadcast from the park," Lechuga went on, "with your approval."

"Certainly! Listen, that's a journalist's job you're doing. We'll definitely have to raise your pay."

Everyone laughed. Fidel continued, "This speech is important. Sierra and I will talk. Lechuga, what do you consider the main problems? What would be your focus, Sierra?" I started to answer, but Fidel continued, "It should not be a speech to praise the town. In such a time, when there is some uncertainty, the people have to be told what their duties are. We have to tell them that the revolution must be the responsibility of everyone. Only in that way can we triumph definitively."

He jumped out of bed and began to pace the narrow room in his bare feet. He continued, "Yes, advancing the revolution is everyone's responsibility."

Lechuga and I remained seated on the bed, listening to the beginnings of what would be a transcendent speech.

"You will have to speak, Sierra, you will have to speak," Marcelo shouted at me through the thunderous noise as we arrived at the main plaza in Santa Clara.

"Who, me? You're crazy. Faced with a crowd like this I wouldn't know where to start."

We were on the stage by the entrance to the provincial government building. In front of us the park was filling up with people. Fidel raised his arms in constant salute. The nearest people on stage

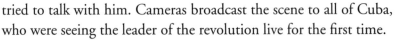

tried to talk with him. Cameras broadcast the scene to all of Cuba, who were seeing the leader of the revolution live for the first time.

The cameramen made signs for us to begin, and someone pushed me to the microphones. I felt a great slowness in my arms and legs. I had spoken in public many times before, but never to a crowed of fifty thousand people on national television. I tried to follow the old formula of choosing someone in the audience and speaking as if I were talking just to that person.

"People of Santa Clara . . . emotion overcomes us . . . how many times have we dreamed of this moment. And today, when it has become real, our minds cannot arrange our thoughts. . . ."

Applause gave me more confidence—enough to finish quickly. Fidel approached the microphone, and a mood of collective hysteria took hold of the crowd. After several attempts he managed to speak his first words. Then I observed for the first time that mystical communion between Fidel and the people. The crowd applauded the one who expressed what they were feeling, the one who spoke everything they held inside.

"Fidel, Fidel, Fidel . . ."

That was like being drunk with happiness. The sun was overhead, and there was so much light that you could distinguish the smallest details. If you looked closely, you could see the features of any face in the crowd. Each leaf of the trees in the park stood out clearly, reflecting the sun's rays as if made of metal, and overhead was the cloudless sky of a winter that was spring.

Then at my side the voice of Teresita Caballero, my old compañera of the Movement, interrupted the communion.

"Pardo Llada is on stage stealing the camera."

Pardo Llada was a popular radical commentator who, seeing the coming triumph of the revolution, had gone up to the Sierra in order to return as a hero, despite having done nothing.

"How terrible. Pull him!"

In a little while Teresita returned. "They had to wrestle him off the stage!"

Fidel was continuing to speak as I tried to keep track of all the upcoming plans and details with Teresita.

"How is lunch coming along?"

"Very well."

"You got in touch with all the members of the leadership?"

"They've all been told."

"Let's go and take a look at the house. Is your car there?"

"Yes."

"Let's go."

We left the stage, pushing our way. We took Teresita's car and went to the house where we were going to have lunch with Fidel. Everyone was at work. Some were marinating the pig, others loading boxes of refreshments. Barrels of ice were unloaded from a truck. Everything was going well. I sat down in front of the television to watch the rest of Fidel's speech on the air, as all the nation was now seeing it.

"It is not enough to give you a living revolution. . . . Batista and all that he represents . . . are gone! . . . Everyone shares responsibility. . . ."

The crowd applauded deliriously. Fidel was speaking now as if he were winding up his talk, and we decided to return to the stage to pick him up and lead him back to the house. We arrived just in time.

There was a delegation of supporters from Cienfuegos who insisted that Fidel visit Cienfuegos before continuing on to Havana.

Fidel looked at me, as if unsure what to do. The afternoon was getting late.

"Fidel, the food is almost ready, and everyone is waiting for you. Better to go afterward."

We got down from the stage, and Fidel got into his car. We went ahead to show him the way to the house. Shortly after we arrived, a line of automobiles appeared. In the first we saw Fidel. We made arm signals to him, but the caravan went on by.

We stood with open mouths. Marcelo arrived and said, "Fidel says that we should go with him to Cienfuegos, that there is no time to eat now, and that we will get together afterward."

Such was the chaotic, unpredictable life of Fidel during that intense period. It was probably disappointing to those who had made all the preparations, but everyone understood as we got in our cars and took off behind the caravan, which was already disappearing in the distance.

I had made that trip to Cienfuegos many times during the insurrection. Then I was always worried and tense, always watching for danger. I always tried to go unnoticed. How different was the trip we made now! When we passed by a small village, or entered a town, the people came running out of their houses and cried, "Fidel! Fidel!"

Emotion gave us goosebumps. But then memories returned and with them new concerns. We went on in silence. The road now seemed longer than ever.

On both sides could be seen the chimneys of the factories and the presence of train cars, next to the sugar refineries, indicating that the sugar processing was about to begin.

We reached Cienfuegos. As elsewhere, the people ran out to the sidewalks, abandoning their work. The people of Cienfuegos competed for Fidel's attention. This city was in the hands of the Second Front of Escambray, which had come down from the mountains after the flight of Batista.

William Morgan, the American who was comandante of the organization, was acting as the military head of the plaza. He insisted that Fidel accompany him to Cayo Loco, an island in the bay where the main naval base on the southern coast was harbored. It was now the headquarters of Morgan, whom we distrusted profoundly. Morgan had once disarmed the forces of the 26th of July in Escambray, betraying existing agreements. To be in Cayo Loco with Morgan was like entering a mousetrap. I managed to get close to Fidel and whisper to him, "Don't accept! Morgan can't be trusted."

"Don't worry," Fidel answered, with a smile that did not succeed in reassuring me.

We went to Cayo Loco. There was an air of tension. The legions of sailors who had been loyal to Batista were still intact. Morgan's men were mixing with them. Fidel got up on something, and his figure stood out above the rest, offering a magnificent target.

There was silence.

"What has been the role of the navy in a country that lives by the sea? Nothing!"

Interest intensified the expressions on the faces.

"What should be the role of the navy in the new Cuba? A powerful arm for the defense of the country!"

Thunderous applause.

"We will create a navy that will be the pride of the Americas."

"Fidel! Fidel! Fidel!" cried the sailors.

"The sailor will be a man useful to society. . . . He will not be the instrument of the enemies of the people but the armed fist of the people."

The sailors looked at one another and patted each other on the back.

"The merchant marine, the fishermen—Cuba will return to the sea."

Hundreds of sinewy arms, toasted by the sun, were lifted up to Fidel as they walked passed the small plaza where we found ourselves.

We had lunch at the Covadonga, and the hours passed. We went through the whole town to the plaza in front of the city council building, where people were gathering. Despite many hours without sleep, Fidel was transformed when he faced the crowd. Then he seemed to forget his fatigue, and again I saw, as I had already observed in Santa Clara, his powerful communion with the people.

When his speech was over, we entered the city council building. Finally we were going to have our meeting with Fidel. It was very late at night, and everyone was very tired, but we had to take advantage of that opportunity.

We settled into wide leather armchairs in a large office. Fidel sat behind a desk in a revolving chair and spun around as the meeting developed. He didn't speak more than he had to. Fidel had said all that he had to say, not only to us but to the people: in Santa Clara, in Cienfuegos, in Cayo Loco.

The light was indirect and not very strong. Fidel leaned on the table and rested his forehead on his forearm. We looked at each other and all got up respectfully.

Fidel lifted his head, and seeing us on our feet he also called it a day. "Let's go," he said, and we went outside.

The fresh air of dawn revived us. The Cienfuego night was clear, and the stars shone in the sky. I breathed the pure air and felt something strange, as if a new life were now beginning, an unknown but exciting life.

The next morning Fidel left for Havana.

## chapter 18

# Government Minister

I received a telephone call from the office of the new president Urrutia in Havana summoning me for an appearance at the secretariat of the Council of Ministers. The taxi left me in front of the presidential palace.

"Which way is the entrance?" I asked the driver.

"That way," and he pointed to an open door, whose entrance was guarded by two rebel soldiers.

"Look, I am the coordinator of the 26th of July Movement in Las Villas, and I have an appointment in the secretariat."

"This way," said the man. "Officer of the guard!" he cried.

Nobody answered. Many rebel soldiers were talking in the little room that led to an interior patio.

"Officer of the guard!" the rebel cried again.

Nobody paid him any attention.

"He's sure to be back. Wait here," and he went back out to the street to take up his position.

Nobody paid any attention to me.

Fidel had passed through Las Villas on January 6, just two days before, on his way to Havana. He had invited me to come with him, but I insisted on remaining in Santa Clara, where I was working to achieve the normalization of life in the province.

"Besides," I told Fidel, "I have completed my duty, and in a little while I can return to my work as engineer."

"So you think you are already done," Fidel had answered. "Don't you know that now is when the real work of the revolution begins?"

It had been only a few days since Fidel had left, and now I was being called to Havana. Why? What had I done?

The rebels were talking about their recent experiences in the capital. Their heads had already passed through the hands of the barbers of Havana. Their beards had been trimmed, and their hair was cut short. Their uniforms were like new, and some beautiful red-and-black bracelets were fixed to their sleeves.

I took advantage of the fact that one of the rebels was looking at me to address him: "I have an appointment in the secretariat, but I don't know how to get there."

"The best thing would be to go up to the second floor. It's full of people. There is a meeting of the Council of Ministers today."

"Where is that?"

"Go through the patio, and on the right you will find an elevator."

I looked at the walls as I went through the patio. There was no evidence remaining of the attack on the palace by the students months before. Batista must have patched up the bullet holes before he fled. Who would have imagined that I would be here today, I thought, and among my victorious comrades who had won the battle against the dictator.

I took the elevator to the second floor, and when the doors opened I saw a large hall in front of me. There were many people and a great murmur of conversation. Groups gathered around the armchairs. Some dozed. Some men were constantly sweeping cigarette butts up off the floor. Others carried immense trays, loaded with cups of coffee and glasses of water.

I looked around for someone I knew and didn't find anyone. I decided to go over to another door guarded by two rebels, and I went into a kind of waiting room full of people. There I saw many faces known to me from the newspapers. I went to a girl behind a desk.

"I am Enrique Oltuski, the coordinator from Las Villas."

The girl knitted her eyebrows.

"Many know me as Sierra, my nom de guerre."

A smile appeared on her wide mouth. "I've heard of you. Pleased to meet you." She gave me a sweaty hand. "I worked in Pepe Blanco's group, here in Havana. You know him!"

"Yes, yes," I said.

With that the door of the council chambers opened, and Armando Hart and Faustino Pérez appeared. They warmly shook hands with me. Some of those present drew near to try to talk to them, but Faustino and Armando led me back to the council chambers.

"Let's go so you can greet Urrutia."

"But isn't the council in session?"

"Yes, but it doesn't matter. Come on!"

We entered a long, narrow room. In the center, filling the whole space, was a large table, where the ministers were seated. At one end I recognized Urrutia, who stood up when he saw me, interrupting the speech he was making. The ministers also stood up as I crossed the room to where Urrutia was, and he gave me his hand.

"Glad to see you."

"And I you. How are you, señor Presidente?"

"Very well, thank you. I want to give you some news."

Everyone around me smiled.

"Go ahead."

"We have just appointed you Minister of Communications of the revolutionary government. My congratulations!"

I was stunned. "But señor Presidente, you must be mistaken; I don't even know where the Ministry of Communications is, nor what they are doing there."

No one paid attention to what I said. Instead, Armando and Faustino embraced me and introduced me to the other ministers, whom I didn't know.

"And now, señores Ministers," said Urrutia, "if you will be so good, we will resume the council."

Everyone sat back down, and I also took a seat, at twenty-eight years old the youngest man around the table.

"The number of laws that we are passing is overwhelming," began Urrutia, "and it is impossible for the council to dedicate its precious time to analyzing the technical aspects of each one. That is why we designated Dr. Osvaldo Dorticós, whose competence in this area is disputed by no one, to fill this function. We have been unable to carry out this idea because, not having attended the councils and not knowing the details of our discussions, Dr. Dorticós's access has been limited to the hour when the laws that are passed here are written up. That is why the idea of appointing him as Minister for Law Revision has come up. That way he can participate in the discussions, and the function of his ministry will be to give legal form to what the council approves."

Some ministers spoke in support of the merits of Dorticós as a lawyer and a person.

"Oltuski can speak to his revolutionary merits," said Faustino. "Dorticós worked with him in Las Villas."

I made a brief account of Dorticós's work during the insurrection. First he had directed the Civic Resistance in Cienfuegos. After the failure of the strike of April 9 and faced with the desertion of some of the directors of the Movement, Dorticós assumed the leadership of that area. He participated actively in the transfer of Bordón to Escambray. Later his participation was discovered by the police, and he had to flee the country.

The council unanimously approved the appointment of Dorticós as Minister for Law Revision. Dorticós, who had just flown back from exile, was called to the hall, and the previous scene was repeated. We exchanged an embrace.

"Always together," Dorticós said to me.

"Yes, always together," I answered him.

Urrutia called a recess for lunch. As we were leaving the council room, the other people in the waiting room approached the ministers, raising all manner of problems. We succeeded in making our way to the palace dining room. All the chairs around the large table were occupied by the people who had filled the rooms and corridors and now were talking and pestering the ministers. We had to wait until some chairs became available.

"This is a plague of lobsters!" exclaimed Armando. "We will have to do something about it."

"The bad thing is that many were invited by Urrutia himself," explained Luis Buch, who had been named Secretary to the Cabinet. "They are his compañeros from exile."

"Well, Luis, I'd like you to explain how one assumes one's role as minister," I asked.

"You show up there and shake hands."

"But what if they don't let me in? Can you give me a paper or something?"

"What's a paper going to do? Walk in the door as if you owned the place, and you will see that there are no problems."

"OK, if you say so. I'll go. One more question. Where is the Ministry of Communications?"

The next day I got up early. Fernando, a compañero from Havana who had worked with me at Shell, came to take me to the ministry. When I went down to the street to get in the automobile, he said, "You're planning to go like that, in shirtsleeves?"

"And why not? Besides, I didn't bring any other clothes with me."

On the corner a newspaper salesman shouted, "New cabinet ministry appointments!"

We stopped to buy a paper. My name appeared on the front page. It gave me a strange sensation—it was the first time my real name had appeared in print.

The car went through unfamiliar streets until it entered an avenue I knew, Rancho Boyeros.

"That's the building," Fernando said.

In front of us was a building with modern lines that I had seen on post office stamps.

"Not bad," I said.

We had gone up the ramp, and Fernando stopped the car in front of a stairway that led to what must have been the main entrance, with glass doors everywhere.

I opened the door and began to climb the staircase when a group of 26th of July militia blocked my way. Fernando had quickly gotten out of the car and run behind me, waving his arms and crying, "It's the minister! It's the minister!"

The soldiers didn't know what to do. I acted as though I was not to be stopped, and following the advice of Buch I began to cross the immense full hall of windows and bags of mail.

A young boy in civilian dress but carrying the band of the 26th of July on his arm reached out to me.

"You . . . you are the minister?"

"The same," and I kept walking to some elevators that could be seen at the other end of the room.

"We read about it in the papers. I am Captain Martínez, of the 26th of July militia. We're the ones who occupied the ministry on the first of January."

We had reached the elevators.

"Surely you will want to go to your office?"

"Yes."

"This way, follow me."

We entered the elevator and went up to the sixth floor. We crossed some rooms with carpets and simple but elegant furniture. Captain Martínez dug in his pockets and pulled out a ring of keys and tried one after another, but the door wouldn't open. I began to get impatient, and the captain was getting more and more nervous. He went through the whole ring and none of them worked.

"It can't be," he said in an anguished voice, and he began again, but this time the first key opened the door.

I walked in. The first thing that caught my attention was a large wooden desk, so massive that it led me to reflect on the way that furniture was made to instill a sense of power in its owner. Behind it was a revolving chair with a high back, of Carmelite leather. And behind that was a long window revealing a landscape in which government offices shared the grounds with an elaborate garden of native Cuban plants.

My feet sank softly into the plush carpeting as I went to the ministerial chair and sat down. It was comfortable. In front of me were armchairs of red and green leather, providing a touch of color that was exciting amid the sober furniture and the walls covered with mahogany. I swiveled in the chair: behind me were telephones and the intercom. Through the glass I gazed out over the nearby buildings to the Havana skyline. Automobiles were traveling along the wide avenues. Pedestrians were walking in shirtsleeves; it was surely hot outside. I became aware of the air conditioning and felt a little cold. I turned back in the chair to put myself in the normal position. The captain was still standing in front of me.

"Sit down," I said.

"Thank you."

"Tell me, what do you know about this ministry?"

"I've learned a lot, señor Minister. The former minister and all of his staff have disappeared, but in the past few days we have restored the ministry's regular activities, and practically all the services are now working normally. You should know that we have already brought in 14,000 pesos from the postal and telephone services!"

"And all the employees are back to work?"

"Yes, señor, except for the biggest supporters of Batista, who have gone, but we have already replaced them with people we are confident in, from the 26th of July Movement."

"Are there many of them?"

"Well, so far we are just beginning, but there are going to be many."

"Come here; explain to me how the ministry works."

"It's pretty complicated . . ."

"But what is it all about? What services does it render?"

"Well, you're talking about the mail, the telegraph, the radio . . . it would be better for me to call señor Collado, who is the one who has been advising me."

"Who is he?"

"He showed up here on the first day and offered his help. He is a man of a certain age, and he knows a lot about all this. They had forced him retire against his will, because he wasn't in agreement with Batista."

"Are you sure?"

"I asked several employees about him."

"OK, tell him to come."

Martínez went away, leaving me alone. I got up and began to open all the doors in the office. One led to a closet, another to a little private elevator. A third went to a small bathroom, very simple and all in white. I went back and sat behind the desk and began opening the drawers, which were unlocked. There were personal letters, almost all letters of recommendation requesting jobs, signed with names I recognized from the newspapers. That's the way it had worked in government before: patronage for friends; jobs that required no work but brought in high pay. It had been a very corrupt system of useless and inefficient bureaucracy.

I swung around in the giant chair to look out the large window. Life went on, and I thought, What the hell do I do now?

I heard a knock at the door. It opened, and the captain entered with a tall, elegant gentleman of about fifty years, who had gray hair and a pleasant face.

"Señor Collado," announced Martínez.

"At your service, señor Minister," said Collado, shaking my hand with a firm grip.

"Sit down, Collado. That will do for now, Captain."

Martínez left the office.

Collado began, "First of all, I want you to know that I am unconditionally at your service."

"Thank you."

"This is like a dream. You should know that I had retired to my house—unwillingly!—but now my twenty years of experience in the postal service are at the service of the revolution. I have occupied several—"

"Can you explain to me how the ministry functions?" I interrupted.

"It's very complicated. It is an important ministry. Things go on here that people never imagine. You should know—"

"There's no manual or procedures list? No organizational chart?"

"What you want, señor Minister, is the Statutory Law of Communications, which the ministry produces, but you should know that it dates from the time of the American intervention at the turn of the century. Since then it has been modified by hundreds of laws and dispositions dictated by subsequent governments. They form a body of law that only an expert can interpret. I—"

"So this ministry takes care of the mail and the telegraph."

"No, much more than that. It regulates the radio and the television. It grants broadcast frequencies. It provides services for navigation. It regulates public utilities."

"Public utilities?"

"Yes, the telephone service, electric power, services of all kinds."

"How interesting . . ."

"You should know—"

"And what would you say are the most immediate problems to be resolved here?"

"Well, we have done some things already, señor Minister," he smiled with a smile that tried to be modest.

"That is good, but I want to know what remains to be done."

"The most urgent is the telegraph. In the last days of the fighting against the tyranny, hundreds of miles of line were destroyed. Many towns are cut off. The government must grant an extraordinary credit. It would have a great effect if you would announce the credit during the coming taking of possession." Now the smile was malicious. "One could think of another popular measure, such as a reduction in the cost of the postal service."

Collado was dressed in an impeccable Prussian blue suit. His blue-and-white-striped necktie was held in the middle by a large white pearl. The sleeves of his coat showed heavy yokes of gold. His legs were crossed elegantly, revealing tight stockings no doubt held with garters. His shoes shone. I raised my eyes and saw the eyes of Collado also appraising me.

"There's no organizational chart?" I asked.

"The organizational chart will only give a general idea. What you need to do is to consult someone with experience. You should know—"

"The organizational chart will give me an idea of the positions and the functions."

"I will be right back."

Collado returned with a notebook in his hand. "Here it is," he said, putting it on the desk. Standing, he looked over my shoulder. I asked him about the functions of each job and took notes.

Collado insisted, "The key position is the undersecretary. That is the man who makes it all work. The minister is a political figure who has national responsibilities. He has to attend the Council of Ministers, take care of his followers, take care of his political base. He cannot dedicate a lot of time to the ministry. He must delegate the administrative work to the undersecretary, who must be a man of experience whom the ministry knows."

"Yes . . . I will think about what you have told me," I said, rising.

"I will be in the ministry all day and in my house at night, at this number." He removed a card from the pocket of his coat. "And don't worry, señor Minister, the secret is in knowing whom to consult."

"Yes, yes."

I was alone again. Now I had an idea what the Ministry of Communications did. I reviewed my notes. What to do now? I thought that the next step had to be to name the heads of the various activities, and each one would learn on the job. I didn't know anyone to trust other than my companions of the 26th of July Movement in Las Villas, but they were all very young. They were students, workers, a few academics. But they were good, honest, and full of enthusiasm. There was no other way: it had to be them.

I went over each one in my head, their knowledge, their character, their occupational experience—little as it was—and I began selecting whom I would assign to each job and writing their names in the organizational chart.

I called Teresita in Santa Clara.

"Tere, have you heard?"

"Yes, we are very happy here."

"Happy? I'm swamped; I know nothing about this stuff. Look, everyone is going to have to pitch in on this. I've decided to name as directors our compañeros from the Direccion del Movimiento. Tell them all to get ready to come here right away, with you at the head."

It was late at night the next day. The door of the office opened, and Teresita's plump figure appeared.

"They're here!"

"I'm on my way."

In the large anteroom, all the members of the Direccion Provincial of Las Villas were waiting. Hugs, jokes, enthusiasm.

"Well," I began, "this responsibility that the revolutionary government gives to me cannot be looked at as a personal recognition. It is a recognition of all our work. The triumph of our management here is the triumph of the 26th of July of Las Villas. That means that we will have to decide who will come to work with me and who will remain in Las Villas."

Everyone followed my words with great interest. I was reading off the functions of each department and the names of the proposed individuals, adding my reasons for each assignment. Everyone agreed with my decisions.

Teresita, now functioning as secretary, came in with a tray full of coffee, and the formal part of the meeting came to an end.

## chapter 19

# The Revolution Takes Power

I looked at the clock. It was already midnight on February 12, 1959. We had been meeting since two in the afternoon, as on the previous day. As on the days before that. Interminable discussions. Results—modest.

The Council of Ministers was not functioning well. From the head of the table, Urrutia presided. He was radical in everything that had to do with the criminals of the dictator, but conservative in respect to social change and politics.

Miró Cardona was the Prime Minister. The only thing he seemed to be interested in was making a crisis for Urrutia so that he could take over as president. He was obsessed with that idea; it was the great ambition of his life. Because of it he tried to get in good with this group and that. He badmouthed Urrutia behind his back and said that he was an incompetent.

Rufo López Fresquet, the Finance Minister, was a representative of reaction. Because he handled the state securities, he dedicated himself, under the pretext of not squandering money, to holding back all progressive ideas.

Agramonte, the Foreign Minister, was the image of the innocuous, the so-called empty shell.

Then there was a group of ministers who came from our revolutionary ranks. Ideas among us were not yet clear, so we acted "on our own," not having a leader in the council to coordinate our actions.

Ill feeling grew among us. Faustino, Armando, Julio Camacho, Luis Buch, and I—who had been more united during the insurrection—began to question what the others were doing.

I looked again at the clock: 1 A.M. Fortunately the council was reaching its end. As we gathered up our papers, we looked at each other's faces, our eyes reflecting a shared understanding.

"That does it," said Faustino.

"Let's go!" everyone said, and we went out to the street.

Luis Buch, as Secretary to the Cabinet, had to stay behind to put in order the agreement reached by the council and to write up the press notes. The rest of us took our cars and went to the Havana Hilton, where Fidel, who was still commander in chief of the rebel army, frequently held meetings and planned activities.

It was almost two in the morning when we located Fidel in one of the corridors of the hotel. There was a swarm of people in the lobby and on several floors. Rebel soldiers, labor leaders, and heads of the 26th of July and other organizations formed groups to discuss all manner of problems. Although the government in power was nominally that of Urrutia, Fidel still had enormous prestige and influence as the leader of the revolution, so a clear distinction could not be made between the government and the 26th of July Movement. In the council, ministers were seated who came from our ranks, so everyone knew that power resided wherever Fidel was and therefore constantly went looking for him in search of guidance at times of decision making. This created a complex situation: there was a government that was not his, yet any decision that was made affected the revolution, which really was his. The heart and the head of the revolution were here and not in the presidential palace.

Fidel never rested. "What are you doing here?" he asked on seeing us.

"We want to talk with you," said Faustino.

"What is it?" insisted Fidel.

"We can't go on like this," returned Faustino. "The Council of Ministers isn't functioning. All we do is talk for hours on end. There are many interests at play and no authority. You must assume the reins of the government!"

"Fidel, this is not our government," I said. "If you don't take charge, we do not want to go on being ministers."

The shadows of the hall were filled with silence. Everyone looked expectantly at Fidel, who leaned thoughtfully against the wall.

"So you want me to take the reins of the government," he said at last. "I don't want to, but, all right, we will talk. Where can we go?"

Someone suggested going to our offices.

"No, not to an office."

Then it occurred to me: "Fidel, why don't we go to my house?" Martha and Frank had moved with me from Santa Clara, and we had rented the ground floor of a house not too far away in the Havana woods.

"To your house? That's not a bad idea, let's go!"

We left in the night. Twenty-third Street was deserted, and we arrived quickly. Fidel ordered more compañeros to be called to the meeting. When we were all gathered together there were not enough chairs in the room; some people sat on the floor, others on the stairs that led to the floor above.

Nobody had eaten, and Martha, who was pregnant with our second child, went to the kitchen and began to cook.

Everybody looked at Fidel, who stood and faced the center of the room. All the lights had been turned on, and Fidel was a handsome figure in his youth and strength.

"Since you want me to take the reins of government, all right, but first let's see what kind of a government we are talking about," he said, putting his hand in the left pocket of the shirt and pulling out a small blue notebook.

He cast his glance over everyone present. "The first thing on my list of important policies is agrarian reform." He gave a long, detailed, and deep exposition of the concept of agrarian reform, to which we all listened with great attention. It was not necessary to discuss much, since we all shared the views expressed by Fidel.

He continued through the pages of the notebook, ticking off important policies, priorities, and issues with which he wanted to deal: high rents; the population suffering from lack of the material necessities of life; the cost of electricity; the need for education and health care; the various sources of employment; the fight against poverty, corruption, and prostitution; economic development; the rebel army; foreign policy.

Hours went by. Martha served a light supper. People chewed automatically—the words of Fidel were the real food.

Dawn came, and light entered through the windows. Nobody was sleepy, even though most of us had gone twenty-four hours without sleeping. Some people were sitting in armchairs, others on tables, others on the floor. Fidel had little room to move. When he stopped, everyone wanted him to go on talking.

"Is that the government you want?" he asked.

"Yes, Fidel, yes," said everyone.

"In that case . . . I accept."

People began leaving, and only those of us who were members of the government remained.

"We have to talk with Urrutia and especially with Miró Cardona, since the job of Prime Minister is the one I must assume."

Shortly thereafter, Miró agreed to resign, and on February 16, Fidel took on the position of Prime Minister.

After the act was official, the ministers sat around the large table in the council chambers. Urrutia presided, sitting at the head. Fidel was seated on one side.

"Let the council begin," began Urrutia.

Fidel interrupted him. "Pardon me, señor Presidente; I would like to make some things clear."

"Go ahead, Comandante."

"The people are waiting for us. There is no time to lose! We have fought to transform this country. We must be deep in our analysis, bold in our decision making, and responsible in our execution of the governmental agenda for which we are reclaiming the corresponding authority."

Then Fidel articulated the agenda of the revolutionary government. He continued, "If I am going to be responsible for fulfilling this program, I must have, I repeat, the necessary authority, and that is why I must preside over the government."

Urrutia was changing color.

"But . . . Comandante . . . then I, as president—what will I do?"

There was a pause, in which everyone remained silent.

"You will remove me if I don't do the job," Fidel finally answered with a smile on his face.

We all felt lifted by that unexpected and brilliant answer that broke the dramatic quality of that historic scene.

But Urrutia got up and left the room.

"Buch, follow him!" ordered Fidel.

After a while Luis Buch returned and said that Urrutia had calmed down. Fidel got up and looked at the chair that had been vacated at the head of the table.

"And where did Batista sit?"

"At the head of the table," someone said.

"Then I will sit in the middle," announced Fidel, while the ministers who were sitting in that part of the table made room for him.

Fidel sat down, and he began the first real council.

# Epilogue

Years passed, and that group of young people took charge of the country, in the same way that I took charge of a ministry whose functions I didn't know, Che assumed the presidency of the National Bank, and Armando Hart became the Minister of Education. A new ministry was created to recover the goods stolen from the state by Batista and his cohorts; it was directed by Faustino Pérez. Other ministries were placed in the hands of figures from the past who were not compromised by Batista.

The Agrarian Reform law, the most important and distinctive revolutionary law, was enacted barely four months after we took power. The lands of the large estate owners were nationalized, among them North American agroindustrial consortiums, and given to the farmers who worked them, with the promise that the lands would be amortized to their former owners. But that promise was not good enough, and so began the exodus of the landowners, and with them the administrators and the technical personnel.

Blows and counterblows soon followed. The government of the United States substantially reduced Cuba's sugar quota in the North American market. Something similar happened with the petroleum provision, which was intended to paralyze the country. The Soviet

Union offered to sell us petroleum and in addition to buy sugar, which saved the Cuban economy from collapsing.

The message from the United States was, Back off or we destroy you. We never doubted which path to follow—to fight. Faced with this state of affairs, we took the second great measure: the nationalization of all foreign and domestic companies and banks. If we wanted to save the revolution, there was no other way.

Faced with the abandonment of the country by the owners, administrators, and technicians, we promoted to those positions young people from the ranks of the rebel army or from the revolutionary organizations, along with some technicians who joined our side.

This process radicalized our positions. We wanted to change the old unjust society, but we did not all agree on how to do it. Disputes arose between us, and some participants left our ranks and even opposed us. Such was the case of Bosch, of Franqui, of Guitérrez Menoyo.

Even among those who stayed the course there were serious disagreements that could only be resolved over the course of time. Such was my own case. I, like so many others, did not go to any school where they taught me how to be a revolutionary. We were young people who saw the injustice that surrounded us: poverty, hunger, prostitution, children begging in the street, the rich growing more and more rich and more and more removed from these problems, and politicians who said that politics was the fastest way to get rich. Batista was the best example of all of this, a poor railroad worker who left a fortune of a billion dollars when he died.

My awareness of this injustice, as well as my readings of Marx and the Russian Revolution, led me to the left.

The Cuban Communists, following the international line of their organization, were against armed warfare, but at heart they sympathized with our cause, and joined our revolution early on. That created division among us, not so much about strategy as about tactics. This happened within several groups, and even in my own ministry. I defended several compañeros who had been my collaborators in the years of fighting, people I trusted to evolve toward correct positions, against those who alleged they were not proper revolutionaries.

Finally, however, I was replaced as minister on the grounds that I was unable to resolve the difficult situation that had been created. The president of Cuba, my old friend Osvaldo Dorticós, said to me, "In recognition of your work as head of the Ministry of Communications and the advances you have achieved there, you have the right to choose the place where you want to work next."

I thought to myself, In case any doubt has been cast on my revolutionary commitment, I am going to show them who I am, so I answered, "I want to work with Che."

"With Che?" My old compañero was surprised.

"Yes, with Che. Don't they say that he is the most radical of all of us?"

And so it was that I worked with Che for five years, until he left to fight in other lands.

In the past, back in the mountains of Escambray, Che and I had disagreed about many things and frequently argued far into the night. We had always liked each other, though, and he was glad to have me come and work for him in his position as Minister of Industries during those early and crucial years when we were first building the new government and the new society of Cuba.

It has been said and written elsewhere that eventually Che and Fidel had a falling out and that Che was forced to leave, but this is a lie. I know firsthand from having been there during the day-to-day activities and many meetings of the period that Che had always planned to leave, from the very first time he met Fidel in Mexico before they set out on the *Granma*. For Che the mission had always been to bring revolution to all of Latin America, not just Cuba, and after the triumph of the 26th of July Movement, he eventually knew that it was time to leave.

"I'm thirty-nine years old now," he said to me one day, "and you know how bad is my asthma. I have to go before my lungs and my legs give out."

Since Che's death, people have asked me many, many times, "What was he like? Please tell us about Che."

I have written several articles that have appeared in our magazines and were quoted in books about Che that were published around the world. I plan to write my own book just about my personal experiences and years with Che at the Ministry of Industries, so this is not the place to tell the whole story.

Nevertheless I will offer again, for those who have not read them elsewhere, just a few thoughts taken from my previous writings about my first reaction to news of Che's death:

What can I say? What can I say about Che that has not already been said?

I can talk about that first night by the fire at our rebel camp in the mountains when I put my hand on his shoulder as a sign of affection. He said to me, "Who has given you such confidence to put your hand there?" and the hand fell down.

I can say that later when we came to know each other well and work together he said to me, "Maybe you are not such a son-of-a-bitch as I was told."

I can say that on a walk along an old stone road through the countryside during one of our regular meetings in the Escambray, we were so engrossed in our conversation that we didn't notice a small enemy plane until it was practically upon us, flying down so close to the open field where we were crossing that I could see the pilot and his machine gun pointing at us.

I ran so fast to hide behind a big tree that if my speed had been measured, it would have broken the world's record. Then there was a barrage of shooting. I looked back to see the pilot strafing the road and Che standing straight and tall in the middle, firing his rifle as the plane approached and flew over him. Miraculously, the bullets missed him, and perhaps he was able to hit the pilot, because the plane kept going and did not return.

Then I saw him looking all over for me and said to myself, How the hell can I ever face this brave man again?

But when I walked back to join him on the road, he saw how distressed I was, and he put his hand on my shoulder, saying, "Don't worry, little Polack (he always called me little Polack), no one will ever hear about this."

I can say that I asked him, "Have you ever felt fear?"
"Yes," he answered. "Very strongly. Many times."

I can say that when he heard our compañeros complaining that they were hungry and did not have enough to eat, he said, "There is plenty."

"Sure, of course, but you have an additional quota," they told him.

And when he found out they were right, he put a stop to his additional ration and told our compañeros, "Yes, until yesterday."

I can say how we waited together after a long day at the Ministry of Industries to be taken to our volunteer work. Che introduced the idea and set the example of volunteering many hours of hard labor in addition to our regular jobs. We would go to build houses, for example, or cut sugarcane together.

I can tell you how we played chess late at night. How Che could sing only out of tune and was famous for being not such a good dancer. How strict he was at first about forbidding any intimate relations among our staff, but then how he became more flexible as time passed.

I can say that Che gave my father a job, appreciating the skills and personality of the older man and appointing him as an inspector of quality for shoe components, a job for which my father was eminently qualified and that made him feel quite happy and useful, traveling around the island to visit the tanneries and other sources of supplies that he knew so well.

I can say that on the night my mother died he came to the funeral home and put his hand on my shoulder, as I had done to him years before. We spoke together that night until dawn.

I can say that Che would often say to me, "Go away, little Polack. You are making me waste time with all this talk," though even then we would keep talking on and on for hours.

I can say that he would often open the windows of our offices during an all-night marathon session and take off his shirt. He would lie on the floor smoking a cigar, and we agreed together that we would take good care of the world and solve all the world's problems.

Years later when I saw the terrible photograph of his dead body lying on that table in Bolivia, his eyes still open, and with the gunshot wounds visible in the bare flesh of his chest, I remembered those nights we spent together when he took off his shirt and lay on the floor, smoking a cigar, talking with me until dawn.

While all our efforts at home continued, it was also necessary to defend the revolution in the international arena; the young people had to learn to run banks, farms, and industries; and we had to fulfill our agenda of eliminating hunger, educating the people, and guaranteeing their health. It was always clear to us that the first human right is the right to life.

But how was all this to be done?

Without trying to make an earthly man into a divine being, I must say that the greatest merit of Fidel was that he knew how to lead us along this intricate path; to unite us while continuing the economic, political, and international struggles; and to find the right decision at each step.

I might be wrong, but I think to change, or even to evolve history, it's not enough for the popular conditions to exist. You also need the man who strikes the spark and knows how to lead people along the right path in the midst of as complex a situation as a revolution.

And that, fortunately, is what Fidel did for Cuba.

How can I tell about those first years after the triumph of the revolution when we worked day and night to improve our people's economic conditions and everyone wanted to be in the forefront of the new battles?

I was vice president then of what is today the Ministry of the Economy, and at the end of one long work session that Fidel had presided over, in which we discussed measures for increasing food production, I went to him and said, "Fidel, I do not want to continue working in an office. I want to work outdoors; I want to work in agriculture, producing the food that our people need."

He looked at me, surprised, and finally answered. "You know, it's not a bad idea. You will start tomorrow."

The next day, I took charge of a large company that had to produce meat and milk for a whole province. Instead of living in the city, Martha, the children, and I went to live in a small cabin in the country, to be in direct contact with nature and the work that needed to be done.

The workers in the factory, and especially the cowboys, were aware of my past, and I felt that initially they did not completely respect me, which I attributed to my being unable to ride a horse or milk a cow.

So I spent my Sundays at one of the farms where we raised horses, until I learned to ride. And every morning I went to the barns, until I learned how to milk. Then, eventually, I felt that the workers considered me one of them.

When I came back to Havana at the end of this period, Fidel told me to wait until I heard from Celia Sánchez about what I should do next. He was thinking of sending me to another cattle project he was establishing in the province of Camagüey, so I stayed at home for several months. It was during that time that I began writing the first few chapters of this book.

Months went by. I would call Celia, and she would tell me, "Fidel wants you to be patient." But I couldn't wait any longer, so I talked to my old friend Orlando Borrego, who was by then the Minister of the Sugar Industry. He talked to Fidel, and Fidel agreed to have me work in the sugar industry.

This was in 1966, a time when we all began working to achieve the goal of producing ten million tons of sugar by 1970. With Fidel's approval I was sent to be the head of the sugar industry in the province of Matanzas. Martha and I closed the house in Havana, took the children, and moved together to the province, as we had done when I went to work on a farm in the cattle business. Other comrades of mine would leave their families behind when they were posted far from home, but Martha was a different kind of person and wouldn't let me live alone.

At that time I knew about the economic aspects of the sugar industry from my work with Che when I was the vice president of the Ministry of the Economy, which was in charge of agriculture, industry, trade, and the like. But I had no idea from a technical point of view how a sugar mill worked or how the sugar was actually produced. I decided that we should live right there where I could see and understand everything that was going on, so we moved the whole family to a small house at the middle of a mill.

Of course, as we all know now, that goal of 10 million tons of sugar was not accomplished in 1970. We achieved only 8.5 million. This was extremely good of course, the biggest amount ever, and Matanzas, the province for which I was responsible, did make its goal of one million tons. But others did not, and the national goal was not achieved. As a result, there was a change of ministers, who brought new people, and even though I had been successful, my old friends at the ministry who hadn't accomplished their goals began to be discriminated against by the newcomers. I didn't like that, and that's why I left.

So in 1971 I joined the Ministry of Fisheries, where I had many friends, and I have been there ever since. The fishing industry has always been very important to Cuba's economy, international relationships, and domestic food supply. Consequently, I have participated in building up our fishing industry, negotiating treaties for fishing rights around the Caribbean, developing many relationships with other countries, and establishing foreign investment in our fish farming industry.

As the deputy minister over the past thirty-one years, I have traveled to and done business with Japan, China, Israel, the Philippines, Spain, Portugal, France, Italy, Germany, Belgium, Poland, England, Switzerland, Greece, Russia, Bulgaria, Czechoslovakia, Egypt, Yemen, South Africa, Guinea, Namibia, Angola, Cape Verde, the United States, Canada, Mexico, Nicaragua, Panama, Columbia, Ecuador, Peru, Chile, Trinidad, Tobago, Jamaica, Norway, and elsewhere.

During the past forty-three years of my service in the government, it has been my responsibility and my pleasure to meet many people from these other countries, either in their land or when they visited us here in Cuba. And how many wonderful people I came to know over those years: for example, Jean-Paul Sartre and Simone de Beauvoir, with whom I formed a close friendship. They came to find out what had happened in Cuba shortly after we took power and began the great revolutionary changes. For them, the success of a revolution created by so many young people who had made such great social changes was not only important but attractive to them as writers, intellectuals, and activists of the left. I was familiar with their work and considered them revolutionaries by virtue of their philosophical theories and their ideas.

One thing that impressed me was the dedication with which Sartre worked. Although we would travel and work together while he was in Cuba, Sartre was never available before eleven in the morning. Why? Because he rose early and started to write.

285

"But why not take advantage of the beautiful mornings while you are here?" I asked him.

"Because I am a worker in literature, and we workers must labor every day," he answered with a smile.

That was a great lesson about discipline and the hard work involved in being a writer, and it has been an inspiration to me in my own work as a novice writer ever since.

Many people are asking me these days about the future of Cuba. Maybe it's because I am a member of the older revolutionary generation. In fact, I am now the oldest vice minister serving in the government.

In any case, let me say this: Karl Marx wrote in the prologue of *Das Kapital* that everything evolves. So the first thing we have to do is evolve our ideas, according to the situation in the world.

The Soviets made a religion out of Marxism. That was their mistake, because the founder of Marxism was entirely against such dogmatism. For Fidel and the rest of us, the basic principles that made us revolt against the old regime, the old society, are still present: man cannot be the exploiter of man. The main principle that should rule our lives is to work for the happiness of everybody in our society.

That doesn't mean that everybody has to be equal. Those who are better workers, who work harder, should be rewarded. But we don't want any billionaires. We want to have a limit to how different you can be. We don't want you to be so rich that you own a factory or become a large landowner. So those principles—which may be difficult to understand if you are an American—are still important, and they still guide us.

We are trying to live out these principles in Cuba, and we make our voice heard in all international meetings. We believe that those who have wealth should help the poor and developing countries and their people to live better, to fight illness, and to save children's lives.

For me, I could have been a rich person by now if I had left Cuba, as did so many others among whom I grew up. But that's not the way I could be happy. I will be happy when everybody in my country has everything that he needs.

After the Soviet Union collapsed in 1989, our economy began to decline dramatically. From 1989 to 1993, it decreased 37 percent. But in 1995, the downward curve stopped and began to go up again. It took us five more years to return to the same level that we had in 1989. And we have evolved; we have changed: now tourism is a bigger industry than sugar, and we hope that eventually people from all over the world will come to visit our beautiful island—as they did before the revolution, when Cuba was the number one tourist destination in the Caribbean—and see we are not such bad people.

As for the U.S. embargo, we didn't feel it so strongly in the early years of the revolution, since the Soviet Union bought our sugar and provided us with cheap oil and other resources. But with the dissolution of the socialist camp we became more alone in the world, and the embargo felt very painful to us. We can't understand how a nation like the United States, a nation that talks about human rights, can create such inhuman conditions for us. This embargo has resulted in great shortages in food and medicine for Cuba. And every time the U.S. government discovers that we are trying to do business somewhere in the world, they use their embassy people to pressure potential partners and investors not to work with us. They threaten that these potential partners and investors will lose crucial economic arrangements with the United States if they do business with Cuba—blackmailing them really—in order to deprive us of opportunities. This tactic doesn't always work, but in most cases the economic power of the United States is so great that when one of these companies in Europe has to choose between the United States and Cuba, the decision is quite clear. Just a few stand with us.

So this is my view of the future: to continue to think and evolve and change and work as I have in the past, for not only these forty-three years since we took over but from the time I was a teenager who believed in social justice and the necessity for revolutionary change. Part of our objectives is also to fight as much as we can against the destruction of the world's environment. The world appears to be marching toward the pollution of its atmosphere, its waters, all of its ecology. Changes are taking place in nature of such importance that we cannot understand how the rest of the world is not more conscious of this grave situation. So this also is one of our great concerns for the future, and at many international meetings throughout the world Fidel has constantly been a leading voice in the struggle for the salvation of our planet's environment.

People also always ask me what will happen to the Cuban government and society when Fidel dies. The answer is, nothing. Nothing will happen, because all Fidel has been doing these last few years, what we all have been doing, is preparing the next generation to substitute for our generation. As a result, most of the ministers and the leaders of the national and provincial governments are young people. We are also paying much attention to educating the masses of our people through new radio and television shows analyzing the daily news and through new programs to fill the libraries with the literature of the world, not only of Cuba—all this is intended to let them know what is really going on and prepare our young people to keep evolving our revolutionary society.

In my ministry, we are very conscience of the age of our members. I am the exception; the rest of our deputy ministers are much younger people, between thirty and thirty-five. We are promoting the young people, because the revolution must be in their hands. For if they are not in charge, they may stand against it. This is what happened in the socialist camp, where the old guard would not leave their posts and the young ones had to rise up against them. Thus 95 percent of the positions in the government today are filled with young people.

I feel an obligation to tell the history of our revolution in its human sense, not just for scholars but for the people, especially the young people.

Che once said to me, when I made some criticism of his literary work, "I am Minister of Industries, head of the western army, international conspirator, and author. You are a simple vice minister, and all you do is criticize me." Fidel, who writes very well, spends his life lamenting that he has so many things he wants to write about but no time to do it. Raúl constantly exhorts us to write about our experience.

Yes, I will keep on writing, not simply as an obligation but also for the pleasure writers feel in making their work—the same pleasure I felt when I worked as an architect and saw buildings constructed that I had conceived in my mind.

My beloved mother died when she was only fifty-four. My father lived until eighty. Martha and I have known each other now for fifty-three years, have been married for forty-six, and are blessed with four children: Frank is now the vice president of a tourist enterprise; Carlos is a department manager; Haydee works as an architect in a government agency; and Sylvia manages a kindergarten. And we have five granddaughters and three grandsons so far.

None of our children or grandchildren have the blue Polish eyes of my mother and me, and most of them are a little darker than I am, because Martha's grandmother was a light mulatto and her father a Creole. In this I achieved my goal of mixing all the races in Cuba: Polish, Jewish, African, Spanish.

We live in a neighborhood of Havana called Nuevo Vedado. Right now my daughter Sylvia, her husband, and two sons live in the house with us, along with Haydee and other members of our family who come and go. Frank and Carlos and their families also live nearby, so the house is always filled with children and guests.

I'm very happy to have a garden next to our house, in which there is a royal palm, many banana trees, fruits and vegetables growing, and chickens wandering about. And in our backyard there is an arbor where we can sit to eat and drink and talk with many visitors in the shade and cool air of the evening.

It was José Martí who said that to be a man you have to have a child, plant a tree, and write a book. So this is what I have tried to do in my life.

# Glossary

**Almeida, Juan**—Was with Fidel for the attack on the Moncada barracks, then jailed and exiled to Mexico. He returned with Fidel on the *Granma* and led a column of troops in the Sierra Maestra. Almeida is currently vice president of Cuba.

**Auténticos (Partido Revolucionario Cubano Auténtico)**—Anti-Batista revolutionary organization organized in the mid-1930s by Grau San Martín. Although the organization was originally known for its idealism and devotion to revolutionary change, its reputation was later tarnished by violence, gunmen, and gangsterism. Nevertheless, the Auténticos were one of the many various revolutionary organizations Castro managed to cooperate with and incorporate at various times.

**Batista, Fulgencio (1901–1973)**—Working-class, mixed-blood cane cutter, water boy, tailor, carpenter, and railroad brakeman who joined the army at twenty, learned shorthand and typing, was promoted to sergeant stenographer, and emerged as a strong-arm leader during the Sergeants' Revolution of 1933. After this successful revolt, he became commander of the army and eventually president from 1940 to 1944, during which time he presided over a corrupt and oppressive regime while amassing a fortune of $20 million. Retiring for a time to Miami Beach, he returned to seize power by force in 1952 and assumed a totalitarian dictatorship notorious for its corruption, gangsterism, and assassination of its opponents. With the triumph of the revolution, he fled the country on December 31, 1958, with an estimated fortune of $300 million, ultimately dying in Spain.

**Bolívar, Simón (1783–1830)**—Sometimes called the George Washington of Latin America. A Spaniard born in Caracas, Venezuela, he inherited a fortune as a child when both his parents died. After traveling as a young man throughout Europe, he returned to

Venezuela and joined a group of revolutionaries who seized Caracas in 1810. Eventually he led an army that defeated Spain in Colombia, Venezuela, Angostra (now Bolivia, after him), and Peru. Also known as El Libertador, by 1825 he had helped every country except Cuba and Puerto Rico gain independence from Spain. His integrity, high morals, and perseverance in the face of overwhelming odds have made him a hero and role model to Latin American revolutionaries ever since.

**Campesinos**—Peasant farmers.

**Castro, Raúl**—Younger brother of Fidel. He was with Fidel at the attack on the Moncada barracks and returned from Mexico with him on the *Granma;* he led a column of guerillas in the Santiago de Cuba area of the Sierra Maestra and eventually became commander in chief of the army.

**Chibás, Eduardo**—President of the Ortodoxo party. He was a fiery, charismatic, brilliant but also mentally unbalanced revolutionary leader during the post–World War II period who accidentally killed himself in 1948.

**Cienfuegos, Camilo**—Heroic leader of one of Castro's original columns of guerrilla fighters in the Sierra Maestra, who walked across Cuba to eventually take Havana. He became commander in chief of the army during the early years of the triumph of the revolution but was lost over the sea in a flight from Camagüey to Havana in October 1959.

**Civic Resistance**—Clandestine group of largely middle-class professionals who donated money, expertise, and connections to the revolutionary effort in urban centers like Havana, rather than taking the more direct action of the 26th of July Movement.

**Compañeros**—Companions, comrades.

**Directorio Revolucionario (Revolutionary Directorate)**—Revolutionary organization founded primarily by university students, organized in opposition to the draconian regime of Batista during the early 1950s.

**Dorticós, Osvaldo**—Prominent attorney from Cienfuegos who in 1959 became president of the republic in the early revolutionary government.

**Franqui, Carlos**—Anti-Batista journalist who interviewed Castro while he was a prisoner on the Isle of Pines in 1955, then helped organize the 26th of July underground weekly *Revolución* (later called *Granma*). He later helped organize and produce *Cubano Libre,* the newspaper Castro himself published in the Sierra Maestra, and the rebel radio station Radio Rebelde.

**García Barcena, Rafael**—Opponent of the dictator Machado as a student; later, as a university professor, he founded the Movimiento Nacional Revolucionaria (MNR), which advocated armed revolt. Among his early followers were Armando Hart, Faustino Pérez, Frank País, and Enrique Oltuski. He was arrested, tortured, imprisoned, and sent into exile by Batista in 1953, effectively ending his political career.

*Granma*—The 58-foot boat Fidel Castro bought from an American. Castro sailed with eighty-one compatriots from Mexico to Cuba in November 1956 to launch his guerrilla movement in the Sierra Maestra. The boat is now on view in the War Museum at the former presidential palace in Old Havana. The name of the revolutionary newspaper of record was changed to *Granma,* which it is still called today.

**Grau San Martín, Ramon (1887–1969)**—Originally a fashionable doctor, as Dean of the Medical Faculty he joined the Sergeants' Revolution against President Cespedes in 1933 and became president later the same year. His tenure was marked by exceptional violence and corruption, as well as by continuing conflicts with Batista, who gradually became the real power of the regime. Grau enriched himself greatly while president, and left office in 1934 when Batista assumed power.

**Guevera, Ernesto "Che" (1927–1967)**—Mythical hero of the Cuban revolution. Born in Argentina, he became a medical doctor who traveled and practiced throughout Latin and Central America. Radicalized by the CIA intervention in Guatemala, he joined Castro in Mexico and came with him to Cuba on the *Granma.* Originally the guerrillas' doctor, he eventually assumed military command and led a column of troops down from the Sierra Maestra to win major battles in the plains. A prominent leader of the revolutionary government, he served as president of the National Bank and Minister of Industries, before leaving Cuba to lead revolutionary insurrections in Africa and later Bolivia, where he was killed in 1967.

**Hart, Armando**—Important early organizer of the 26th of July Movement, who later became the Minister of Education in the early revolutionary government.

**Machado, Gerardo (1871–1939)**—President of Cuba from 1925 to 1933, a period of intense corruption and brutality. He was eventually forced from office with the intervention of U.S. ambassador Sumner Welles.

**Martí, José (1853–1895)**—Heroic martyr and icon of Cuban revolutionary spirit. Exiled at eighteen for his revolutionary writings, he spent many years in the United States producing a large, enormously influential body of writing, raising money, and training revolutionaries. When he finally returned to lead an armed revolt, he was nearly immediately killed in a random skirmish. His life and work has had tremendous impact on all Cuban revolutionary movements since, and images and statues of him can be seen in many Cuban cities, towns, schools, and homes to this day.

**Movimiento Nacional Revolucionaria (MNR); National Revolutionary Movement**—Revolutionary organization, popular primarily among university students and young professional people, founded by professor Rafael García Barcena. The MNR advocated armed revolt rather than working within the political system.

**País, Frank**—Baptist schoolmaster and leader of the revolutionary movement in Santiago de Cuba who coordinated local commando raids in Santiago with Castro's landing on the *Granma*. Later, in 1957, he was shot down by the police on the streets of the city, and died at twenty-three.

**Partido Socialista Popular (PSP); Popular Socialist Party**—Name chosen in 1944 by early Cuban Communists for their revolutionary organization, changed from the previous name, Union Revolucionaria Comunista, when they decided that their goal was "not the establishment of Communism but the struggle for complete liberation . . . to culminate in the . . . establishment of socialism."

**Pérez, Faustino**—Baptist former medical student who became an early member of the National Council of the MNR, then one of the men who came on the *Granma*. He later escorted Herbert Matthews of the *New York Times* to see Fidel in the Sierra Maestra. Pérez eventually became a minister in the early revolutionary government.

**Plains, the (Il Llano)**—Cuban term for the lowlands that extend from the eastern edge of the Pinar del Rio mountains to the western border of the Sierra Maestra, including all the farmlands in between. Most of Cuba's major cities—for example, Havana, Santa Clara, Cienfuegos, Sancti Spíritus, and Camagüey—are in the plains.

**Prío, Carlos**—Originally a student leader in the struggle against Machado, he was in the Grau San Martín government as senator, Prime Minister, and Minister of Labor. Prío was elected president of Cuba in 1948; his tenure was notable for its hypocrisy, greed, and corruption. He was overthrown by Batista's coup in 1952 and fled the country.

**Sánchez, Celia**—Heroine of the revolution, personal secretary and lifelong friend of Fidel Castro. She died in 1980.

**Santamaría, Haydée "Yeyé"**—One of the rebels who attacked the Moncada barracks, she continued to be an important leader of the 26th of July Movement throughout the revolution. She fought with Frank País during the uprising in Santiago de Cuba in coordination with Castro's landing on the *Granma* in 1956, and worked underground in Havana. She was later the wife of Armando Hart, a member of Castro's Central Committee, and president of the Casa de las Americas cultural institute and literary magazine.

**26th of July Movement**—Large underground revolutionary movement, founded by Castro in 1955 just before leaving for Mexico, and named after the date of the attack on the Moncada barracks.

**Urrutia, Manuel**—Municipal judge in Santiago de Cuba who in 1957 acquitted a group of one hundred supporters of Castro, including several who had come with Fidel on the *Granma*. He was rewarded by being made the first president of the republic under the new revolutionary government, but was ineffective; eventually forced to resign, he then left the country.

**Ventura, Esteban (police chief)**— Notorious chief of police in Havana and henchman of Batista, known as a legendary death-dealer of students and revolutionaries. Indicted for murder by a courageous Havana magistrate in 1958, even before the defeat of his patron Batista, he fled Cuba in January 1959, taking exile in the United States.

# About the Author

**E**nrique Oltuski was born in Havana in 1930. He went to school in Santa Clara, Cuba, before attending college in the United States at the University of Miami to study architectural engineering. He returned to Cuba to join the fight against the Batista dictatorship. He was part of insurrectionary efforts in Havana and later headed the 26th of July Movement in the province of Las Villas, where he met and worked with Che Guevara when Che was leading invasion forces in the mountains of Escambray.

After the triumph of the revolution, Oltuski assumed the position of Minister of Communications in the first revolutionary government, and later served as vice minister, under Che, of the Ministry of Industries and in the Central Planning Committee. He is currently Deputy Minister of the Fisheries and Merchant Marine in Havana.

# About the Translators

Thomas and Carol Christensen translated the best-selling *Like Water for Chocolate,* by Laura Esquivel, as well as works by Alejo Carpentier, Julio Cortázar, Carlos Fuentes, Senel Paz, Virgilio Piñera, José Manuel Prieto, and others. Their translation of Louis-Ferdinand Céline's *Ballets Without Music, Without Dancers, Without Anything* was a finalist for the 2000 Pen America West Translation Award. The Christensens are also authors of *The U.S.-Mexican War* and other books.

# Index

## A

Acosta, A., 147, 148
Agramonte (Foreign Minister), 269
Agrarian reform, 69, 196, 271–272, 277
*Aldabonazo,* 93
Almeida, J., 113, 159, 181, 213
Amaro, A. S., 9
American police, 144
Andrade, E., 30
Arcos, G., 77–79, 101, 102
Argüelles, J., 67–69, 73, 74, 80, 85, 127, 246
Auténticos (Authentic Revolutionary Movement), 145, 148, 149
"Autumn Leaves" (Mercer), 11

## B

Baire, 214, 215
Banco Continental, 210
Barletta Motors, 96
Batista, F., 18, 30, 43, 51, 58, 60, 65, 72, 78, 92, 96, 98, 101, 103, 113–115, 123; coup d' état of, 6–13; flight of, 231–237
Batista, P., 9
Bayamo, 207–209

Beauvoir, S. de, 183, 285
Biltmore, 47–48
Blanco, A. E., 42, 256
*Bohemia,* 6
Bolívar, S., 9, 37
"Bonifacio," 127
Bordón, V., 128, 133, 143, 149, 159, 153, 169, 195, 224, 258
Borrego, O., 284
Bosch, O., 157–159, 170, 171, 246, 278
Boti, R., 95, 183
Brest, Poland, 71
Buch, L., 215, 216, 218, 207, 260, 270, 273; as Secretary to Cabinet, 259
Buchanan, J., 27–33, 165, 166
Buenaventura, Colombia, 40
Bueycito Mines, 113

## C

Caballero, T., 126, 132–137, 248, 249, 265
Caballete de Casa, 202
Caibarién, xxxiii, 128, 145, 159
Camacho, J., 270
Camagüey, xxxiii, 113, 195, 284
Cantillo (Batista general), 222, 234

Capote, F., 111, 112

Carbonell, F., 141, 142, 145

Cardona, M., 116, 163, 269, 272

Carratalá (Batista police henchman), 113

*Carteles,* 91

Castro, F., xxviii, xxix, 58, 60, 72–73, 78, 79, 97, 99–101, 103, 96, 112, 143, 158, 159, 182, 184, 185, 207, 247; on action at Guisa, 207; arrives at Santa Clara, 244; and attack on Moncada barracks, 50–53; at Cayo Loco, 250–251; decrees general strike, 235; detention of, in Mexico, 96; as environmentalist, 288; exiled in Mexico, 65; first encounter with, 216–218; greatest merit of, 282; letter of, regarding sending troops to Las Villas, 191; and march on Havana, 241–252; at Rinconada, 220; in Sierra Maestre, 107; speaks at Cienfuegos, 249–250; speaks at Santa Clara, 248; takes on position of Prime Minister, 270–273; treatment of prisoners by, 213; on Urrutia, 221

Castro, L. (sister to Fidel), 100

Castro, R. (brother to Fidel), xxix, 102, 158, 159, 183, 220, 221

Catholic University, Chile, 33, 42

Cayo Loco, 250–251

Charco Redondo, 218

Chavarry, P., 95, 103

Chaviano, J., 163

Chibás, E., 47, 50, 92

Chile, 37, 38, 40–44; Catholic University, 33; Chilean Catholicism, 43; Federation of Chilean Students, 42

Christian Socialists, 41, 43

Cienfuegos, xxxiii, 128, 133–135, 166, 169, 224, 225, 258; Castro stops at, 249–250; uprising at, 124

Cienfuegos, C., 181, 196, 200, 201, 221, 222, 234, 237, 242

Civic Resistance movement. *See* Resistencia

Civil Coordinating Committee, 114

Club Telefónico (Guanabo), 117, 118

Cobrin, Poland, 71

Collado (ministry advisor), 261–264

Colón, Panama, 38

Communist Party, 66–68, 95. *See also* Cuban Communist Party; Partido Socialista Popular (PSP; Popular Socialist Party)

Condado, 150, 191, 192

Contramaestre sugar mill, 222

Contreras, P., 47

Contreras, Y., 47

Council of Ministers, 136, 255, 269, 271

"Crazy Horse," 211–213

Cuban Communist Party, 132, 278–279. *See also* Communist Party; Partido Socialista Popular (PSP; Popular Socialist Party)

Cuban Jewish community, 17–18, 51

Cuban Medical Association, 115

**D**

*Das Kapital* (Marx), 30, 34

Diaz, A., 144, 145

"Diego." *See* Paneque, V. M.

Direccion Provincial, 77, 78, 129, 133, 235–236, 245, 265

Directorio Revolucionario (DR), 72, 128, 143, 165, 166

Dorticós, O., 135, 136, 166, 167, 181, 182, 224; as Minister for Law Revision, 257–258; as president of Cuba, 181, 279

DR. *See* Directorio Revolucionario

**E**

El Pedrero, 202, 203

Escambray, 159, 163, 166–169, 194, 195, 200, 258, 279; Second Front of, 164, 169

*Escopetero,* 210–211, 216, 217
Esso, 68
Estrada Palma, 113

**F**

Faure, 169
Federation of Chilean Students, 42
Fernández, M., "Zoilo," 134,
    141–143, 145, 243–245, 247, 249
Fernández, P., 116, 119
FEU. *See* Students Federation
"Fico," 97, 98
Fleites, A., 168, 169
"Fofo." *See* Gutiérrez, A.
Fontanillas, M., 108
Franqui, C., 91, 92, 94–99, 102, 103,
    111, 112, 207, 278
Frei (Leader of Chilean Phalange), 41
Fresquet, R. L., 269
Frías, L. C., 208
Frías, N., 166, 167
Frio (Santa Clara), 67

**G**

Gálvez, W., 201
Garay, S., 68
García Barcena, R., "Professor," 18,
    20, 21, 23, 24, 48, 51, 58–63, 65
García, G., 113
General strike: of April 9, 141–154;
    failure of, 113–120, 258
González Abreu, J., 136, 137, 224
*Granma,* xxviii, 93, 102, 104, 235,
    279
Guanabo, 117
Guevera, E., "Che," xxviii, xxix, xxx,
    57, 113, 125, 126, 143, 178, 221,
    222, 224, 231, 235, 236, 242; and
    alleged falling out with Fidel, 277;
    in Las Villas, 191–204; letter of,
    from Santa Lucia, 198–199; as Min-
    ister of Industries, 279, 280; as pres-
    ident of National Bank, 181, 277
Guillén, N., 42, 208

Guisa, 207, 209
Gutiérrez, A., "Fofo," 100, 102
Gutiérrez Menoyo, E., 164, 168, 169,
    195, 278

**H**

Hart, A., 48, 49, 60, 72–73, 91, 92,
    94–97, 110, 163, 257, 258, 270;
    as Minister of Education, 277
Havana, xxxiii, 51, 71, 80, 83, 84, 91,
    107, 109, 113–115, 235; delivery
    of order to advance on, 234; Fidel's
    march on, 241–252
Hernández, M., 101, 213, 214
Hernández, P., 145
Herzl, T., 18
Holguín, xxxiii, 113, 127
Hormiguero Sugar Mill, 231

**I**

Ibáñez, C., 41
Iglesias, J., 92, 123
*Iskra,* 93
Israel, 18

**J**

Jiménez, N. N., 147
Jiménez, P., 10
Junquera, R., 109, 111, 117

**L**

*La Carta Semanal* (Partido Socialista
    Popular), 132
La Lata, 213, 214
La Plata, 112
Las Villas, 77, 142, 145, 159, 200,
    221, 255; Che in, 191–204; fight
    in, 123–137
Lechuga, C., 246, 247
Lenin, V. I., 34, 93
Lima, Peru, 40
Llanusa, J., 163, 164
Llanusa, P., 108
Llerena, M., 95, 109
López, O. F., 246

Lubián, C., 127
Lubián, G., "Toto," 127, 246
Luis Hernández bakery (Santa Clara),
    149

**M**

Machado, G., 72, 108
Machado, R., 160–163
Maffo, 213, 218, 221
Marcelo (guide), 203, 204, 218, 220
March, A. (wife to Che), 126, 127, 199
Marcia, 141, 143
Mariana Grajales, 209
"Mario." *See* Salvador, D.
Martí, J., 18, 21, 37, 271
Martínez, 146, 154, 260–262
Marx, K., 30, 34, 278
Marxism, xx, xxxi, 34
Masvidal (Batista police lieutenant),
    129, 130
Matanzas, xxxiii, 113, 284
Menéndez, Doctor, 67
Mercado, S., 41, 42
Mesa, L., 108
Mexico, 65, 96; Mexican Police, 101
Mexico City, 99
Miami, 6, 23, 58, 60, 144, 162–164,
    176
Minerva (Miami), 27–28
MNR. *See* Movimiento Nacional Rev-
    olucionaria (MNR)
Moncada barracks, 95, 219; attack on,
    50–53
Morales, C., 234, 235, 241, 244, 245
Morgan, W., 168, 169, 250–251
Movimiento Nacional Revolucionaria
    (MNR; National Revolutionary
    Movement), 18–20, 27, 37, 41,
    43, 50, 58, 65, 66, 195

**N**

Naranjo, J., 183
National Association of Lawyers, 116,
    135, 136

National Bank, 277
National Directorate, 145, 158, 159
National Revolutionary Movement.
    *See* Movimiento Nacional Revolu-
    cionaria (MNR)
Nazis, 72
"Neno," 160, 161
Neruda, P., 42, 201
Nieves, 193, 194
North American market, 277
Núñez, Father, 80–82

**O**

Oltuski, B. (father), 10, 18, 108, 174,
    175, 177, 241, 242, 281, 271
Oltuski, C., 111, 184, 271
Oltuski, E.: assumes command of Las
    Villas, 157–172; bar mitzvah of,
    109, 174; in Chile, 40–44; chooses
    nom de guerre (Sierra), 109; finds
    job at Shell, 80; goes to work in
    production, 283; goes to work in
    sugar industry, 284; goes to work
    with Che in position of Minister of
    Industries, 277–280; as government
    minister, 255–265; hands order to
    advance on Havana to Che, 234; in
    Havana, 91–104; joins 26th of July
    Movement, 77–86; meets Fidel,
    207–220; meets Martha Rodríguez,
    21–23; in Mexico City, 99–102; as
    Minister of Communications, 178,
    180, 257; in Ministry of Fisheries,
    285; and nationalization of tele-
    phone company, 180; in Panama,
    38–40; return of, to Cuba, 57–63;
    revolutionary quest of, 65–74;
    secret life of, as Sierra, 124, 125;
    in the Sierra Maestra, 207–224;
    student political activities of, in
    United States, 27–34; at University
    of Miami, 5–13
Oltuski, F. P. (son), 123, 124, 163,
    179, 184, 242, 271, 271

Oltuski, H. (daughter), 184, 271
Oltuski, J. (mother), 70–72, 174
Oltuski, M. (wife), 107, 123, 124, 129, 141, 143, 163, 179, 210, 224, 225, 242, 271, 272, 271. *See also* Rodríguez, M.
Oltuski, S. (daughter), 184, 271
Oltuski, S. (sister), 108, 119, 174, 177
Oriente, 109, 112, 142
Ozacki, J. *See* Oltuski, J.

**P**

País, F., 104, 113, 117, 118
Palma, 222
Palma Mocha, 112
Palmira, 225
Panama City, Panama, 38
Paneque, V. M., "Diego," 127, 143–145, 149, 157, 159, 161, 162, 198
Pantoja, O., 203
*Parallel Lives* (Plutarch), 33
Pardo Llada, J., 48, 49, 248
Partido Accion Unitaria, 9
Partido Socialista Popular (PSP; Popular Socialist Party), 132, 133, 147, 148, 195, 196, 236
*Paso doble,* 72
Pastora Sugar Mill, 232–233
Pazos, F., 95
"Peasant," 129–131
Pedrosa, Doctor, 50
Pérez, F., 20, 21, 24, 48, 49, 72–73, 90, 92, 94–96, 104, 107–110, 113–115, 117, 119, 133, 134, 142, 145, 181, 207, 257, 258, 270, 271, 277
Phosphorus, use of, 103
Piedra, C. M., 231
Pinar del Rio, xxxiii, 200
Pino, O., 100, 101
Pino, Q., 74, 77, 78
Plutarch, 33
Poland, 10, 71

Porro, 110
Prieto, P., 107
Prío, A., 7, 72
Prío, C., 6, 7, 27–28, 48, 58, 59, 143, 149, 170
Prío, P., 7
"Professor." *See* García Barcena, R.
PSP. *See* Partido Socialista Popular

**R**

Radio Rebelde, 201, 207, 218, 207
Rancho Boyeros Airport, 5
Ranchuelo, 231–232
Remedios, 128
*Resistencia* (Civic Resistance movement), 93, 107–120, 136, 144
*Revolución,* 93, 99
Riera, S., 79
Rinconada, 220
Rivas, E. S., 6
Rodrígues, A., 112
Rodríguez, C., 164
Rodríguez, G., "Rooster," 18, 20, 21, 23, 24, 50, 51, 73, 77, 159, 160, 162, 163, 165, 170, 176, 246; picked as direct aid to Oltuski, 126
Rodríguez, J., 31–32
Rodríguez, L., 31–32
Rodríguez Llompart, H., 95, 103
Rodríguez, M., 18, 21–23, 80–82, 85, 91, 95, 103, 175, 176. *See also* Oltuski, M. (wife)
"Rooster." *See* Rodríguez, G.
Rosell, A., 50, 51, 65–67, 72–73, 77–79
Rubiera, V., 116–119
Ruiz do Zárate, S., 134–136, 167, 224
Russian Revolution, 66, 278. *See also* Soviet Union

**S**

Sabadí, 95, 103
Sagua la Grande, xxxix

Sagua, zone of, 77, 128, 133; fall of, 150–154
Salvador, D., "Mario," 127
Samuel, 146, 154, 177
San Pablo de Yao, 113
Sánchez, C., 222, 223, 244, 245, 284
Sancti Spíritus, zone of, xxxiii, 128, 198
Santa Clara, xxxiii, 5, 17–19, 21, 51, 65, 67, 72, 73, 77, 79, 84, 113, 123, 124, 128, 143, 148; battle of, 234, 242
Santamaría, A., 102, 207
Santamaría, H., "Yeyé," 95, 110, 163–165, 172
Santiago, Chile, 41, 43
Santiago de Cuba, xxxiii, 50, 51, 102–103, 104, 113, 141, 209, 223
Sargent, N., 164
Sartre, J.-P., 183, 285–286
Second Front of Escambray, 164, 169, 250
Shell Oil Company, xix, 80, 92, 96, 99, 108, 109, 123, 125, 133, 162, 210
"Sierra." See Oltuski, E.
Sierra de Escambray, xix, xxxiii, 124, 125, 128, 166, 200
Sierra Maestra, xix, xxxiii, 103, 104, 107, 113, 125, 142, 193, 201
Soviet Union, 30, 277–278, 287
Stalin, J., 34
Stein, M., 53, 58, 73, 84–86
Students Federation (FEU), 6, 19, 72

T
Three Who Made a Revolution (Wolfe), 34
Torres, R., 37, 38, 40, 41
Torture, 124
"Toto." See Lubián, G.
Toyo, M., 224
Trelles, C., 191, 192
Trinidad, xxxiii, 128, 166, 191

Trinidad, D., 233
Trotsky, L., 34
26th of July Movement, 72–73, 74, 91, 93, 99, 103, 107, 114, 124, 128, 144, 148, 260, 261, 264

U
United States, 277, 278; activities in Latin America, 43; embargo of Cuba, 287; Embassy, 243
Universidad de Concepción (Chile), 43
University of Chile, 41
University of Havana, 12, 18, 19
University of Miami, 5, 10; Foreign Students Club, 27
Urdaneta, A., 11, 28
Urdaneta sisters, 28
Urrutia, M., 215, 216, 207, 221, 235, 255, 257, 258, 269, 270, 272, 273
Uvero, 112

V
Valdés, R., 195, 196
Valparaiso, Chile, 38, 40
Vecino, E., 211
Vecino, F., 210, 224
Velasco, R. de, 115–117, 119
Ventura (Batista police captain), 107, 108, 111, 113, 133, 171

W
Wolfe, B. D., 34

Y
Yaguajay, xxxix, 128, 143, 159, 161, 163, 165, 200
"Yeyé." See Santamaría, H.

Z
"Zoilo." See Fernández, M.
Zones, establishment of, 127–128
Zulueta, J., 210

Pinar del Río

Havana

Matanzas

Cienfuegos

San

Trinidad

Sierra de

N

10  30  50  70 miles